ARMS AND ARMOUR

ARMS *and* ARMOUR
IN ANTIQUITY AND THE MIDDLE AGES
Also a descriptive Notice of Modern Weapons

Translated from the French of M.P. Lacombe,
and with a Preface, Notes, and
One Additional Chapter on Arms and Armour in England

CHARLES BOUTELL

COMBINED BOOKS

Published by Reeves & Turner, London, in a new edition, 1907.

Combined Books Edition, 1996.

ISBN 0-938289-61-6

CONTENTS.

A

CHAPTER VI.

CHAPTER VII.

CHAPTER VIII.

CHAPTER IX.

CHAPTER X.

CHAPTER XI.

LIST OF ILLUSTRATIONS.

viii   LIST OF ILLUSTRATIONS.

LIST OF PLATES.

PUBLISHERS' NOTE.

THIS edition of M. Lacombe's work, as translated, edited, and expanded by our great English authority, Charles Boutell, has been enriched by the addition of very numerous and interesting illustrations from various sources; and the publishers desire to express their thanks to Lord Zouche, Sir Noël Paton, and Mr. Percy Macquoid for permission to reproduce pieces from their collections that had been given in the two Portfolio monographs on "Armour in England," by Mr. Starkie Gardner, the electros being furnished by Messrs. Seeley & Company Limited.

August 1901.

PREFACE.

THE original work, written in French by M. P. LACOMBE, of which a version is here submitted to English readers in their own language, was published in Paris at the commencement of the year 1868.

The collection of engravings on wood by M. H. CATE-NACCI, which appears with the present English version, also illustrates the French volume. The delicacy and beauty of these wood-engravings must necessarily secure for them a cordial welcome in their present association with English letter-press; their fidelity, too, will not fail to be thoroughly appreciated on the north side of the Channel.

M. Lacombe's volume contains neither Preface, Introduction, nor Index; nor, with a single exception, is his Text accompanied by any Notes. It is evident, however, that his aim and purpose were to give, in a concise popular form, a general sketch of the entire subject of which he had undertaken to treat—consequently, his plan being thus comprehensive, while the space at his disposal was restricted within comparatively narrow limits, M. Lacombe's chapters for the most part are brief, and he rarely enters into many details. Evidently both an earnest student and an accomplished *con-*

noisseur of ancient art, a reverential worshipper of Homer, and
generally well read in classic literature, M. Lacombe is by no
means strong as a mediæval archæologist; nor has he any
sympathy with either the arts or the arms of the Middle Ages.
On the other hand, when he proceeds to treat of periods that
are less remote, his military views have led M. Lacombe into an
apparently unconscious sympathy with that famous northern
soldato, Major Sir Dugald Dalgetty, so far, at any rate, as con-
cerns his profound admiration for Gustavus Adolphus; still,
from some of the Major's well-known sentiments concerning
military service, the French author, as would have been expected from him, decidedly dissents.   And yet, at the same
time, he does full justice to the merits, such as they were, of
those soldiers of fortune—to whatever country they might in
reality have belonged—who, as he says, at certain periods,
played no unimportant parts on the battle-fields of Europe. As
an artist and a lover of art, M. Lacombe is a devotee of the
Renaissance ; and, accordingly, warm and enthusiastic are his
expressions of admiration for some of its wildest caprices and
most fantastic follies.   As it is quite certain that M. Lacombe
has not read the " Stones of Venice," it is much to be desired
that he should do so as speedily as may be possible ; and
meanwhile it might, perchance, exercise a beneficial influence
on Mr. Ruskin, in urging him to return to his earlier and
happier style, were he to study carefully the examples of arms
and armour which M. Lacombe has selected for special
laudation as masterpieces of the armourer's art.

The present volume is a translation and not a paraphrase

of the original French work. It is not an English book,
therefore, but an English version of a French book. It
would not have been possible to have re-cast M. Lacombe's
materials, without destroying their identity in the process of
re-casting ; or, in other words, any attempt to convert M.
Lacombe's book into an English one would have implied
writing a fresh book in the English language. This is not
what I was desired to undertake. Nor would it have been by
any means desirable, either to have built up a popular English
treatise on " Arms and Armour" on a French foundation, or
to have withheld altogether from English readers what M.
Lacombe had written on that subject. And, again, the
greater number of the French woodcuts would have positively
refused to illustrate a new English book ; and there can be
but one opinion as to the desirableness of the appearance of
these admirable woodcuts in England, and their naturalisation
amongst ourselves.

It will be found in the following pages that, except in the
case of two of the French chapters, I have deviated as little as
possible from the original, seldom omitting anything, and still
more rarely adding to the text. In the matter of dates, however, I have habitually inserted such as appear to be of importance, within brackets, in the text itself. One of his
longest chapters M. Lacombe has devoted to detailed descriptions of certain examples of arms and armour, which are remarkable either for their singularity or for the richness of their
ornamentation. The engravings which in the original illustrate this chapter I have arranged to form an Appendix to my

translation; but of this chapter I have not translated the text. In like manner, I have not included M. Lacombe's last chapter in the contents of my own volume; but, instead of his conclusion, I have added a few "concluding" passages to my eleventh chapter. My tenth chapter is altogether fresh— an addition to the work for which I alone am responsible. In this additional chapter I have endeavoured in some degree to supply what M. Lacombe had not provided for English (or, indeed, for French) readers—a sketch, that is, of ENGLISH ARMS AND ARMOUR. In conformity with M. Lacombe's plan, which ought to determine the character of the entire volume, I have not attempted more than a sketch, while I felt that without some such attempt the present volume would be unpardonably imperfect. It has been my good fortune to be enabled to introduce into this new chapter a few English wood-cuts, which, however they may differ in their style from their French companions, in their own style are singularly excellent. They have been engraved from drawings on the wood by R. T. Pritchett, F.S.A. In addition to Chapter X., I have collected together and placed at the end of the volume, in the form of *Notes*, such comments as various passages in the original appeared imperatively to require; and also, as far as possible, I have caused these Notes (which I should gladly have extended very considerably, had space been allowed for that purpose) to take a decided part, both in commending the Text to English readers, and associating English arms and armour with statements and descriptions that, either exclusively or in some special acceptation, are French.

The remarks that appear in the Text upon the Bayeux Tapestry, in its capacity of an historical monument of unquestionable authenticity and authority, proceeding, as they do, from the pen of a French writer, will be regarded with much interest in England. And so, also, in like manner, no slight interest attaches itself to the brief but graphic sketch of the French mediæval military system—suggestive as it is of the feudal ages from a point of view that is not English—with which M. Lacombe commences his seventh chapter. And, again, the same may be said of his statements and observations in the eighth chapter, concerning the great English victories of Crécy and Poictiers, and of the conduct there both of our Black Prince and of our countrymen the yeomen archers of England. All these passages have been rendered with especial care, so that in the translation they might convey the exact sense which they bear in the original.

If any part of M. Lacombe's volume be in a special sense applicable to his own country, and to France alone, and in no way capable of being applied to England, it is that part which treats of the arms and armour of the three successive half centuries which extend from about A.D. 1300 to about A.D. 1450. We are glad to know what a French writer on the subject before us had to say concerning the period in question; and his remarks become the more valuable to us when we observe how completely they differ from what we ourselves, writing about our own country at the same period, should have written.

There now remains for me only the pleasing duty to

record my grateful sense of the truly valuable aid that I have received from two dear fellow-workers in the preparation of this volume in its English costume.

CHARLES BOUTELL.

LONDON, *Easter*, 1869.

Fig. 71.—GROUP OF FOUR ANCIENT GREEK EMBLAZONED SHIELDS. From painted Vases in the British Museum. [*See p.* 45 *and Note* 23.]

ARMS AND ARMOUR.

CHAPTER I.

THE STONE PERIOD.—ANTEDILUVIAN AND PRE-HISTORIC
WEAPONS.

WHATEVER the motive which led to the invention and the
earliest use of weapons, whether the object of the inventor
was to strengthen his hand in self-defence or that he might
be enabled with greater force to strike aggressive blows, it
appears to be certain that almost from the time of his first
appearance upon the earth, man has felt the necessity of
arming himself.   Possibly, weapons were originally constructed for the purposes of defence, and perhaps the first
assailants of primeval man were fierce animals ; but it is
also equally probable that at a very early period mankind
found in their fellow-creatures enemies to be attacked as
well as resisted.[1]

Within the last thirty or forty years fresh opinions have

grown up amongst men of science with reference to the probable antiquity of the human race. The researches in France of M. Boucher de Perthes, and of many other anti-quaries who have followed his example, led to the discovery of primitive weapons, which have been confidently assigned not only to the antediluvian era, but also to a period very far more remote than that which has generally been accepted as the age of the creation of man. At the first it was sup-posed that these relics would be found only in certain locali-ties; but after a while, when the search for them had become more general (and in England it has been carried on with equal zeal and success), it was ascertained that relics of this class were in existence and awaiting discovery in countries widely separated from one another. If the high antiquity that has been assigned to these weapons be admitted, man, the maker of them, must necessarily have been contemporary with the colossal animals, the *bos primigenius*, the *elephas giganteus*, and that great bear of the caverns which was as large as an ox. The hunters of those far away days would certainly have pursued the monstrous animals with which they were familiar; and they would have encountered and de-stroyed them.

In treating of the ARMS and ARMOUR that have been in use at successive periods throughout the world, we commence with the *Stone Period;* still, it is altogether beyond our power to determine the commencement of this period. The knife, the axe, the arrow—either discharged from the bow or thrown as a javelin from the hand—these were the weapons of the first men; and of these weapons, all of them invari-ably made of stone, numerous specimens have been dis-covered in all parts of the habitable globe. Stone, the material thus always employed in the production of these earliest weapons, has very consistently given a distinctive name to the ages during which they were exclusively in use.

And as it is absolutely impossible to date the "Stone Period" from any fixed era, so also serious difficulties attend every attempt to define the exact era of its close. Stone weapons unquestionably continued to be used throughout the whole range of the "Bronze Period"—the second period, that is, during which weapons were generally made of bronze, and which corresponds with the epoch of the earliest traditions of Gaul, and with the Egyptian, the Assyrian, and the Homeric civilisations. And again, the use of stone weapons was still further prolonged into the third or "Iron Period," when bronze generally was superseded by iron; and, far advanced in this "Iron Period," even so late as the eighth century of our own era, lances and arrows of stone were found in the hands of the Normans.

The weapons of the "Stone Period" were made almost exclusively of silex. A stone less hard than flint would have failed to have produced satisfactory results, when subjected to the process of treatment which alone was at the disposal of primitive man. He probably selected a stone which showed a natural tendency towards the form that he desired it should ultimately assume: then, employing a second stone as his working-tool, by a rapid succession of little sharp blows, he struck off splinters from the first stone, until his work was accomplished, and the desired weapon—arrow or lance, knife or axe—was perfected so far as he could make it perfect. It must not be forgotten, that when this primitive armourer struck his blows on the stone that was being made into a weapon, the splinters which flew off did not proceed from the part of the stone that had been struck, but from the side of the stone opposite to that which had received the blows, and consequently from the side which the operator could not see while he was working. It was necessary, therefore, for him to supply the place of sight by a precision and certainty of touch which were indeed extraordinary. Workmen such

as these, savages as in so many respects we must consider
them to have been, gave signs already of that instinctive and
patient ingenuity which is one of the most honourable endow-
ments of the human race. It is also evident that between
different individuals of these workmen there were distinct
gradations of capacity, skill, and experience, relatively as
great as those which in our own times may exist between
artists of various degrees of rank.

At first sight apparently uniform in their excessive simplicity, after observant, thoughtful, and prolonged study these

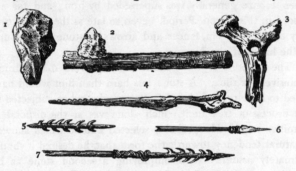

Fig. 1.—ARMS OF THE STONE PERIOD.

productions of the primeval flint-armourer are found to
possess certain distinctive and characteristic qualities, by which
they may be assigned each to their own country and era,
precisely as the same thing may be done in the case of the
most elaborate works of art. Antiquaries also have learned
to declare with confidence that certain countries generally
furnished superior workmen, while the productions of other
countries were almost always of an inferior order; and they
have even succeeded in dividing that vast space of time which
preceded the deluge of Noah into periods of decadence and
renaissance.[2]

Without attempting, and indeed without any desire now

to carry further these preliminary considerations, we proceed to examine some characteristic typical examples of the various weapons of the "Stone Period." Their forms may be clearly understood from engraved representations; notwithstanding that in consequence of the complication of their lines, the inevitable result of the process of their manufacture, an intelligible description of them may fairly be pronounced impossible. The group, Fig. 1, contains seven examples. Of these, Nos. 1 and 6 severally represent an axe-head and an arrow. Now, we may ask by what means flint axes and arrows such as these become hafted? There can be no question as to whether the flint arrow-head should be made with a socket, like an arrow-head of metal, for fixing it to the shaft; for, even if the workman had succeeded in piercing a socket-hole in the flint for the reception of the shaft, the walls or enclosing sides of this socket in the flint would certainly have burst at the first shock. The only available process that would be successful, was the same that still is employed by those races who continue to use arrows as missile weapons, and who arm their arrows with tips of pointed stone; that is, the ancient stone arrow-heads were set in shafts that had been split at the end in order to receive them, and then the shaft with the arrow-head within its grasp was bound round with bands of skin or fibre, as in Fig. 1, No. 6. Of the axes some evidently have been made for the purpose of being fixed to the end of a handle or haft; but in others the equally evident intention was that they should be grasped in the hand without any haft, when in use. On the side where they are to be held these last have received a polish, so that the hand might not be hurt; and sometimes they have a hole through which the thumb may be passed in order to give a firmer grasp. Examples of the earliest hafted axes are represented in the wood-cuts, Fig. 1, No. 2; and Fig. 2, Nos. 8, 9, and 10. It is possible also that the antediluvians may have been acquainted with many of those ingenious methods for attaching their stone weapons to handles, prevalent at a later period, which savage tribes still employ in order to obtain for the two parts of their weapons a solid coherence. We shall have occasion hereafter to treat more fully of the curious and interesting processes, to which here it is sufficient thus briefly to refer.

If it should be asked whether the art of polishing stones was known at the remote period of the antediluvian armourers, the reply would be that almost beyond all doubt it was then known. Such a simple knowledge assuredly was not beyond

Fig. 2.—ARMS OF THE STONE PERIOD.

the intelligence of workmen, who daily executed much more delicate operations than the imparting a polished surface to smoothed stones. However this may be, the smooth stone hatchets that were common amongst the earliest Celts and their contemporaries, are not found amongst the relics of the still earlier antediluvian era: but this circumstance may be explained in a manner which probably will excite some surprise, since the absence of smooth stone hatchets in the most remote ages must be attributed to the fact that the superior utility, for many purposes, of the irregular and splintered weapon was then known and understood. The smoothed axe might be the more pleasing in appearance, but the rough one was the better in use.

On this side of the last geological revolution, and consequently in that period of terrestrial history of which we now proceed to treat—but still, before the dawn of historical ages, that is, before the time (uncertain enough) in which definite human tradition commences—man is found to have been armed in the same fashion that he had been before the flood, the great revolution in question. Post-diluvian man comes upon the scene without any advance in knowledge. To him, as to his predecessors, the use of metals is as a sealed book. He continues, after the fashion of what to him was the olden time, to hunt and to make war, equipped and armed with knives and axes and arrows of flint.

M. Boucher de Perthes, who speaks with the highest authority on all points connected with the weapons of the " Stone Period," positively affirms that weapons of the same class, all of them formed of silex, may be assigned without hesitation, some to the ages anterior to the flood, and others to the post-diluvian pre-historic era. The former, he says, may always be recognised by their surfaces exhibiting the traces of minute splinters of every variety of shape ; while, on the other hand, the latter may be distinguished by the evident fact that they were fashioned by knocking off splinters of a larger size, and always elongated in their form. It might also be added, apparently, that in the second section of the " Stone Period " the weapons have a much neater outline, and that they already indicate (or, at any rate, that they suggest) the contours which prevailed during the " Bronze Period "—typical contours that are universally well known. Thus, the objects represented in Fig. 2, No. 12, are seen at a glance to be the heads of either arrows or javelins. It must be added that these examples belong to the least remote period of the pre-historic age.[2]

Amongst the weapons of the period now under our consideration there are not a few which show their makers to have been endowed with the sentiment of beauty and elegance. The axe, for example, known to antiquaries as the " axe of the dolmen," modelled in the form of a large flattened egg, and polished with the utmost care and nicety, exhibits in its curves a truly artistic contour. So, again, certain stone arrow-heads that are barbed and wrought with minute splinters, convey the idea of firmness and steadiness of hand, combined with a truly extraordinary delicacy of touch.[4]

In conclusion, it must be added, as one of the characteristics which distinguish the first epoch of the " Stone Period " from the second, that in the latter, intermixed with all the varieties of flint weapons, there are found arrows of bone, and clubs made of wood only, or more frequently of stags' horns, as in Fig. 1, Nos. 3, 4, 5 and 7. In Fig. 2, No. 11, is shown a little axe of stone, pierced in the centre for the insertion of the haft : here we have the expression of the first idea of the socket, and also its original form. In this same Fig. 2, No. 13 is a knife of flint.

CHAPTER II.

IT has already been stated that, by common consent, the title
of the "Bronze Period" has been bestowed on those early
ages in which men, in consequence of their still continuing
in ignorance of the nature and working of iron, employed the
mixed metal bronze, an alloy of copper, zinc, and tin, for the
manufacture as well of their implements as of their weapons.
The three successive "Periods" of "Stone," "Bronze," and
"Iron," we may here repeat, in this respect penetrated or
overlapped one another, so that after the introduction of
works in bronze, the old flint implements still continued to
be retained in use; and in like manner bronze weapons and
implements and those of iron, for a prolonged period of time,
were in use together. Thus, when they invaded Gaul, the
Romans always wore defensive armour formed of iron, and all
their offensive weapons were made of the same metal; but, at
the same period, the arms of the Gauls were constructed of
both bronze and iron, and both metals were evidently held in
high esteem.[5]

In this chapter we propose to treat of the weapons, and
also of the defensive equipment of the Assyrians, of the
Gauls, and of the Greeks at the time of the Trojan war.
Our silence concerning the arms and armour of other contemporary nations must be attributed to its true cause—the
absence of historical monuments. Any attempt, therefore, to
include other contemporary nations with the races that we

have specified, could only lead us deliberately to place before
the reader unfounded conjectures in place of authenticated
facts.[6]

Section I.

Assyrian Arms and Armour.

The discoveries made of late years by M. Botta and Mr.
Layard among the remains of the ancient cities of Nineveh
have enabled us to give, with the most gratifying confidence,
various details of the military equipment of the Assyrians.

Fig. 3.--Assyrian Armed Warriors.

We commence with the defensive armour of that great, warlike and restless empire of antiquity.

The *shield* which is represented in the Assyrian monuments is round, and it appears generally to have been formed
in concentric circles; but whether the material was metal or
wood, or any other substance, the sculptures do not indicate
texture with sufficient minuteness to enable us to form even a
probable conjecture. These circles may be observed when
the inner faces of the shields are represented. If any shield
was formed of metal, its outer face was probably covered with

a single plate; or a skin might have been stretched over a
frame-work, and might either have bound together the
circular bands that have been mentioned, or have been
supported by them.   Other shields, also round, have a very
remarkable aspect : they have reticulated outer surfaces, the
net-work sometimes having the appearance of a species of
masonry; and, possibly, they may have actually been composed of small brick-like pieces of wood (*briques en bois*),
which were bound together by an iron frame.[7]   One of the
reticulated shields is shown in Fig. 3.

The Nineveh sculptures exhibit no examples of the *cuirass*
or *greaves*, defences for the breast and lower limbs, such as
were possessed by the Greeks.   The Assyrian warriors appear
generally to have been clothed for defence only in long tunics
of some thick material, sometimes covered with long hair, as
if the material were goat-skin.   Some, however, appear to
have worn a species of *justaucorps*, or tight-fitting coat, having
a more military appearance, which seems to have been constructed of twisted cords—a simple primitive prototype of
mail-armour.   This plaited or matted work would seem to
have been better qualified to resist blows than the common
tunic ; and, perhaps, with strict propriety and accuracy it
may be considered to have been the *cuirass* of the Assyrians.[8]

The *helm*, sometimes simply a close-fitting skull-cap,
was sometimes considerably elevated above the head of the
wearer, and finished in a point.   In some examples, the
raised upper crest-like part of the helm is seen to have been
bent backwards and truncated ; but in others the cap is surmounted by a kind of horn curved downwards to the front,
and not having a very prepossessing appearance.   These
helms were evidently formed of metal, and they were provided with defences to protect the neck at the back and sides.
(See Fig. 3, and also one example in Fig. 4.)

The offensive weapons of the Assyrians were the *sword*,

the *bow* with its *arrows*, the *club*, and the *lance* or *javelin*, of which (with the exception of the bow and arrows) representations are given in the wood-cut, Fig. 4.

Almost all the Assyrian warriors appear armed with the *sword*, which they wore on the left side, passed through a belt girded about the waist, and so adjusted that the weapon was maintained nearly in a horizontal position. The sword itself was straight and short, and it commonly exceeded but little the dimensions of a dagger. As far as can be determined, since it is always represented in the scabbard, the Assyrian sword was broad in the blade, with two edges, and

Fig. 4.—Assyrian Swords, Club, Lance, and Helm.

pointed at the extremity. The hilt, which is shown in the sculptures with minute carefulness, has a peculiar form, which is clearly explained by the examples in Fig. 4. The pommel is elegant in form, well developed, and suitably enriched. There is no guard for the hand, nor is the hilt separated from the blade by any cross-piece. The scabbard terminates in a rich *bouterolle*, which is always decorated in the same style : figures of lions, or other animals, are introduced, having their bodies stretched out in the direction of the sword-blade, while they project to the right and left, and impart a bold and effective finish to a highly artistic composition.[9] (See Fig. 4.)

The *bow*, which evidently was in very general use, was

small. When not actually on the field of battle, the Assyrian archers partly unbent their bows, and slung them over their shoulders, where they remained suspended. The *quiver*, well stored with *arrows*, they carried in the same position, beside their bow, sustained by a cord or quiver-belt.[10]

The *club* or *mace* at first sight is not easily recognised in the Assyrian bas-reliefs. It has the general form of a sceptre, for which it may easily be mistaken. But its true character is determined by a leathern strap coiled into a ring, which is apparent at the end of the handle, and by means of which the warrior doubtless was enabled to grasp his weapon more firmly and with greater security when in action, "as our peasants do now," says M. Lacombe, speaking of the modern peasantry of France, "when using their single-sticks." It must be observed that the club represented in Fig. 4 is altogether an exceptional example.

The *lance*, in length about equal to the height of a man, having a smooth shaft and an oblong head, served at once as a weapon to be held fast in the hand, or to be thrown, after the manner of the famous Homeric javelins.

Two observations we here introduce in concluding this brief section. 1. The Assyrians—that is to say, their chiefs and distinguished warriors—fought, as Homer's Greek heroes fought, in *war chariots*, which were shaped much in the likeness of the chariots of the Greeks. 2. *Military engines* for use in sieges were well known by the Assyrians. One of these engines, which is repeatedly introduced in the bas-reliefs, was a kind of chariot of large size formed of strong lattice-work, which, when it had been filled with soldiers, was driven up close to the walls or to the gate of the enemy's fortification. Through a hole pierced in the front of this engine a large pike is shown to have protruded, and with this the soldiers endeavoured to break through either the masonry of the hostile walls or the woodwork of the doorway.

Whether the pike was moved and driven forward by the soldiers sheltered within the engine, simply by strength of hand, or by some machinery, we have no means for obtaining information.   In the representations of sieges also in the Assyrian sculptures, warriors are seen carrying lances which have some inflammable preparations attached to the lance-heads, and with these they are endeavouring to set the gates on fire.   Here we discover evidence which proves that combustible compositions, designed to be employed in military operations, date back to a remote antiquity.[11]

Section II.
Arms and Armour of the Gauls.

The *axes* that were made and used by the early Gauls exhibit but little variety of form ; and indeed they generally conform to the same type in the shape and structure of their heads or blades, while in their handles they present several interesting varieties.   The heads of these axes, which are of bronze, are oblong, widened on the side next the edge, but having their profile formed by two lines which are either straight or slightly concave.   The axe that is of the most common occurrence, and is without edges or hollows, could have had for its haft nothing but a stick or piece of wood that had been split open at one end, so that the whole might be bound together by narrow strips of leather or by sinews of animals.   Examples of this class are represented in Fig. 5, Nos. 1 and 2.

Savage races are familiar with a process, of which doubtless the ancient Gauls were not ignorant.   When they had inserted an axe-head into a cleft stick, it was not grasped by the wood very firmly.   But if they had inserted the axe-head into a cleft in the branch of a tree, and had left that branch afterwards growing for a year, and without being severed from the tree, they knew that the tree, by the act of growing,

would spontaneously make an effort to heal the injury it had
received; it would strive, so to speak, to bind up its own
wound, or to cause the cleft parts to grow together again;
and thus the axe-head would become almost a part of the
branch which held it, so close and firm would be the growth
of the tissues of the wood by which it was encompassed. Savage
races are well aware of this fact; and it may be assumed that
the ancient Gauls knew and practised it also. This process is
in use at the present day amongst the islanders of the Pacific
Ocean. Their modern war-clubs explain to us the ancient
Gallic war-axes. Habit and necessity have taught to savage

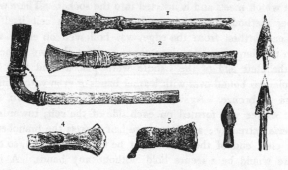

Fig. 5.—CELTIC ARMS.

races various other methods for joining different substances
with great strength and firmness. We ourselves, civilised as
we are, do not suspect to what good account a simple knot
may be turned; and, more particularly, we generally are
altogether ignorant as to the number of the varieties that it
may be made to assume. We, in England, may believe without
any hesitation that our own remote ancestors, in common
with the remote ancestors of the French of the present day,
all of them at least equally endowed with the savage islanders
of the Pacific, understood, as these savages now understand,
all the complicated knots, all the clever methods for producing

good joinings which are able to render to man such signal service.

The axe that bears the name of the " celt," of which a variety is shown in Fig. 5, No. 3, may be defined to be a kind of wedge, sharp at one extremity, and at the other formed into a hollow.   Into this hollow, as into a socket, the haft was fixed; and a few inches below the junction at the socket the haft was bent until the actual handle was at right angles with the axe-head.   Then a leathern strap was secured, both to the axe-head at the raised border of its socket, and also to the upper part of the straight handle just below the curved portion which meets and is inserted into the socket.   There were other methods for making celt-handles.   The celt itself, at the end farthest from the edge, was hollowed on either side into two large grooves; into these grooves the two branches of the cleft end of the handle were placed, and then the whole was bound over with leather bands or even with a single band of bronze.   Again, sometimes, as in Fig. 5, No. 4, a half socket was formed on each side of the celt, towards its reverse extremity ; and into these half sockets the branches of the cleft end of the haft might be fitted and fixed, so that there would be a secure hold without any bands.   A haft which had been fixed on this principle, however, would be liable to split, in consequence of the rebound of the axe when a vigorous blow was struck.   The example of a hatchet of bronze (Fig. 5, No. 5) with a true socket, is without doubt the production of a more modern period than its companions in the same group.[12]

The Gallic sword[13]—the weapon, at any rate, which is exhibited in museums under that name, and of which there are many fine examples in the Museum of Artillery at Paris—was formed of bronze : it is long, sharp-pointed, edged on both sides, and in the graceful curves of its form it somewhat resembles the leaf of the sage plant.   (See Fig. 6,

No. 1.) This weapon was like the Greek sword, and consequently very different from the characteristic national sword of the Romans, with which it was so often brought into conflict. Of the hilt of these swords two types have been observed. In the one, the metal of the blade is continued up to the pommel, and is almost as broad as the blade itself; this, having been pierced with holes, would be placed between two pieces of wood of suitable form and size, and rivets passing through the holes would bind the whole together. In the other type, the blade, instead of being prolonged to form the central nucleus of the hilt, terminates abruptly in a large solid boss; from this, two or three long spikes project in the same line with the blade, and they are fixed into the wooden cylinder which constitutes the handle. This is necessarily not a very secure mode of hilting a sword. It must be added that the swords of both these types are regarded by the most learned and experienced archæologists with grave suspicion. By them, indeed, they are generally suspected to be, not Gallic, but Roman swords, that is to say, manufactured late in the empire by Romans after Greek models. Should this surmise be correct, the decided resemblance of these swords to weapons of the same class that are unquestionably Greek, would be at once explained. One thing is certain, that these bronze swords, which have been assigned to the ancient Gauls, in every particular differ most decidedly from the long, flexible, and pointless weapons that are described by the Roman historians as having been seen in the hands of the same ancient Gauls, when they made their famous raid into Italy.

It was the sword that led to the substitution amongst the Gauls of iron, in the stead of its elder brother-metal, bronze. This was a change that proved to be attended with unfortunate results, since the Gauls never attained to such a knowledge of the treatment of iron as would have enabled them to

C

forge really serviceable weapons from that metal. It was not
from any inferiority in courage, accordingly, but in consequence
of their very decided deficiency in both skill and experience
in the armourer's art, that the Gauls were vanquished in Italy
by the Romans, in the early days of Rome. Thus, when at
Telamone, in alliance with the forces of the Samnites and
Etruscans, for a moment the Gauls appeared to be in the very
act of crushing the growing power of Rome, they eventually
experienced a terrible defeat, which decided the fate of their
colonies in Italy. This arose from the inferiority of the Gallic
swords. At that period the Romans had yet to attain that
eminence in discipline and military tactics, which afterwards
became identified with their name; but, even then, in the
character of their weapons they exhibited a judicious discernment unknown to their Gallic adversaries. Thus, the Gaul,
whose badly-tempered blade had bent at the first blow which
he had delivered, while in the act of straightening his sword
beneath his foot, was instantly struck down by the sharp,
firm, and ready steel of the Roman.

The Gauls were slow to adopt any species of defensive
armour; nor did their chiefs conform in this matter to the
usage of the Greeks and Romans, until after their relations
with those great military powers had become, if not more
amicable yet certainly much more intimate. The *helm* that at
last the Gallic chiefs assumed, was identical with the Roman
head-piece; but the Gauls added horns of goats and bulls, or
the wings of birds, and various other objects—appendages, in
some degree crest-like in their character and object, which
after a very singular fashion changed the aspect of their
helms.[14]

The *cuirass*, at no time in common use amongst the
Gauls, when worn was formed, after the custom of both the
Greeks and the Romans, either of two plates of metal, the
metal being either bronze or iron, or of interwoven mail-work,

The *shield*, which was more generally in use, was constructed of a framework of wicker, covered over with leather;
or it was made of wood; and in either case it was adorned
by having the head of an animal nailed in the centre, after
the manner of a boss; or a flower, or a mask executed with
the hammer (*repoussé*) in bronze, was fixed in a similar
position.

Fig. 6.—GALLIC ARMS.

·In the examples represented in the wood-cut, Fig. 6,
from the triumphal arch at Orange, the shield of elongated
form, in addition to its central boss, has a decorative conventional device, the whole being within a border. All this
decoration appears to have been executed either in colour on
a flat surface, or in low relief. It must here be observed, however, that the Romans in their representations of barbarous
(foreign, that is) nations, while distinguishing very decidedly

C 2

between the barbarians and themselves, took but little care to discriminate between the different barbarous races; accordingly, the Gauls on the Orange arch, and the Dacians on the column of Trajan, appear almost in the same costume, and with scarcely any perceptible difference in their armour and weapons.[15]

Section III.

Greek Arms and Armour of the Heroic Ages.

Such representations of arms and armour as might have been represented upon monuments, do not exist to illustrate the heroic ages of Greece; but, on the other hand, we are able to appeal to Homer, the most exact, the clearest, and the most minutely faithful of the ancient poets. At once, then, and with that profound respect which most justly is due to him, we bid Homer speak. Achilles begins the combat with Hector :—

> " He said and, poising, hurled his weighty spear ;
> But Hector saw, and shunned the blow ; he stooped,
> And o'er his shoulder flew the brass-tipped spear,
> And in the ground was fixed : but Pallas drew
> The weapon forth, and to Achilles' hand,
> All unobserved of Hector, gave it back."

Then Hector spoke, and

> " Poising, hurled his ponderous spear ;
> Nor missed his aim ; full in the midst he struck
> Pelides' shield ; but, glancing from the shield,
> The weapon glided off.   Hector was grieved,
> That thus his spear had bootless left his hand.
> He stood aghast ; no second spear was nigh :
> And loudly on Deiphobus he called
> A spear to bring ; but he was far away."

Then other, and they bitter, words fall from the lips of the Trojan prince :—

" Thus as he spoke, his sharp-edged sword he drew,
Ponderous and vast, suspended at his side ;
Collected for the spring and forward dashed. . . .
Achilles' wrath was roused : with fury wild
His soul was filled : before his breast he bore
His well-wrought shield ; and fiercely on his brow
Nodded the four-plumed helm. . . .
Gleamed the sharp-pointed lance, which in his right
Achilles poised, on god-like Hector's doom
Intent, and scanning eagerly to see
Where from attack his body least was fenced.
All else the glittering armour guarded well. . . .
One chink appeared, just where the collar-bone
The neck and shoulder parts, beside the throat. . . .
There levelled he."

Il., xxii. 320. *

Nearly all the details of the ancient Greek military equipment are brought before us in this brief passage. By the aid
of other passages we may be enabled very distinctly to develop
their several characteristic peculiarities, and, as it, were, to
reproduce them, one by one, in their original identity.

The *offensive weapons*, as we here observe, are the *sword*
and the *lance* or *javelin*. It is the latter weapon that plays
the principal part in the Homeric combats; for, on every
occasion, it is not until his lance has been lost, that the
warrior, whether Trojan or Greek, draws his sword. This
lance is long and ponderous ; and, as a consequence of its
weight, it was invariably thrown only at a very short range—
always, indeed, within conversation distance. In their single
combat Hector and Ajax hurl their lances at each other, but
without effect; then both warriors recover their lances, and
renew the onset; and now their spears are used by them as

* The passages here given from the "Iliad" are from the Earl of
Derby's translation, the sixth edition, published in London, in 1867,
by John Murray, of Albemarle Street : the references denote the lines in
this translation, and not those in the Greek

veritable *lances*, grasped in their hands, and in close conflict
Hector first throws his weapon :—

> " He said : and, poising, hurled his ponderous spear ;
> The brazen covering of the shield it struck,
> The outward fold, the eighth, above the seven
> Of tough bull's-hide ; through six it drove its way
> With stubborn force ; but in the seventh was stayed.
> Then Ajax hurled in turn his ponderous spear,
> And struck the circle true of Hector's shield :
> Right through the glittering shield the stout spear passed,
> And through the well-wrought breast-plate drove its way,
> And, underneath, the linen vest it tore ;
> But Hector, stooping, shunned the stroke of death.
>   " Withdrawing then their weapons, each on each
> They fell. . . .
> Then Hector fairly in the centre struck
> The stubborn shield ; yet drove not through the spear :
> For the stout brass the blunted point repelled.
> But Ajax, with a forward bound, the shield
> Of Hector pierced ; right through the weapon passed."
>
> *Il.*, vii. 273.

The spear-head at this time appears to have been long,
broad, and without barbs; and the shaft we know to have
been made of the tough wood of the ash. Thus, in the
6th " Iliad," Agamemnon is armed with an " ashen spear ;"
and the tree, from which had been obtained the shaft of the
lance of Achilles, we are expressly told was an ash that grew
on Pelion. Thus we read :—

> " The son of Peleus threw
> His straight-directed spear; his mark he missed,
> But struck the lofty bank, where, deep infixed
> To half its length, the Pelian ash remained.
> Then from beside his thigh Achilles drew
> His trenchant blade, and furious, onward rushed ;
> While from the cliff Asteropæus strove
> In vain, with stalwart hand, to wrench the spear.
> Three times he shook it with impetuous force,

GREEK ARMS.

> Three times relaxed his grasp ; a fourth attempt
> He made to bend and break the sturdy shaft."
>
> *Il.*, xxi. 192.

The strength of the ashen shaft is indicated in a striking manner in this passage; and it also shows, in a manner equally characteristic how the use of the sword was reserved until after the effect of the lance had been determined.

To the *sword* Homer applies the epithets "large," "long," and "sharp," or "trenchant ;" and he also tells us that it was "two-edged," and consequently we may assume that it was straight in the blade. It is evident from various passages that this formidable weapon served equally well to deliver blows struck with the edge, and to thrust with the point.

In "Iliad" xxi., we read how

> "Achilles drew,
> And . . . .
> Let fall his trenchant sword ; the two-edged blade
> Was buried deep." *Il.*, xxi. 133

The sword of Agamemnon is thus described :—

> "Then o'er his shoulder threw his sword ; bright flashed
> The golden studs ; the silver scabbard shone,
> With golden baldrick fitted." *Il.*, xi. 29.

And again, in the 2nd Book of the "Iliad," it is said of Agamemnon that he—

> 'O'er his shoulders flung his sword, adorned
> With silver studs." *Il.*, ii. 51.

And, in like manner, of Menelaus also—

> " Around his shoulders slung, his sword he bore,
> Brass-bladed, silver-studded ; then his shield
> Weighty and strong . . . .
> . . . . his hand
> Grasped the firm spear, familiar to his hold."
>
> *Il.*, iii. 390.

Again—

> " Then Peneleus and Lycon, hand to hand,
> Engaged in combat : both had missed their aim,
> And bootless hurled their weapons : then with swords
> They met. First Lycon on the crested helm
> Dealt a fierce blow ; but in his hand the blade
> Up to the hilt was shivered ; then the sword
> Of Peneleus . . . .
>   . . . . deeply in his throat the blade
> Was plunged."   *Il.*, xvi. 385.

And again, when the heralds of the two armies had interposed and broken off the combat between Hector and
Ajax, the Trojan prince thus addressed the sturdy Greek :—

> " But make we now an interchange of gifts . . . .
> This said, a silver-studded sword he gave,
> With scabbard and with well-cut belt complete."
>   *Il.*, vii. 335.

The sword, then, had its hilt enriched with studs; and
when in its scabbard, it hung from a belt that passed over the
shoulder—over the right shoulder, we may assume, since there
is no statement whether the weapon was suspended on the
left side or the right; but the length of the sword must be
considered to imply that it hung on the left side.   Only very
short weapons, such as daggers, can be adjusted to the right
side of the wearer.[16]

Homer, it will be observed, assigns the same weapons and
armour to both the Trojans and the Greeks.

We pass on now to consider, under the guidance of Homer,
the most ancient *defensive armour* of the Greeks.

In the celebrated passage from the 18th Book of the
" Iliad," which will form the basis of our own remarks, the
shield is specified by name, and it is very clearly and fully
described; but a very few words are bestowed upon the other
pieces of the armour, the *helm*, the *cuirass*, and the *greaves*.[17]

In compliance with the prayer of Thetis, Vulcan forges for

the renowned son of the sea-goddess of the silvery feet, a
mighty shield, a marvel of art :—

> " And first a shield he fashioned, vast and strong,
> With rich adornment; circled with a rim,
> Three-fold, bright-gleaming, whence a silver belt
> Depended. "   *Il.*, xviii. 539.

This "shield-belt" is identical with the "guige" of the
middle ages, by which the shield was secured to the
person of the wearer, and also carried by him without
inconvenience, suspended about his neck.   The mediæval
guige crossed over the right shoulder ; but whether Homer
would desire us to assign the same adjustment of their shield-
belts to his warriors, we know not.   The sword-belt, as we
have seen, was adjusted (sometimes, certainly, if not as an
invariable rule) by the Homeric warriors over the right
shoulder.   A belt also appears to have been worn, at any
rate by some of the Greek heroes, fastened below the cuirass,
and encircling the waist; such a belt as this apparently is
intended to be described in the passage from the 4th Book
of the "Iliad" (presently to be quoted), in which the poet tells
how the arrow of Pandarus took effect upon Menelaus.

To return now to the shield of Achilles.   With lavish
hand Vulcan scatters over the entire surface the wonders of
his admirable art.   He represents the earth, the sky, the sea,
the never-weary sun, the moon at her full ; the constellations
also, which crown the heavens, the Pleiades, the Hyades, the
bold Orion, and the Bear, too, by men called the Wain,
which revolves ever in the same regions of space, looking
towards Orion, and at no time has any share in the baths
of the Ocean.

> .   .   .   .   "Of five folds the shield was formed ;
> And on its surface many a rare design
> Of curious art his practised hand had wrought.
>   Thereon were figured earth, and sky, and sea,
> The ever-circling sun, and full-orbed moon,

And all the signs that crown the vault of heaven ;
Pleiads and Hyads and Orion's might,
And Arctos, called the Wain, who wheels on high
His circling course, and on Orion waits ;
Sole star that never bathes in the ocean wave.

And two fair populous towns were sculptured there :
In one were marriage, pomp, and revelry,
And brides, in gay procession, through the streets
With blazing torches from their chambers borne,
While frequent rose the hymeneal song.
Youths whirled around in joyous dance, with sound
Of flute and harp ; and, standing at their doors,
Admiring women on the pageant gazed.

Meanwhile a busy throng the forum filled :
There between two a fierce contention-rose,
About a death-fine ; to the public one
Appealed, asserting to have paid the whole ;
While one denied that he had aught received.
Both were desirous that before the judge
The issue should be tried ; with noisy shouts
Their several partisans encouraged each.
The heralds stilled the tumult of the crowd :
On polished chairs, in solemn circle, sat
The reverend elders ; in their hands they held
The loud-voiced heralds' sceptres ; waving these,
They heard the alternate pleadings ; in the midst
Two talents lay of gold, which he should take
Who should before them prove his righteous cause.

Before the second town two armies lay,
In arms refulgent ; to destroy the town
The assailants threatened, or among themselves
Of all the wealth within the city stored
An equal half, as ransom, to divide.
The terms rejecting, the defenders manned
A secret ambush ; on the walls they placed
Women and children mustered for defence,
And men by age enfeebled ; forth they went,
By Mars and Pallas led ; these, wrought in gold,
In golden arms arrayed, above the crowd
For beauty and stature, as befitting gods,
Conspicuous shone ; of lesser height the rest.
But when the destined ambuscade was reached.

Beside the river, where the shepherds drove
Their flocks and herds to water, down they lay,
In glittering arms accoutred ; and apart
They placed two spies, to notify betimes
The approach of flocks of sheep and lowing herds.
These, in two shepherds' charge, ere long appeared,
Who, unsuspecting as they moved along,
Enjoyed the music of their pastoral pipes.
They on the booty, from afar discerned,
Sprang from their ambuscade ; and cutting off
The herds and fleecy flocks, their guardians slew.
Their comrades heard the tumult, where they sat
Before their sacred altars, and forthwith
Sprang on their cars, and with fast-stepping steeds
Pursued the plunderers, and o'ertook them soon.
There on the river's bank they met in arms,
And each at other hurled their brazen spears.
And there were figured Strife and Tumult wild,
And deadly Fate, who in her iron grasp
One newly-wounded, one unwounded bore,
While by the feet from out the press she dragged
Another slain : about her shoulders hung
A garment crimsoned with the blood of men.
    And there was graven a wide-extended plain
Of fallow land, rich, fertile, mellow soil,
Thrice ploughed ; where many ploughmen up and down
Their teams were driving ; and as each attained
The limit of the field, would one advance
And tender him a cup of generous wine :
Then would he turn, and to the end again
Along the furrow cheerly drive his plough.
And still behind them darker showed the soil,
The true presentment of a new-ploughed field,
Though wrought in gold ; a miracle of art.
    There, too, was graven a corn-field, rich in grain,
Where with sharp sickles reapers plied their task,
And thick, in even swathe, the trusses fell ;
The binders, following close, the bundles tied.
Three were the binders ; and behind them boys
In close attendance waiting, in their arms
Gathered the bundles, and in order piled.
Amid them, staff in hand, in silence stood

The king, rejoicing in the plenteous swathe.
A little way removed, the heralds slew
A sturdy ox, and now beneath an oak
Prepared the feast ; while women mixed, hard by,
White barley porridge for the labourers' meal.

And, with rich clusters laden, there was graven
A vineyard fair, all gold ; of glossy black
The bunches were, on silver poles sustained ;
Around, a darksome trench ; beyond, a fence
Was wrought of shining tin ; and through it led
One only path, by which the bearers passed,
Who gathered in the vineyard's bounteous store.
There maids and youths, in joyous spirits bright,
In woven baskets bore the luscious fruit.
A boy, amid them, from a clear-toned harp
Drew lovely music ; well his liquid voice
The strings accompanied ; they all with dance
And song harmonious joined, and joyous shouts,
As the gay bevy lightly tripped along.

Of straight-horned cattle, too, a herd was graven ;
Of gold and tin the heifers all were wrought ;
They to the pasture, from the cattle-yard,
With gentle lowings, by a babbling stream,
Where quivering reed-beds rustled, slowly moved.
Four golden shepherds walked beside the herd,
By nine swift dogs attended : then, amid
The foremost heifers, sprang two lions fierce
Upon the lordly bull ; he, bellowing loud,
Was dragged along, by dogs and youths pursued.
The tough bull's hide they tore, and gorging lapped
The intestines and dark blood ; with vain attempt
The herdsmen, following closely, to the attack
Cheered their swift dogs ; these shunned the lions' jaws,
And, close around them baying, held aloof.

And there the skilful artist's hand had traced
A pasture broad, with fleecy flocks o'erspread,
In a fair glade, with fold, and tents, and pens.

There, too, the skilful artist's hand had wrought
With curious workmanship a mazy dance,
Like that which Dædalus in Cnossus erst
At fair-haired Ariadne's bidding framed.
There, laying on each other's wrists their hand,

Bright youths and many-suitored maidens danced :
In fair white linen these ; in tunics those,
Well woven, shining soft with fragrant oils
These with fair coronets were crowned, while those
With golden swords from silver belts were girt.
Now whirled they round with nimble practised feet,
Easy, as when a potter, seated, turns
A wheel, new fashioned by his skilful hand,
And spins it round, to prove if true it run ;
Now featly moved in well-beseeming ranks.
A numerous crowd, around, the lovely dance
Surveyed, delighted, while an honoured bard
Sang, as he struck the lyre: and to the strain
Two tumblers, in the midst, were whirling round.
　About the margin of the massive shield
Was wrought the mighty strength of the ocean stream.
　The shield completed, vast and strong, he forged
A breastplate, dazzling bright as flame of fire ;
And next a weighty helmet for his head,
Fair, richly wrought, with crest of gold above ;
Then last, well-fitting greaves of pliant tin."

Il. xviii. 542—695.

If we should be disposed to inquire by what expression of Art the figures were rendered in all these varied groups, and what processes Homer himself understood to have been employed in the production of them, we are led by the terms that the poet has adopted, as well as by what we know of the contemporaneous civilisation, to believe that the whole of the composition was executed by engraving. However that may be, in this description of the shield of Achilles we have proof that the arts of drawing and composition were in existence when Homer wrote. At that same period also, men had discovered the decorative processes of plating, gilding, and enamelling. (See Note 18.)

The shield of Agamemnon, briefly described as follows, in the 11th Book of the " Iliad," unlike that of Achilles, is formed of ten circular plates of brass, which are studded with twenty bosses of a white metal; and the whole is bound together, doubtless by a metallic band ·—

> .   .   .   .   "Next his shield
> He took, full-sized, well-wrought, well-proved in fight;
> Around it ran ten circling rims of brass;
> With twenty bosses round of burnished tin,
> And, in the centre, one of dusky bronze—
> A Gorgon's head—with aspect terrible—
> Was wrought, with Fear and Fright encircling round.
> Depending from a silver belt it hung;
> And on the belt, a dragon, wrought in bronze,
> Twined his lithe folds, and turned on every side,
> Sprung from a single neck his triple head."
>
> *Il.*, xi. 31.

As we have already seen, the shield of Ajax is made of seven tough bull's-hides, covered over in front with a plate of burnished brass.

Homer, who is desirous to give a grand idea of the prowess of his heroes, certainly exaggerates when he describes the weight and dimensions of their shields. In these descriptions he indulges himself with a free use of poetic license. From his descriptions, however, we obtain two certain facts; one of them arising out of the other, and consequent upon it. First, we find that the Homeric Greek shield, as a general rule, was constructed of metal (the metal sometimes being backed with leather), and not of wood, as was the prevailing custom amongst other nations; and secondly, it is evident that this shield was massive and ponderous. The great weight of these shields is shown in a striking manner in the incident, when Ajax himself, the strongest of the strong, for a moment is overwhelmed by the weight of his own shield, and is unable to use it without difficulty. And, again, on another occasion, we have an expressive illustration of the magnitude of these shields, which is not the less clearly described because the description is indirect rather than in express terms.

Hector, in the 6th Book of the "Iliad," is said to have quitted the battle-field for a brief space of time, and to have turned his footsteps towards Troy :—

> " Hector of the gleaming helm,
> Turned to depart ; and as he moved along,
> The black bull's-hide his neck and ancles smote,
> The outer circle of his bossy shield."

Il., vi. 137.

Thus the shield of the Trojan prince, when slung at his back for convenience in walking, covered his entire person from neck to heel. Even with such dimensions it might have been comparatively light, had the shield been long and narrow : but it was circular, or, at any rate, a rounded oval. It is easy to imagine how great must been the weight of such a shield, round or a rounded oval, when carried for defence upon the arm. At later periods, so far as we may judge from their monuments, the Greeks considerably reduced the dimensions of their shields; but even then they still continued to be of very great weight.[18]

It is more difficult to obtain a definite and clear idea concerning the form and structure of the Homeric *cuirass*. The one worn by Agamemnon is described by the poet in terms such as these :—

> " Himself his flashing armour donned.
> First, on his legs the well-wrought greaves he fixed,
> Fasten'd with silver clasps : his ample chest
> A breastplate guarded. . . .
> Ten bands were there inwrought of dusky bronze,
> Twelve of pure gold, twice ten of shining tin ;
> Of bronze six dragons upwards towards the neck
> Their length extended, three on either side ;
> In colour like the bow, which Saturn's son
> Placed in the clouds, a sign to mortal men."

Il., xi. 16.

Hector, as we have seen, wore a linen tunic beneath his cuirass ; and, from a passage presently to be quoted, we learn

D

that beneath his richly-wrought breastplate Menelaus wore a shirt of mail.

The military equipment of the Greeks of the era ot the Trojan war will not be complete without some notice of the *bow*, the *sling*, the light *dart*, the *helm*, and the *greaves*. The archers and the slingers formed the common soldiery of the Greek army, on whose courage in action the commanders could rely with comparatively little confidence. The warriors, on the other hand, who had achieved renown, and were well known by name, are represented as being armed with lance and sword, but they have neither bow nor sling. Paris, it is true, is an expert archer; but we know what character it is that Homer ascribes to him; and certainly, whatever his other qualifications, he is not distinguished amongst the Trojans for his personal bravery. Teucer, again, who ranks with the Greek heroes, has a bow; he is very young, however, so that in him, without any deficiency of courage, physical power is yet scarcely equal to bear the heroic arms. Meriones on one occasion, discharges an arrow which strikes Menelaus: still this would seem an exceptional attack, since at all other times he appears in the strife armed with the lance. The same may be said of some others of the heroes, who, as in the remarkable instance of Pandarus, use the bow occasionally, in order to show their extraordinary skill and address in the management of that weapon. It is not the less true, in consequence of the existence of these exceptional examples, that in the Trojan war, the archer, as a rule, performs a subordinate part. Not being able to carry a shield himself, the archer of that era was constrained to seek shelter in the rear of his comrades, or he would implore some hero to cover and protect him; and it is by no means difficult to understand how, in accordance with the sentiments of those times, such a procedure would imply something of degradation. One passage in the " Iliad " in a remarkable manner illustrates the

GREEK WARRIOR. From a fictile vase.

Greek Warrior. From a statue.

estimation in which the bow then was held.   It shows that
a shaft shot from a distance from a bow was sometimes
employed to strike down a warrior, who might be too formidable to be attacked hand to hand; and, consequently,
this use of the bow, while demonstrating its value, also
deprives that weapon of any heroic character.   (See Note 19.)

Æneas, observing the havoc that was made in the Trojan
ranks by Diomedes, seeks for Pandarus, the skilled archer:—

> " Him when Æneas saw amid the ranks
> Dealing destruction, through the fight and throng
> Of spears he plunged, if haply he might find
> The godlike Pandarus ; Lycaon's son
> He found. . . .
> . . . and addressed him thus :
> ' Where, Pandarus, are now thy wingèd shafts,
> ' Thy bow, and well-known skill, wherein with thee
> ' Can no man here contend ?   Nor Lycia boasts
> ' Through all her wide-spread plains a truer aim.
> ' Then raise to Jove thy hands, and with thy shaft
> ' Strike down this chief, whoe'er he be, that thus
> ' Is making fearful havoc in our host ! ' "
>
> *Il.*, v. 196.

On another occasion, before the effect of his arrow upon
Menelaus is described, the poet tells us what the *bow* of
Pandarus was like :—

> "Straight he uncased his polished bow, his spoil
> Won from a mountain ibex, which himself,
> In ambush lurking, through the breast had shot,
> True to his aim, as from behind a crag
> He came in sight ; prone on the rock he fell
> With horns of sixteen palms his head was crowned.
> These deftly wrought a skilful workman's hand,
> And polished smooth, and tipped the ends with gold.
> He bent, and resting on the ground his bow,
> Strung it anew. . . .
> His quiver then withdrawing from its case
> With care a shaft he chose, ne'er shot before,
> Well-feathered, messenger of pangs and death.

The stinging arrow fitted to the string. . . .
At once the sinew and the notch he drew ;
The sinew to his breast, and to the bow
The iron head ; then, when the mighty bow
Was to a circle strained, sharp rang the horn,
And loud the sinew twanged, as toward the crowd
With deadly speed the eager arrow sprang—
              ——it struck
Just where the golden clasps the belt restrained.
And where the breastplate, doubled, checked its force
On the close-fitting belt the arrow struck ;
Right through the belt of curious workmanship
It drove, and through the breastplate richly wrought,
And through the coat of mail he wore beneath,
His inmost guard, and best defence to check
The hostile weapon's force ; yet onward still
The arrow drove."

Il., iv. 119.

This is a passage which enables us to form a just conception of the exact, clear, and minute accuracy of Homer's descriptions; and to see in how remarkable a manner he conveys in a few words a multiplicity of details. It may be desirable for us to observe particularly certain points, that are set forth in this description of the bow of Pandarus with such careful and vivid distinctness. In the first place, this bow was made of horn; which, by a singular coincidence, was also the material that, in later times, formed the bows of the Moslemin whom the Crusaders encountered in Syria. The bow of the Greek hero, when in the field, was carried in a bow-case from which, when it was required for action, he brought it forth; and it was strung with a sinew, or with a bowstring formed of twisted sinews. The arrows, which had iron tips, were flighted with feathers: here is one of the rare occasions in which iron appears in the midst of the prevailing bronze of the Homeric age. That these arrows might, with the greater ease be adjusted to the bowstring, they were notched at their base. The adjustment of the arrow-heads is not noticed here; but, some few lines in advance, there follows a description of the manner in which they were inserted within a split in the head of the shaft, where they were made fast by a ligature of sinew. The *quiver* here described does not appear to resemble the classic quiver, as we are familiar with it in association with the archer divinities, Apollo and Diana. Instead of being an arrow-case, to be slung upright (or nearly so) over the shoulder, from which the heads of the arrows projected, the quiver of Pandarus certainly was an oblong box, covered with a skin which was drawn over the aperture in it; thus, it is said, that he "uncovers his quiver." It is remarkable that Homer describes the bow to have been used by placing one end of it on the ground, and holding the other end in the left hand, while with the right hand the string was drawn to the breast of the archer, whenever it was desired to secure for the aim the highest possible degree of precision. When bending his bow under such conditions as these, it is evident that the archer must have placed one knee upon the ground, if he did not discharge his weapon when actually sitting down."[19]

Concerning the *sling* but little can be said. It was made of a woollen stuff. The slingers formed the lowest rank in the army. Their position was in the rear of the men-at-arms, from whence they discharged stones from their slings; and, in order to avoid the heads of their comrades in their front, their aim must necessarily have been high.

The men-at-arms themselves, however, including the most dignified chiefs and renowned heroes, were skilled in hurling with their hands heavy stones—missile weapons of a truly primitive character, yet by no means devoid of effective power in the *mêlée* of battle, and even in single combat. As Homer tells us, they used to select the largest stones that they were able to carry, and fling them by sheer strength against their enemy. And many a shield which lances had failed

to penetrate, was crushed by a blow from a stone; or, even
if the good shield could resist such an assault as this, the
ponderous stone when thrown with great violence would beat
down and seriously injure the combatant by whom the shield
was carried.[20]

Thus in the combat between Hector and Ajax :—

> " Yet did not Hector of the gleaming helm
> Flinch from the contest : stooping to the ground,
> With his broad hand a ponderous stone he seized,
> That lay upon the plain; dark, jagged, and huge,
> And hurled against the seven-fold shield, and struck
> Full on the central boss ; loud rang the brass :
> Then Ajax raised a weightier mass of rock,
> And sent it whirling, giving to his arm
> Unmeasured impulse ; with a millstone's weight
> It crushed the buckler ; Hector's knees gave way ;
> Backward he staggered, yet upon his shield
> Sustained, till Phœbus raised him to his feet.
> Now had they hand to hand with swords engaged,
> Had not the messengers of gods and men,
> The heralds, interposed."   *Il.*, vii. 296

Again, Diomedes in his attack on Æneas :—

> "A rocky fragment then
> Tydides lifted up, a mighty mass,
> Which scarce two men could raise, as men are now,
> But he, unaided, lifted it with ease.
> With this he smote Æneas."

The Grecian festive games in reality were training exercises, carried on in a systematic manner, with a view to preparation for the military profession ; and it was from the game
of the *discus*, or quoit, that the Greeks learned to accustom
themselves, when engaged in warfare, to throw great stones
from a considerable distance with extraordinary force and
precision.

The *dart*, or true *javelin*, a light spear always to be distinguished from the lance, was shorter, and in every respect

slighter than that weapon. It was always used as a missile, and was thrown from the hand. The Greek warriors would hold several of these javelins in their hand, like a quiver of arrows, when they entered into the strife of battle ; and some of them were able to throw their javelins as well with their left hand as with their right. Agamemnon carried with him to battle two lances.

Homer gives to the *helm* or *casque* the epithet "long," which has been supposed to indicate either a long mass of horse-hair hanging down from the head-piece over the back of the wearer, or a lengthened covering to protect the back of the neck, and in front to have a projecting peak. The latter supposition seems to be the more probable. The helm was surmounted by a "long" crest, to which was attached a cluster of horse-hair, apparently fan-shaped. In addition to this decoration, which may be seen on some of the later monuments, on the sides of the Homeric Greek helms there were one or more small conical projections, designed to hold plumes. Agamemnon appears to have had four of these plume-bearers attached to his helm :—

> " Then on his brow his lofty helm he placed,
> Four-crested, double-peaked, with horse-hair plumes
> That nodded, fearful, from the warrior's head." *Il.*, xi. 42.

In like manner of Menelaus Homer says, that—

> " On his firm-set head
> A helm he wore, well wrought, with horse-hair plume
> That nodded, fearful o'er his brow " *Il.*, iii. 390.

Casques of a simpler kind are described in the 10th Book of the " Iliad :" they are worn by Diomedes and Ulysses :—

> " Then on his brow a leathern head-piece placed,
> Without or peak or plume ; a simple casque,
> Such as is worn by youths to guard their head."
>
> *Il.*, x. 287.

And Ulysses—
> "On his brows a leathern head-piece placed,
> Well-wrought within, with numerous straps secured ;
> And on the outside with wild boars' gleaming tusks
> Profusely garnished, scattered here and there
> By skilful hand ; the midst with felt was lined."
>
> *Il.*, x. 292.

The *greaves* ("*cnêmides*") completed the defence of the
body. They are leggings formed of a pewter-like metal,
which covered the lower limbs down to the instep ; and they
were fastened by clasps, as we have seen in the case of
Agamemnon. Homer designates them as " flexible;" and he
frequently speaks of the Greek soldiery as being well-equipped
with this important defence—not only, that is, well provided
with greaves, but also having them so well formed and
adjusted, that they would protect the limbs of the warrior
without in any degree affecting his freedom of movement
and action.

These greaves, as has been stated, appear to have been
formed of a metal resembling the alloy that we know as
pewter. The rest of this early armour with all the offensive
weapons (certain arrow-points excepted) used by the warriors
who wore it, whatever the mixed metal of which they were
composed, certainly were not of iron. With the exception
of a few arrow-heads, they were made of the alloy that may
be entitled bronze or hardened brass, an amalgamation, that is,
of copper with tin, not unlike the best kind of " latten" used
in the middle ages. The ancients sometimes added to this
all-important mixed metal some particles of silver, and even
of gold. This almost universal use of bronze does not imply
that in the Homeric age iron was altogether unknown. This,
indeed, is far from being the fact. The Greeks of that age
had discovered by what process iron might be brought into
use ; they were able to temper it, and they had actually commenced working in it; but it is certain that their knowledge

of the treatment of this great metal was very far from being
sufficiently advanced to enable them to produce in it their
weapons and armour. Homer speaks of iron as difficult to
work.

It is not possible, when taking a general survey of the arms
and armour of the Greeks of the Homeric age, to determine with any degree of exactness, their relative capacities
for injury and defence—the penetration of the one, and the
resistance of the other. Sometimes, in the many conflicts
in the " Iliad," lances, swords, and arrows were blunted or
broken upon either a hostile shield, or helm, or cuirass ; and,
on the contrary, sometimes the weapons pierced through the
armour, and even when one defence covers another, both are
occasionally penetrated. We may suppose, however, that those
warriors were generally in safety behind the shields, which
they were so careful to have made of such ample dimensions,
and which they always carried with them whenever they
went into action.

But the sketch of the military appliances of the heroic
era of Greece which Homer has given, is incomplete without a glance at the preliminary proceedings of the combatants
before they advance actually to blows. The grand incidents
of every battle are the single combats of the most formidable
and renowned warriors on either side ; around them the
interest is concentrated ; and upon their personal victory or
defeat the result of the day's engagement mainly, if not
absolutely, depends. Two chiefs advance in front of the
lines for a single combat : as they approach each other, they
hold a parley ; perhaps they discourse of many things, or
possibly at once and without any preface, they enter upon
mutual defiance and exasperating insult.[22] This occurs every
instant in Homer. It has its motive ; and the motive is
strictly in keeping with the matter in hand. Each hero
makes the same calculation, based upon the words he may

address to his adversary: as his speech proceeds, he will slightly draw back his shield, and in some degree lay himself open to an attack; he will tempt the foe to take the initiative; he will watch his own opportunity to strike at a favourable moment, when his enemy, by an injudicious, or unwary, or precipitate movement may be tempted in some measure to forsake his sheltering shield, and so may be attacked with a better prospect of success. And all the time the strange dialogue is sustained, until at length a blow is struck, and the struggle commences in earnest. All this proves in what high estimation these warriors held their shields, and how entirely they trusted to them for their defence. It is remarkable that when two warriors meet who are pre-eminent in military renown they pride themselves on departing from such vulgar tactics as these, and they fight at once, boldly and gallantly, without any attempt at a feint or *ruse* of any kind.

Thus, without any previous prolonged speech, Hector and Ajax, at Hector's bidding, commence their combat.

When these warriors challenged and strove to provoke one another by that pantomimic performance that has just been described, the motive of which may so easily be understood, they brandished their lances vehemently with their right hands, and with their left hands they raised and lowered and moved their shields to this side and to that. This would be an exercise attended with great fatigue, and particularly to the left arm. So that the warriors who on these occasions indulged in the longest discourses, may be supposed to have felt justified in trusting to their own superior strength and power of endurance ; and consequently they would calculate upon taking advantage of the exhaustion of an enemy less robust than themselves.

In the conclusion of this chapter, a few brief remarks upon the art of decorating arms and armour may consistently

be introduced. The arms of Achilles have led us to surmise
that the Homeric Greeks understood how to employ for this
purpose the art of engraving, with singular effectiveness. The
arms of Agamemnon, simpler in the style of their decoration than those of the son of Thetis, were adorned by the
introduction of various metals, which were worked in combination. In several passages, Homer speaks of a metallic
composition under the name of "*cyane*," which was greatly
in favour for the ornamentation of cuirasses and of the bosses
of shields. What this decorative composition or process may
have been, is not now known with any certainty; still, it is
highly probable that it may have been a species of enamel
of a bluish black colour: and, as the antique bronze of
which the arms and armour were composed was of a golden
hue, it is possible that this favourite decoration may have produced results not unlike what we now know as *niello*.

CHAPTER III.

THE IRON PERIOD.—ARMS AND ARMOUR OF THE GREEKS OF
THE HISTORIC AGES; AND THOSE OF THE PERSIANS AND
THEIR ALLIES IN THE GRECO-PERSIAN WAR.—ALSO THE
BRONZE ARMS AND ARMOUR OF THE ETRUSCANS.

WHEN now we enter upon this period it will be kept in remembrance, that the use of both armour and weapons of
bronze by no means ceases; but, on the contrary, that armour
and weapons of both bronze and iron during this period are
in use together. As the period advances, the bronze gradually falls into disuse, and the iron as gradually becomes
more general. Thus, in the "Iron Period," from the first,
in arms and armour iron aspires to reign; and, after a while,
the supremacy of the iron is fully established.

SECTION I.

Arms and Armour of the Greeks and Persians.

It is desirable that we here should introduce a slight description of the three classes of ancient Greek soldiers, for
whose use arms and armour had to be provided.

1. The *Hoplite*, or man-at-arms, a heavily-equipped soldier,
who never went into action except in his own proper position
in the phalanx. With the remarkable and celebrated aggroup-
ment or formation known under this term "phalanx," all
readers of history are familiar; still, it may be as well to
make a few remarks upon it. At different periods the
phalanx varied greatly in the numbers of the soldiers by
whom it was composed. In its earliest condition, its numbers

scarcely exceeded 200.   At the period of the Persian wars, on
the other hand, the number of men who formed the phalanx
had risen to 5,000, thus giving to this formation the weight
and importance of a " division " of an army.   Still later, in
the wars of the Greeks with the Romans, the phalanx embodied an army 16,000 strong.   But notwithstanding these
very decided changes in the numerical force of this body,
from first to last the Greek phalanx maintained unchanged
the same tactics and the same manner of fighting.   The
hoplites were formed sixteen deep; the soldiers in the same
rank stood firmly pressed one against the other, helmets
touching helmets, shields partly covering shields (as Homer
tells, for already, in his early time, the idea of that close and
deep battalion, the phalanx, had dawned upon the Greeks);
and grasping their long spears (*sarisses*), they strove to resist
and defeat the attacks of the enemy by compactness and
cohesion.   Later, when treating of the Roman legion, we
shall see both the advantages and the disadvantages of this
system of fighting very clearly set forth by a master of ancient military tactics, the historian Polybius.

For offensive weapons the Greek hoplite had the *sword*,
and the *spear, pike,* or *sarisse,* of which latter mention has
just been made.   This last term " sarisse," is particularly
applicable to the pike when it was in use in the Macedonian
armies; but under whatever name it might have been known,
this long pike, with some slight variation in its length, was
always the same weapon.   In the time of Polybius the length
of the pike was twenty-one or twenty-four feet; so that in
the phalanx formation the pikes of the front rank projected
at least sixteen feet in advance of the line ; while those of
the second, third, fourth, fifth, and sixth ranks severally projected about thirteen, ten, seven, four, and two feet; and so
the head of each file presented to the enemy the points of
six levelled pikes, each one of them about three feet in

advance of the next in the series. Some examples of Greek weapons are represented in the woodcut, Fig. 7.

The *sword*, long when compared with that of the Romans, but rather short than long if placed side by side with the swords of the middle ages, is pointed, double-edged, swelling with graceful curves in the middle of the blade, and nar-

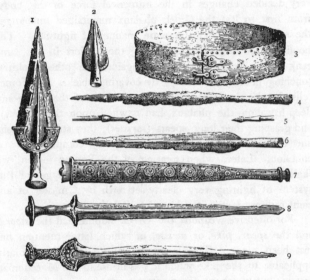

Fig. 7.—GREEK ARMS.

1. A Dagger.   2. A Javelin-head.   3. A bronze Belt.   4 and 6. Lance-heads.
5. Arrow-heads.   7. Sword-scabbard.   8 and 9. Swords.

rower as the blade approaches the hilt. Thus, like the earlier weapon represented in Fig. 6, No. 1, it has some resemblance in its contour to the sage-leaf. It is fixed to the hilt by rivets passing through a long and strong spike. The scabbard, in form an attenuated oblong, constructed of metal and variously adorned, generally is guarded at its extremity with an enriched button or bouterolle.

The defensive equipment of the hoplite consisted of a *leathern tunic* (not a corslet or cuirass), a *helm, shield,* and *greaves.*

The *shield* was generally round, but occasionally oval. Its exact dimensions are not known, for in the early monuments shields appear of very different sizes; none, however, are seen to cover the whole man from head to heel, like the Homeric shield of Hector. It is probable that the ancient shield, in consequence of its excessive weight, did not remain very long in fashion. Some Greek shields of the period now before us are seen to reach from the shoulder to the knee; and another, a more common type, is of still smaller dimensions, and covers but little more than the breast. The largest of these shields may be considered to have been borne by the hoplites, and to be the true battle-shield of all the Greek soldiers. The feature which is common to all these shields is the bold convexity of the external surface; and they also are alike in having their circle bounded at its circumference by a flat band or border: an example of such a shield as this is given in Fig. 16.[23]

In Greek monuments three distinct varieties of *helms* are depicted. One, which appears to date back from a remote antiquity, consists of a close-fitting cap, a lengthened neck-guard, pendant guards for the face which are attached to the cap on each side by hinges to give free movement, and an elevated visor or frontlet of a triangular pediment-like form, which in reality is simply a decoration for the front of the helm. (See Fig. 8, Nos. 2 and 4.) The crest, with the panache or plume, appears under a great variety of forms; but the prevailing arrangement is for the prolonged crest to be carried from the visor to the neck-guard, and to be covered with a plume or tuft displayed like a fan. This gives that fine military aspect to the helm, with which all are familiar who have studied either the original ancient monuments, or

E

pictures and engravings which give faithful representations of them.   (See Fig. 16.)

The second type of Greek helm may be described as a deep head-piece with a long projecting peak, visor, or "nasal," and at the back a deep neck-guard (*garde-nuque*); upon the peak or visor, the nose and eyes of a human

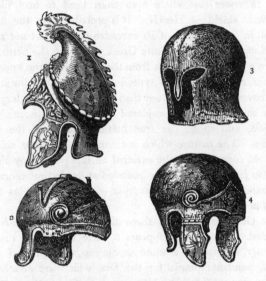

Fig. 8.—Nos. 2, 3, 4. GREEK HELMS.   No. 1. A LYDIAN HELM.

face are indicated with more or less distinctness.   There seldom is any crest, but some examples are surmounted by the figure of a bird or animal, as the figure of an owl, a lion, a horse, &c.   This is the well-known helm represented on figures of Minerva (Pallas Athené), to which we shall again advert when we come to treat of decorated armour.

The third variety, distinguished as the " Bœotian Helm," was preferred to all others by warriors—a preference easy to be understood when we consider the characteristic qualities of the helm itself. It is a deep head-piece, with neck and cheek-guards (*jugulaires*), the whole being wrought into a simple solid mass, which would cover and effectually protect the wearer from the shoulders upwards, with the exception of the face only; and even here the nasal, seconded by the projection of the cheek-guards, would afford an almost perfect defence—a defence, indeed, nearly as perfect as was consistent with freedom for sight and breathing. This helm is shown in Fig. 8, No. 3. In front, this helm, from the arrangement of the nasal and of the cheek-guards,

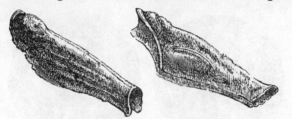

Fig. 9.—GREEK GREAVES.

has somewhat the appearance of the human countenance in its essential features of eyes and nose. It is the true military helm of the Greeks; and it may be assumed as certain that it was universally adopted, soon after its introduction, by all the *élite* of the Greek warriors, including the whole array of the hoplites. In Fig. 8, No. 1, an example of a Lydian helm is given.[24]

The *greaves* (*cnémides*) at this period, instead of the pewter of the Homeric age, were made of bronze. They were fitted to the limbs, so that in consequence of their form, and aided by the elasticity of the metal, they were worn without requiring any clasp or other fastening. It appears also that his greaves were made specially to fit each warrior. Examples are given in Fig. 9.

2. The *Peltaste*, or javelin-man, a soldier lightly armed.
for weapons of offence had a *sword* and a *javelin, pelta,* or
dart, which weapon in his hand represented the spear or
pike of the hoplite; but as a general rule it was used by n.m
as a missile to be thrown from the hand. This *javelin* was
provided with a leathern strap (*amentum*), fixed about the
middle of the shaft, and into this the first two fingers of the
hand were inserted, in order to give both greater force and
a more sure certainty of aim, when the weapon was thrown.
The *shield* of the peltaste was considerably smaller and
lighter than that of the hoplite; probably it was identical

Fig. 10.—A GREEK SHIELD.

with the smallest of the shields that have been already described. In Fig. 10, a representation of a small circular
Greek shield is given, and both the inside and the exterior
face of it are shown. The *helm* of this warrior, and his
greaves, differed but little, if they differed at all (except perhaps in being lighter), from those of the hoplites.

3. The *Knight,* or mounted warrior, who was armed with
a *sword* and a long *lance,* wore a *cuirass,* which, better
known by its Roman name of *thorax,* or *breastplate,* than by
its Greek name, was so modelled as to conform to the figure
of the bust of the wearer, as appears from Fig. 11. In this
respect the Greek cuirass differed from the corresponding

piece of Roman armour, that it generally was finished at the waist; and from this point it was continued by pendant straps of leather, *lambrequins*, cut square at the ends, and set close together, which fell over the lower part of the body and reached as far as the thighs in double and sometimes in treble ranks. The cuirass was made of two pieces, breast and back plates, united by hinges on one side, and on the

Fig. 11.—A GREEK CUIRASS, BREAST AND BACK PLATES.

other side closed with clasps; over the shoulders it was sustained by thick straps of leather, which we may entitle *épaulières* (*shoulder-straps*, or *shoulder-guards*).

A weapon which appears to have been in general use by all classes of Greek soldiers, is a short sword or *dagger*, called *parazonium* (belt-companion), which sometimes was reduced to the proportions of a knife. Like the sword itself, this smaller weapon has a blade shaped like the sage-leaf; or, occasionally its blade, as in Fig. 7, No. 1, tapers in straight lines from the hilt to the point. The same weapon we shall find again in the armoury of the Romans, who borrowed it from the Greeks. [See Fig. 15, No. 4.] It was adjusted at the waist, as was the mediæval *misericorde*, on the right side, while the sword hung on the left side; but the ancient dagger

*

had its own short shoulder-belt, by which it was held in an oblique position, the pommel of the hilt being level with the breast of the wearer.

It is not possible thus to take a survey of the military equipment of the ancient Greeks at the grand period of their history, when they repelled the successive invasions of the Persians, without calling to remembrance the famous battles of Marathon, Salamis, Platæa, and above all of Thermopylæ. Our knowledge of those battles and of the Greek and Persian war, being derived entirely from Greek sources, at least must be considered in some degree imperfect, since we can scarcely suppose the narratives of the Greek writers to be strictly impartial when treating of such a subject. Possibly, as we see all the incidents of that memorable strife only from a Greek point of view, the forces of the enemy may appear to us greater and more formidable than in reality they were, the chances of successful resistance may appear more desperate, and both the struggles more severe and the victories more glorious than we might be disposed to regard them, were we able to compare Persian chronicles with those of Greece.[23] Be this as it may, having now just passed before us in review the armed Greeks who fought in that war, it certainly cannot fail to be interesting to enquire what may have been the military equipment of their Persian adversaries. In his army, which, according to Herodotus, numbered 1,700,000 men, Xerxes included contingents from every realm and race of his vast empire ; and, accordingly, if we are enabled to collect sketches of all the various costumes and arms which thus were brought together, many of them by most unwilling wearers, in the expedition of the Persian king, we shall have seen something of almost every nation at that time known to have been in existence. Herodotus, who has described the enormous army, will be found ready to give us many striking details of their equipment.

First, the *Persians* themselves. On their heads they wore turbans, or caps of compressed felt, which they called "tiaras," and consequently they were without helms; sleeved tunics of various colours they had; laminated corslets also of iron or steel—corslets, that is, formed of rows of metal scales sewn upon garments of leather or linen, in such a manner that the scales in each row would overlap those in the row below them; their shields, called *gerrhes*, were made of wicker-work, and were rhomboidal in form; short darts, large bows, cane arrows, and daggers hung from the right-side (it will be observed that no swords are mentioned), completed their equipment.

The *Medes* were armed and accoutred after the same fashion.

The *Assyrians* (it will be understood, as a matter of course, that we now shall specify only the weapons that are peculiar to each people; certain weapons, such as the dart, the bow, and the dagger, being common to all races and nations, it would be superfluous to mention them in every instance again)—the Assyrians were distinguished by their brazen helms, which are described to us as being interwoven or interlaced; and by their defensive tunics of flax. It is by no means easy to form a correct idea of these interwoven Assyrian helms; but, it is probable that the historian intends his words to convey the impression, that he was describing head-pieces formed of brass mail—of rings or chain-work, which might be interwoven or interlaced, precisely after the manner of the mediæval "mail coif;" such defences for the head are still in use in the east; and who shall assert that they have not been transmitted, in true conformity with oriental unchangeableness, to the present day from a far distant antiquity? The cuirasses, or defensive tunics of flax, were in use also, as Herodotus himself informs us, amongst the *Egyptians;* they were formed of several strips or layers of

woven flax, sometimes as many as eighteen, which were glued
together one above another, after they had undergone a long
maceration in a composition of wine and salt. These cuirasses, it seems, would resist a heavy blow struck with the edge
of a weapon, but they were not proof against a well-delivered
thrust of the point of sword or spear; notwithstanding this
imperfection, they were held in great favour amongst the
nations of antiquity. The Greeks themselves adopted them,
and wore them, contemporaneously with the metal corslet,
until a late period. Pausanias says, that in hunting the flaxen
cuirass was peculiarly serviceable, since, if it would not afford
against weapons held in human hands so sure a defence as the
corslet, against the attacks of savage animals it was at once
convenient and thoroughly efficient. Perhaps, being much
less costly than the corslet of metal, the flaxen cuirass was
often adopted when the more valuable piece of armour was
not to be obtained. As we shall see hereafter, the Romans,
like the Greeks, included the flaxen cuirass in their defensive
equipment.

The *Ethiopians*, clothed in the skins of lions and leopards,
had bows, at least six feet in length, made of palm-tree wood ;
long cane arrows that were tipped, not with iron, but with
sharp pieces of stone ; and darts headed with the pointed
horns of roebucks. Here are evidences of a much less advanced civilisation ; and, indeed, all these weapons, precisely
as Herodotus has described them, are still to be found amongst
many savage tribes of the natives of Africa.

The *Lydians* in their arms and armour resembled the
Greeks.

The weapons and armour that were characteristic of the
Phrygians were the shield and the axe. The shield, circular,
or nearly so, at the base, was cut off in two slopes to the right
and left at its summit. The axe, or *bipennis*, was double-
edged, having the edges set back to back, and between them

the long shaft or handle is produced until it ends in a point; or, sometimes, this axe has an edge on one side only, when on the other side it has either a hook or a hammer. This Phrygian shield, of very elegant form, and this same axe, are found in all the combats of the Amazons which antiquity has bequeathed to us; and, in consequence of the eminent popularity of the subject, representations of these singular combats are very numerous. It is not for us here to investigate, and much less to endeavour to determine, the accuracy of the legend which describes the existence of a race of warlike women who lived on the banks of the Thermodon in Asia Minor. Still, without any question, by the universal consent of antiquity, the Phrygians were considered to have been descendants of these Amazons; and, consequently, the Phrygian arms, in representations of the Amazons, are assigned to those celebrated warrior-ancestresses, as they were supposed to be, of the Phrygians themselves. The Amazons, perhaps, are fabulous; but the weapons and armour of the Phrygians, whether their descendants or not, are real.[26]

Section II.

Arms and Armour of the Etruscans.

The relics that have come down to us of the arms and armour of the Etruscans we might have correctly and consistently grouped with those worn and used by other races during the bronze ages; but it has appeared to be preferable, on the whole, that they should be placed after the arms and armour of the Greeks of the historic period, and in immediate connection with them, in consequence of the evident alliance that exists between the Greek and Etruscan armories. The weapons of the Etruscans that remain to us are, it is true, but few in number; still some examples are preserved in the various museums of Europe, and what is deficient in actual relics is amply supplied in the compositions represented upon innumerable painted vases, and also in the decorations of various Etruscan sepulchres.

The first glance at the ancient pictorial representations of Etruscan armed warriors shows that they can be distinguished from Greeks, only by certain eccentric details of their equipment, while in more important particulars no difference whatever can be detected.

The *cuirass*, like that of the Greeks, is formed of conjoined breast and back plates, which never descend below the waist; but the *épaulières*, or shoulder-guards, of this Etruscan cuirass, which are very thick and large above and narrowed below, are joined together over the chest of the wearer, and they have some resemblance to that arrangement in a modern waistcoat which is entitled "double-breasted:" this is one of

Fig. 12.—ETRUSCAN HELMS.

the eccentricities of which we have just spoken. Amongst the most decided points of resemblance may be specified the habit of the Etruscan warriors to carry, almost invariably, in their hands the short Greek sword or dagger, the *parazonium;* and the Etruscan *shield*, which, exactly in accordance with the Greek usage, resembles a large circular globose dish with a flat rim.

Of the *helm* there are many varieties. Two, which are the most frequently to be seen, it will be sufficient for us to describe. One is a helm of a deep bell shape, after the Greek fashion, such as Fig. 12, No. 1. Sometimes this helm is surmounted by a narrow crest, excessively elevated, and bent down so as to droop; and expanded wings are added on both sides, rising from the bell of the helm. The other variety, Fig. 12, No. 2, has the bell of a more conical form; it is crested, and has wings of extravagant proportions, which impart to the head-piece a wild and fantastic appearance.

CHAPTER IV.

THE ARMS AND ARMOUR OF THE ROMANS.

SECTION I.

Defensive Armour.

ALREADY it has been incidentally stated, while describing its
Greek prototype, that the *Roman cuirass* from its earliest period
was formed of two pieces of metal, breast and back plates,
which, being adjusted with *épaulières* and joined together
with hinges and clasps, were modelled to represent with
a greater or less degree of fidelity those parts of the
human frame which they covered and protected. In examples
of the Roman cuirass of the highest order this modelling is
very perfect, and the exact form of the chest and of the lower
part of the body is expressed with the most careful precision;
consequently, when no additional ornamentation is introduced,
the Roman warrior armed in his cuirass, when represented in
sculpture, can scarcely be distinguished from a nude figure.
The modelling of the cuirass, however, was not considered to
preclude the introduction of various decorative figures of
animals and birds, with foliage and arabesques, which were
executed either by engraving or in low relief.

This cuirass is shown to have been supported on each
shoulder by a strap, which in front fastens to a ring fixed in
the cuirass itself, and behind upon the back plate it buckles
over the shoulder-blade. From the upper edge of the
hollow, through which passes the arm of the warrior and the
half-sleeve of his tunic, there hang short straps of leather,
plaited or knotted at their lower extremity, which fall over
the upper arm. From the bottom of the cuirass there fall

two thick borders, generally of leather, jagged, of which the upper one partially covers the lower; and from below this double border there issue the leathern *lambrequins*—a shield-like defensive covering reaching nearly to the knee, formed of very many curled or plaited straps, of the same shape as the shoulder-straps, but broader, and sometimes plated with metal.

The cuirass was put on over the *tunic*, of which the half-sleeves, as has been stated, appeared covering the arms; and the skirt, without falling quite so low as the knee, was seen descending a little from within the lambrequins. Over the cuirass was worn the military *mantle*, the *paludimentum*, which the ancients draped in an endless variety of folds and in the most picturesque style. It is frequently exhibited in Roman statutes so adjusted, that it is tied by the two ends over the right shoulder; the neck of the wearer passes through the open space between these two ends; the right arm is free; the mantle covers the left shoulder, falls over the front of the left arm in graceful folds, and flowing the length of the body, hangs down as far as the middle of the leg. Such is the Roman military equipment, which obtained until the era of the first of the emperors.

If we are to accept the authority of Polybius, in his time (about B.C. 160) the plate cuirass was the armour of the private soldiers in the ranks of the legions, and the laminated or scaled cuirass was worn in its stead by men who had attained to some military rank. The most ancient monuments, upon which naturally we see represented only the figures of generals and other military chiefs, show us the cuirass only, as we have described it; but, subsequently, when private soldiers are introduced into the representations, notwithstanding the statements of Polybius, they appear either without any body-armour, or equipped in a cuirass of a very different form. On the columns of Trajan and Antoninus, in every instance, from the emperor to the centurions, the cuirass is worn by chiefs alone; and as it is worn by them it has undergone a decided and marked change, since, instead of entirely covering the body, and having the form of the human frame, as at earlier periods was the case, here it is seen to stop short at the waist, after the old Greek fashion; the jagged border also has disappeared, and there only remain two rows of the lambrequin-straps, one above the other, and they both descend much lower than was the earlier Roman usage.[77]

The cuirass of the private soldier, such as it appears in the bas-reliefs of both the Trajan and the Antonine columns, is composed of three perfectly distinct parts, the cuirass proper, and the two shoulder-pieces. The cuirass itself is a garment of leather or linen, upon which are sewn circular plates of iron. Each of these circles or discs is made of two half-circles, joined at the back by a hinge, and closing in front by a clasp. The shoulder-pieces, formed of four plates, and smaller than those of the cuirass, to which . hey are fixed at their extremities, pass over the shoulders like straps. Sometimes, from the bottom of the cuirass there fell four small oblong plates adjusted vertically, which cover the middle of the body below the waist. This armour left the upper part of the chest without any protection. Some indications, which are by no means so clear and satisfactory as we should have desired, in the Trajan column, lead to the supposition that the part of the chest otherwise unprotected was covered with a piece of stout leather, or with an iron plate. The cuirass, as it is here described, was not the appointment of the private soldiers, but only of the *élite* of their rank, the regular legionaries.

As it is so well known, there were in the Roman army three distinct orders or classes of soldiers : first, and in their dignified rank in a manner resembling the knights of the feudal ages, the *equites*, whom we style by the mediæval title of *knights*, who formed the cavalry ; second, the *legionarii*, the soldiers of the legions; and third, the *velites*, or light infantry, whose entire equipment was in exact conformity with their distinctive denomination. The arms, armour, and appointments of the *legionarii* we have already considered.

The *velites* did not wear any corslet or cuirass, but their tunic appears to have been formed of leather, which would account for the rigid aspect which it presents in representations; it was generally escalloped at the bottom. It is possible also that the velites sometimes wore, instead of leather, a tunic of quilted linen.

The *knights* sometimes are depicted equipped with scale-armour (the *squammata*), consisting of a tunic of leather or of linen, upon which are sewn scales of steel which overlap so as to cover the entire surface; or, sometimes, their cuirass, instead of scale-work, is covered with a species of mail formed of metal chains (*hamata*). Very commonly, also, the knight appears, habited like one of the velites, in that flaxen cuirass of which mention was made (page 51) when we were giving descriptions of the armour of both the Egyptians and the Greeks. This same military defensive garment was also unquestionably well known to the Romans, and habitually used by them; and, though on the monuments, as would naturally be the case, we may not be able to distinguish this from other defensive garments that were made of woven fabrics, the linen cuirass we may feel sure has its place amongst the appointments that are represented.

Polybius speaks of short boots of metal, *ocreæ*, which were worn by the Roman soldiers of his time; but on the monuments of later times no vestige of them is visible, except only in the statues of the emperors.

The Trajan column, to which we always must recur whenever we desire to obtain exact and minutely accurate information upon Roman armour, gives us examples of two varieties of *shields*. In its form, one of these shields is an elongated and convex oblong, somewhat resembling a hollowed water-course tile; many soldiers are seen holding this shield uplifted, to cover their heads, and when in that position it is exactly the length of the left arm which is carrying it. As it evidently was narrow in order to prevent its being oppressively heavy or cumbersome, by the dexterity of their movements the soldiers would have to make good for their own defence whatever deficiency might otherwise have arisen from the small proportions of their shields. Moreover, we know in what manner this shield was constructed. It was made of two plates of metal dovetailed together; and both at the head and the base of the shield an iron border was fixed, in the one case that the shield might be stronger to resist blows, and in the other that it might not suffer any injury from resting (as frequently it would have to rest) upon the ground. As its only ornament this shield bore on its outer face the insignia of the legion; so, for example, the soldiers on the column of Trajan, whose legion bore the title of "the thundering," display upon their shields a thunderbolt, of the same familiar form that is represented in his statues held in the right hand of Jupiter.[28] This variety of shield is peculiar to the legionaries.

Fig. 13.—ROMAN SOLDIERS : from the Column of Trajan, A.D. 114.

The other variety of Roman shield, now to be described, in shape is an elongated oval, and its convexity is considerably less than in the former shield. Its decoration varies. The ornament of most frequent occurrence is a device somewhat

resembling a vine-branch entwined about a rod or staff. This
shield was carried by both the knights and the velites. Here
and there, besides, but always upon the same monument
with the two varieties of shields that have been described,
some hexagonal bucklers may be seen; but this piece of
armour, which certainly is not Roman, belongs to some
auxiliary corps of barbarians. In Fig. 13, a group of three
Roman soldiers is shown, as they are represented upon the
column of Trajan.

When we direct our attention to monuments of an age
later than that of the Trajan column, we no longer find the
rectangular shield; but, in its stead, the shield of oval contour is found to have been assumed by the legionaries themselves. The dimensions of this oval shield are also seen to
have been enlarged, at the same time that the Roman sword
became a considerably longer weapon than of old it had been.
Hence it is evident that as their former high discipline
gradually relaxed, the soldiers of the Roman legions abandoned the small shield and the short sword, which required
in the men who were armed with them consummate cool-
ness and admirable dexterity, and inclined to the adoption of
the arms of the barbarians.

The Roman *helm* is distinguished at once from the Greek
by its remarkable want of depth. It is, in fact, an iron (or
steel) skull-cap, strengthened by two cross-bands, furnished
with a hollowed neck-guard at the back, and in front finished
with a narrow band, or having a small bar (*bagnette*) acting
as a visor. Cheek-pieces of iron fastened this helm under
the chin; and a ring, placed at the crossing of the two
strengthening bands, took the place of a crest. Such was the
helm of the legionaries in the time of Trajan. On the march
the soldiers slung their helms by the clasped cheek-pieces
from their right shoulders, and they advanced bare-headed.
The helm that was worn by both the *equites* and the *velites*

F

was considerably widened at its base and also much flattened
in its contour.   The chiefs always appear having their heads
uncovered, nor in any single instance do we see them wearing
any helm.   [See Fig. 15, Nos. 2 and 3.]

In the declining days of the empire the Roman helm
conforms in many particulars to the early Greek type.   The
head-piece itself is deeper, and it is furnished with a long
lowered visor or nasal.   In all other respects this is the era in
which uniformity and precision appear to have ceased to exist.
Swords very long in the blade were in use at the same time,
and apparently by the same corps, with others that were very
short; small shields, some of them circular, and others hexagonal, were intermixed with other circular shields of such
extravagant size, that their counterparts can be found only in
the old Homeric descriptions of heroic equipment; and so,
in like manner, similar incongruities and inconsistencies were
universally prevalent.   All these things declared but too significantly the character and the tendencies of those times.   And
of those times there exist but a very few monuments, nor is
the number of the written records either greater or more
richly stored with graphic information.   Thus, it is not possible
for us to determine the precise period of particular pieces of
of armour or of certain weapons, nor are we able with more
decided certainty to fix the corps to which they ought to be
assigned.   The good old Roman traditions then had passed
away; and the fine discipline and the strict order of earlier
and better days, having fallen into contempt, speedily passed
away with them.[29]

SECTION II.

Offensive Weapons.

The *Pilum*, that most formidable spear, which, according
to Montesquieu, subdued the world, of which Polybius has
given an elaborate description, and which might have been

found in abundance upon every Roman field of battle, strange
to say, at the present time still continues to be amongst the
most experienced archæologists a subject for discussion. Like
the famous Trojan ancestor of the equally famous founder of
Rome, the Roman pilum, the most renowned weapon of antiquity, remains enveloped in a cloud of uncertainty. In this
condition of doubt, we turn to Polybius, and observe what
he has recorded concerning the pilum. It was, according
to him, a spear having a very large iron head or blade, and
this was carried by a socket to receive the shaft. The socket
itself in length about nineteen inches, which was almost one-
third of the length of the entire weapon, was strengthened
towards its base, until it became not less than three half-
fingers in thickness. The swelling which thus was caused by
this formation of the socket, together with its extreme length,
were peculiar to the pilum. It bore no resemblance to any
other weapon of the same class, either lance, pike, or javelin.
At present we have been able to discover no ancient example
which in every particular corresponds with this description.
The nearest approach to it is a kind of pike, which is represented borne in the hands of two Roman soldiers of the
fifteenth legion (the *primigenia*) upon a funeral *cippus* at
Mayence.[30] These figures are in bas-relief. The striking
feature in the pike in this monument is, that at about three-
quarters of its height from its base it has a swelling which
presents the appearance of a large knot, or a ball of thread
pierced by a needle; and, besides this, the blade has the
dimensions that are specified. It is probable that this was
intended to represent a pilum of a later age than that of
Polybius, if not a weapon of that class of his own age; and
thus it may have experienced some modifications in its form
and its peculiarities.

Concerning the use and management of this famous
weapon we have not been left in any uncertainty. By the

soldiers of the legions, to whom the use of the pilum was restricted, this weapon was both hurled from the hand as a javelin, and grasped firmly, as well for the charge as to resist and beat down hostile attacks. The weight of the pilum caused it to be regarded rather as a spear than as a dart; and, from this same circumstance, when it was to be used as a missile weapon, the pilum could be thrown with effect only from a comparatively short distance, and by strong and skilful hands. When in use as a spear or lance, the pilum not only discharged the duties performed by the modern bayonet, but it also was equally efficient to ward off sword-blows with the long and strong socket, which was made, indeed, for that very purpose. The blows of the Gallic sword, much more violent than dangerous, the Roman legionary received with cool steadiness upon his strong pilum; and in so doing he notched the hostile blades to such a degree that, as Polybius has said, he changed them into mere *strigiles* (skin-scrapers) such as they used in the baths.

If the pilum, in Roman hands, was really the instrument which wrought a change in the apparent destiny of the world, it must have acquired this great power, as it would seem, not from its own intrinsic excellence as an offensive weapon, but from the fact that its use implied careful drill and constant exercise and practice on the part of the soldier. Unlike the Greek hoplite, who stood or moved in his dense phalanx, an armed automaton rather than a living warrior, the Roman legionary with his pilum was a true soldier—brave, cool, self-reliant, well qualified alike for the skirmish and the close combat, able to act independently, and always ready to take a part with his comrades in displaying both the firm solidity and the steady movements of a highly disciplined force.*

* *Note in the original French, by the author, M. Lacombe.*—" At the moment in which I was writing these remarks upon the Roman *pilum*,"

The exact shape of the Roman *sword* earlier than the time of Scipio,[31] is not known (about B.C. 150); but after his era, and we may thank him for the fact, the Roman sword is

says M. Lacombe, "I learned that the eminent professor of the school at Chartres, M. J. Quicherat, had discovered the lost form, or forms (for without any change in its essential and characteristic peculiarities, the pilum had more than one established and recognised form) of this celebrated weapon. I am indebted to his obliging communication for the following facts:—'For the future it may be accepted as certain, that the pike represented in the hands of the soldiers of the "legio primigenia," in the bas-relief at Mayence, of which mention has just been made, is the *pilum ;* but the weapon shown on this monument belongs to a later age than that of Polybius, and it is not the pilum which that author has described. The true original pilum, however, is found to have been represented on the monument at St. Rémi, in Provence, which, after having long been considered to belong to the era of the lower Latinity, at length has been recognised as undoubtedly a genuine work of the age of the first Emperors.' It is this original figure of the *pilum,* now that its authenticity has been thoroughly established by M. Quicherat, which has enabled that judicious observer to follow the career of the weapon, to trace it through the various modifications and degradations which during the lapse of time it experienced, and to detect its presence here and there with positive certainty under a number of forms which till now had appeared to be strange, and capricious, and unintelligible. These fanciful and exceptional weapons at length have ceased to be perplexing, and now are capable of receiving a consistent classification. I had myself made a collection of these very examples," remarks M. Lacombe, " with the intention of adducing them as specimens of eccentric arms ; but, instead of this, the discovery and researches of Professor Quicherat have determined their proper rank and place in the armoury of Rome.

"In order that we may be enabled clearly to understand the tenacity with which the one peculiar characteristic of this weapon, its massive iron socket-rim, was retained in every variety of form that the pilum assumed, it will be necessary for us to consider the special object which the pilum itself was desired to accomplish in the act of conflict. This object was that, after being thrust through the shield of an enemy, the pilum should bend by its own weight and drag along the ground, without permitting the enemy to shake it off or in any way to liberate himself from so distressing an embarrassment ; the consequence would be

found to have been identical with the well-known Spanish or Iberian weapon of the same order. This sword was worn on the right side, a mode of

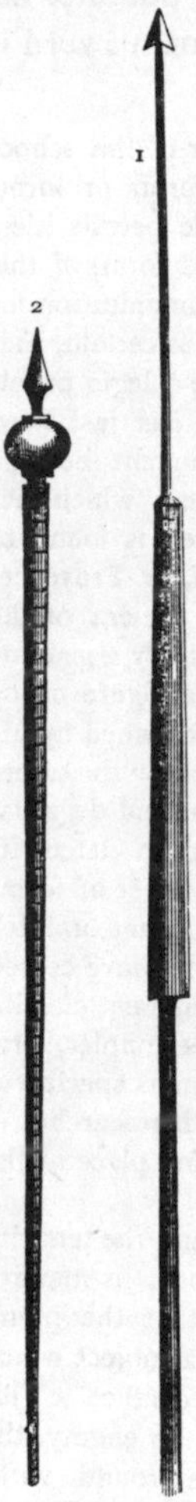

that the enemy would find his shield no longer of any service—it would paralyse his movements if he retained it, and it would leave him unprotected should he cast it away ; and, in either case, with his shield pierced by a bent pilum, the enemy would be exposed to the assault of the terrible sword of the legionary. It was the thick heavy band of iron (*bourrelet*) which strengthened the socket of its head or blade not far from the centre of the shaft of the weapon, that aided in giving momentum to the blow of the pilum, and then both caused it to bend and prevented it from breaking. It was with precisely the same object in view, in later times, as hereafter we shall observe more particularly, the Franks made use of a lance having a boss at the base of the lance-head, and of the ' angon' —the barbed javelin, which was a favourite weapon amongst that people. In Fig. 14, are shown two examples of the ' pilum,' both of them of degenerate eras, and which give only an approximate idea of the original weapon. No. 1, however, approaches deci- dedly nearer than No. 2 to the original type."

The account given by Polybius of the *pilum* that was in use, in early times, in the armies of Rome, is too obscure to enable us to derive from his words any very clear ideas concerning that famous weapon of antiquity.

Vegetius, in his essay *de re militari*, says that the javelins, or missile spears, used by the soldiery in the Roman army of the Lower Empire, were called *pila ;* and he adds one remarkable particular concerning the *pila* of that period, to the effect that they had slender iron heads of *trilateral* form—*ferro subtili trigono præ- fixa* are his words. The *pilum*, having a head such as this, measuring from 9 to 12 inches in length, also had its trilateral head *barbed*, in order to prevent its ready extraction from a hostile shield—so that *in scuto fixa non possent abscindi* (lib. i., c. 20). And, again,

Fig. 14.
Two Varieties of
the Pilum.

adjustment possible only when the weapon, contrary to the prevailing character of its form, is short in the blade. Accordingly, all the monuments concur in giving evidence, that, at and about the era of Cæsar, the Roman sword was remarkable in the highest degree for the shortness of its blade. Suspended from a baudrick, or scarf-like shoulder-belt, this sword reached from the hollow of the back to about the middle of the thigh; and thus we are enabled to compute its length at about twenty-two inches. The blade was straight, of uniform width, double-edged, and cut at an obtuse angle to form the point. In process of time this point-angle becomes more and more acute; and it is this formation of the sword-point which enables us to distinguish with certainty the relative antiquity of the various Roman swords, that at different times may be brought under our notice. A good and characteristic example is engraved in Fig. 15, No. 1.

Upon the column of Trajan, the ordinary Roman sword already appears considerably longer than it is in the statues of the earliest Emperors. Nevertheless, it still is very short when compared with the weapons of the same class that have been in use amongst other nations. Under the Flavian Emperors, when the decadence of the empire to which we have alluded had commenced its downward course, and the arms and armour had begun to degenerate, the Roman soldiers

---

subsequently (lib. iii., c. 15) the same writer states that there then were Roman *pila* of two kinds : the one just named, with a shaft 5½ feet in length, which, when impelled by a strong arm, was able to transfix a foot-soldier through his shield, or a horseman through his breastplate —this weapon, "formerly called *pilum*, is now *spiculum;*" and a second kind, distinguished as *verrutum*, which was similar in character but smaller in size, the trilateral head being 5 inches long, and the shaft 3½ feet.

Some small trilateral spear-heads have been found in the Roman encampment on Hod Hill, near Blandford, Dorset. (*See Note* 43). C. B.

appear provided with long swords, edged on one side only, and sharp at the point. This weapon is the *spatha*, which the Romans first borrowed from some barbarous tribes, and then introduced amongst others. Its presence does not prevent the contemporaneous appearance of the short swords, of which some are very short; but amongst them it always is easy to recognise the *spatha*.

Fig. 15.—ROMAN ARMS : 1. The Sword; 2. Early Helm; 3. Late Helm; 4. Parazonium and its Scabbard.

The short sword or sword-dagger of the times of the republic, suggests the same reflections as the pilum. Its form suggests at once that the warrior who is armed with so short a weapon must of necessity qualify and prepare himself for the closest hand-to-hand conflict. The short sword, then, implies personal bravery in the soldier. Averting, as best he might, the thrusts and blows of hostile spears and swords, the legionary, with his short sword in his hand, would have to take one additional step in advance, which would deprive his adversary of whatever advantages he might have gained from his longer weapons. In addition to this most characteristic weapon, the Romans under the empire used the *parazonium*, of which mention has been already made (p. 49). It appears to have been reserved for the most part for the military chiefs. Some emperors are represented with this weapon, figured in No. 4, Fig. 15, resting in the hollow of their hand, in an attitude of peaceful command. It was generally worn on the left side.

The first occasion on which the Romans and the Greeks encountered each other in battle was 280 years before our era [B.C. 280], when Pyrrhus invaded Italy. At that time the Romans can scarcely be said to have emerged altogether from a state of barbarism, while the Greeks then had already been long living in a condition of civilisation that in many important particulars was of a high order. At first Pyrrhus obtained some successes; but they were obtained at a disastrous cost, and eventually he was compelled to retreat, vanquished, from Italian soil. About a century later, in their turn, the Romans became invaders of Greece, and especially directed their attacks against the kings of Macedon, at that time the sole representatives of the military prowess of the Greeks. Several fortunate campaigns were crowned by the victories of Cynocephalæ and Pydna, which led to the eventual overthrow of Greek independence. The phalanx then had to yield to the legion.[32]

In a celebrated passage, Polybius endeavours to set forth and explain the causes which brought about the supremacy of the Roman legions. This passage belongs by right to our present subject, in consequence of the details which it gives of the armament of the two great hostile nations, together with its descriptions of the reciprocal advantages and disadvantages resulting from their respective military systems, by which they were affected on the field of battle. It is as follows :—

"Now that these different orders of battle (the phalanx and the legion) are discovered in hostile opposition, it will be desirable for us to consider in what they differ, and to investigate what the causes were which brought the advantage to the side of the Romans.

"The result of this inquiry will be, that we no longer attribute the success of the Romans to prosperous fortune; but, on the contrary, that our commendation of them will be just and reasonable, and based upon their own merits and deserts.

"Proofs abound on every side, which demonstrate as a fact without a single exception, that so long as the phalanx maintained its own proper and natural condition, no power whatever could resist its charge or sustain the violence of its shock.

"In this formation, three feet of ground is allotted to each armed soldier. The 'sarisse' (spear or pike), at first twenty-four feet in length, was subsequently reduced to twenty-one feet in order to render it more easy to be managed. When of this reduced length, six feet of the shaft of the sarisse, measured from the point where he holds it, pass beyond the soldier to the rear, and act as a counterpoise, leaving fifteen feet (including the spear-head) which advance in front of him; and this he thrusts forward, with his full strength with both his hands, against the enemy. Consequently, when the formation of the phalanx is perfect, and when each soldier gives a proper support to the next to him in both rank and file, the sarisses of the second, third, and fourth ranks project in advance of the front rank by graduated distances, all of them more than the sarisses of the fifth rank, the projection of which would be only three feet. And, as the phalanx is formed sixteen deep, it is easy to estimate the weight, force, and power of such an array. It is a necessary consequence of this disposition of the ranks, that the sarisses of the ranks to the rear of the fifth are useless for either delivering a charge or receiving the charge of the enemy. The sarisses of the sixth and of the succeeding ranks, accordingly, are not levelled to the front ; but the men of each rank rest them on the slope, on the shoulders of the men in the rank in advance of them, their points elevated high above the heads of all, and inclining towards the enemy : and thus, in compact order, they check the flight and break the force of any hostile missiles that may have passed over the front ranks, and might fall heavily upon the centre or rear. The rearmost ranks also have their proper duties and contribute their becoming share to the solidity and power of the whole body ; besides keeping their sarisses elevated on the slope, and besides standing firm, for them it is, if need be, to push forward their comrades who are in front of them, or to deprive them of the possibility of facing about and falling back."

Here we have brought vividly before us the formation of the phalanx, and the disposition and duties of its component ranks. Now, therefore, we may reverse the picture, and on the other side may examine into the equipment and formation of the Romans, that so we may be enabled to draw a comparison between them and their Macedonian foes.

"The Roman soldier," continues Polybius, "when in fighting order does not cover more than three feet of ground. But since it is necessary for him to move as well as to stand, in order that he may be enabled to cover himself with his shield and to deliver blows with both the point and the edge of his weapon, each legionary requires to have a space of at least three feet about him on every side clear and free from every obstacle.

"Each Roman soldier in line in the legion, then, when engaged against a phalanx, has directly opposed to him in

the front rank, two men of the enemy, and no less than ten
levelled sarisses; and, in hand-to-hand conflict, it is not possible for him either to break or to cut his way through such a
hostile array. And, again, his own supporting ranks in this combat could render him no aid : their most violent onset would
be ineffectual, and his own sword would become powerless.

"My statement, therefore, was altogether correct, when I
affirmed that the phalanx, so long as it maintained its own
proper formation, would continue invincible, front to front;
and also that no other array could sustain and resist the shock
of its charge.

"By what means, then, does it come to pass that the
Romans are victorious?   How happens it that the phalanx is
vanquished ?

"Now, in war, the time, the place, and the circumstances
of every battle may vary far beyond all calculation; and,
indeed, to the possible changes in each one of these all-
important conditions there positively is no limitation.   But the
phalanx is invincible and irresistible only at one particular
time, only in one well-defined place, also only under one
felicitous combination of circumstances.   When a decisive
action is imminent and must be fought out at a time, and
on ground, and under circumstances, all of them such as
are favourable to the phalanx, few, indeed, and slender are
the chances of success which attend any attack upon that
formidable body.   Very different, however, is the prospect,
if the attack be made, as so easily it may be made, when for
the phalanx in both time and place and circumstance, there
are not advantages, but disadvantages.

"For a phalanx to act with good effect it is necessary
that a piece of ground should be found on which it may
be formed, that is flat, open, level, without any ditches
or swamps, without defiles or eminences, and also removed
from every river.   This is universally admitted.

"On the other hand, without any question, if not impossible except under very rare circumstances, it certainly must always be most difficult to discover and to secure the possession of a piece of ground of sufficient extent, which possesses all the required qualifications and is absolutely free from every obstacle.

"What good service will the most perfect and the most powerful of phalanxes be able to accomplish, if the enemy instead of advancing upon it and closing with its array upon a singularly fortunate piece of ground, should break up his force into small yet strong parties, should spread himself over all the adjoining country, should ravage the towns, and lay waste the territories of friends and allies? The invincible corps, which would continue to be invincible only so long as it should hold its advantageous position, having already failed to protect its friends, would speedily cease to be able to secure its own safety.

"The enemy, master of the adjoining country, meeting none to resist him, would cut off every convoy; while the phalanx, if it should attempt any enterprise, would so seriously impair its own strength and solidity, that it would excite the derision of the enemy.

"But, again, grant that an attack is made on the phalanx in its own territory and on its own ground; even then, if the enemy should not concentrate his entire force and bring up the whole at one and the same time to the attack, or if at the moment of the combat he should draw off, and, avoiding the hostile shock, should retire once more, what will become of the redoubtable formation in phalanx?

"It is easy," continues the ancient historian, "to form an opinion on all these points, by observing the strategy of the Romans at the present day. Thus our argument is built up, not even on the most conclusive reasoning, but on facts that are still recent and fresh.

" The Romans' do not employ all their troops to form a front equal to that of a phalanx; but, while they oppose one division of their force to the enemy, they always hold a second division in reserve.

" Again, whether the phalanx should break the line that is opposed to it in its front, or should itself be broken, it still maintains its own proper formation. But, if it should attempt either to follow up an advantage by pursuing any fugitives, or should it seek for itself safety in retreat or flight—in either of these cases, the solid formation of the phalanx, in which its strength and its consequent security consist, must in some degree be broken up, even if it be not altogether dissolved. Openings are made in the serried ranks, which the reserve of the enemy quickly discern, and upon them they deliver their attacks in flank, in rear, wherever there may be the slightest encouragement or any prospect of success.

" Finally, since it always is easy to turn aside from whatever would be for the advantage of the phalanx, while it is scarcely possible at any time to escape from everything which must act for its disadvantage, these considerations alone appear to be even more than sufficient to show how decidedly inferior the celebrated military formation of the Greeks was to that which was brought against it by the Romans.

" But, it must be added," Polybius continues, " that the troops who are under orders to join in the formation of a phalanx may be required to march to their rendezvous through every variety of country; they may have to encamp on their route, to take possession of advantageous positions for their halting-places, to besiege hostile towns, or to have their own encampments besieged; they may have to attack, or to resist the attack of an enemy, suddenly and unexpectedly, while on their march; and, in a word, they must be prepared to encounter and to surmount every contingency. These all are the chances of war; on them victory frequently depends, and almost invariably they contribute to it in no slight degree. On all occasions such as these it is scarcely possible to bring the phalanx, as such, into action; or, if it were possible, it could act to but little, if to any advantage, in this irregular and desultory warfare. Not so with the Roman armies. All places, all times, all circumstances by their soldiers are regarded with equal satisfaction. Always in readiness for prompt and decided action, they cannot be embarrassed by any particular form or aspect of the hostile demonstration. Whether formed up in the ranks of the legions, or in small detachments, or in open skirmishing order, when man might be opposed to man, the soldiers of Rome are prepared, as they are qualified, to go gallantly into action.

"With an order of battle in which the combatants could act with such ease, such promptness, and such complete efficiency, it cannot be a matter for any surprise that the Romans in their enterprises easily and certainly triumphed over enemies, who had been trained and who fought under a system, at once so different and so inferior.

"I have felt constrained," concludes the historian, "to treat this subject thus at length, because at the present day it is common with the Greeks to assign the overthrow of the Macedonians to something which they would fain have to be esteemed as bordering upon the miraculous; and also because I am well aware that there are other persons besides Greeks who have yet to learn what is the true character of Roman warfare, and who consequently at present are unable to appreciate the vast superiority of the legion over the phalanx." [33]

CHAPTER V.

THE DECORATION OF ANCIENT ARMS AND ARMOUR.

At all periods in the history of arms and armour the decorative arts have been invited by the armourer to take a part with him in the adornment and enrichment of his works; and, on the other hand, the great demand for the works of the armourer, and the high estimation in which they have universally been held, have acted as a powerful impulse to promote the best interests of the decorative arts. Some brief notice of the decoration of ancient arms and armour, accordingly, appears to be not only consistent with the general aim and purpose of these pages, but also of necessity to be comprehended within their range.

The corslet and cuirass of the Greeks sometimes show no other decoration than the bold flutings at their base, while at other times a rich foliage is introduced and expressed by effective outlines. Again, in other and more elaborate examples, the *plastron* or breastplate is divided by horizontal bands into several fields, which are covered with foliage and arabesques in relief. The uppermost field in these examples generally displays a Medusa's head.

Contrary to what might have been expected, it appears that the least decorated pieces of ancient Greek armour were the corslet and the shield, and that the greatest amount of ornamentation was lavished upon the helms and the greaves (*cnemides*). Fine and characteristic examples of greaves still exist in considerable numbers. They often are divided by several bands that are set back one upon another, an arrangement which, with a very happy effect, imparts to the piece of armour a pervading curvature of form. Numerous figures of men and of animals, with scroll-work, executed in tolerably high relief, decorate each of these bands.

The decoration of the helm generally consists of figures of men and animals, which are executed in full relief for the crest, and on the sides of the bell of the head-piece are highly relieved also.

The shield, as it would seem, was generally adorned only with painted figures and other enrichments. A circular wreath of foliage, the leaves most in favour being those of either the laurel or the olive, or circles traced out with small studs or discs—these form borders ; and the central figures and devices are either a tripod, or a serpent, or a head of Medusa, or some other object of a somewhat similar character. In Fig. 16 a Greek warrior is represented with his shield bordered, and charged with a serpent.³⁴ We must keep in remem-

Fig. 16.—GREEK WARRIOR.

brance, however, that the Greek poets, as in the pre-eminently famous instance of the shield of Achilles (see page 25), have bequeathed to us descriptions of shields that possess far more scientific and elaborate ornamentation. If we suppose that the ancient monuments have preserved for our information only such examples of shield-decoration as were most prevalent and in general use, while the poets have written their brilliant descriptions of a few exceptional specimens of rare magnificence, it will not be difficult to reconcile these two distinct authorities. It does not follow, however, that in this matter of highly-enriched shields we

G

should form our judgment concerning the usage of antiquity from what we know of the Renaissance. At that period the taste for luxurious armour, when armour was in the act of ceasing to be worn, was widely prevalent, and, indeed, it became a fashionable passion; and this sentiment delighted to find a consistent expression in the production of numerous shields, most magnificently adorned with admirable artistic skill, but which for all genuine practical shield uses were of as little value as possible. Very many of these remarkable Renaissance shields are still in existence in perfect preservation.[85]

The Greek sword, in addition to the happiness of its form, which is in itself a beautiful decoration, on its blade exhibits various lines forming elongated chevrons and other figures of characteristic contours. The hilt, besides, receives the base of the blade between two flat bands that are carved in half-circles, where the blade is fixed by a group of large round-headed studs, the simple effect of which is not deficient in elegance. The scabbard, rectangular in its outline, at its four angles was enclosed by bands of metal, and at its extremity it was finished with a bouterolle, of which the terminal line formed a half-circle extending beyond the thickness of the scabbard itself. A trail of foliage, executed apparently in inlaid metal-work or in enamel, filled the space between the angular bands.

The heads of javelins present those correct lines which render all other decoration superfluous. The wings of these javelin heads are rounded, and their sockets are prolonged and finished with a circular raised fillet, which is both elegant and effective. This form of javelin-head has been transmitted from Roman antiquity to the times of the barbarians.

The breast-plate or corslet of the Romans is always ornamented upon a very simple system. There generally are two animals, or two figures, which are placed symmetrically at the base of the bust, where they form the principal element of the decoration. Foliage, geometrical figures, arabesques, objects borrowed from their worship, such as altars or braziers, and other devices, are added ; but these are always arranged in such a manner that a considerable space is left plain and altogether free from ornamentation. This enables us instantly to distinguish the works of antiquity from those of the Renaissance, when the luxurious taste of the time delighted in covering the entire surface of the material with a super-abundance of details.

In direct opposition to the usage of the Greeks, amongst the Romans the helm was the piece of armour which received the least enrichment. We have seen how simple and how devoid of adornment was the helm of the legionary. It would be difficult to find amongst all the known representations of emperors and famous warriors any considerable number of remarkable helms, for this very simple reason, that they were almost invariably represented bare-headed.

To the general rule there is one decided exception in the splendidly adorned helms that were worn by the soldiers of the Prætorian corps. The bas-relief which is preserved in the Museum of the Louvre at Paris, and now is fixed into the pedestal of the statue of Melpomene, contains a figure of one of these soldiers. His helm is ornamented with a coronet of laurel in high relief, conforming to the contour of the bell of the helm itself, which in other respects is plain ; the visor is elaborately enriched with a pile of various arms ; and the throat-piece has thunderbolts, which are either embossed or executed in hammer work.

The shield of the legionary, as we have already stated. was painted, and that of the knight, which was made of *cuir bouilli* (boiled and moulded leather), would not admit of any other form of decoration. The military chiefs were generally without shields. This last circumstance explains the otherwise

singular fact that Roman shields are very rarely to be found
with rich decorations. The shields of the Prætorians, on the
other hand, in the monuments, are almost always represented
adorned with splendid carving.

Upon the pommel, or at the two extremities of its massive
rectangular hilt-guard, the Roman sword commonly displays
either the head of a lion or the head and beak of an eagle.

At this place it is desirable that some remarks should be
introduced upon a piece of defensive armour, the use of
which, in its true original capacity, as an important member
of the military equipment, appears to have been lost at an
early period. We refer to the *ægis*, which in sculpture is
retained to this day as an attribute of the warrior goddess,
Pallas Athené, or Minerva. When it is represented in statues
or other figures of this divinity as a cuirass, it is evident that
the artist was not aware of the origin and true character of
the ægis. Its correct form is that of a large épaulière (shoulder-
guard) of untanned leather, which is placed upon the left
shoulder. We know, indeed, that the ægis itself, which was
given to Minerva by Jupiter (Zeus), was formed from the
skin of the goat, Amalthea. Accordingly, when any sculptor
has been faithful to the tradition of Greek Mythology,
Minerva appears bearing, over her cuirass, the ægis in its
proper form and in the position that has just been described.
Then the ægis so far discharges the duty of a shield that it
guards the left arm and shoulder, while it leaves the right arm
to wield the lance or sword. We should not have thus permitted our attention to have been attracted to this curious
piece of very ancient armour, had there been reason for considering it to be only an element of a mythological fable ;
but the fact is, that in all probability we here have a relic of
a primitive usage, and perhaps the prototype of the earliest
shield. What, indeed, can be more natural than that the idea
of armour should have been first expressed amongst certain

races by placing upon the left shoulder and wrapping round the left arm a piece of leather, or of some tough woven fabric, in order to obtain that defence which in later but still early times men desired to secure for themselves by making shields from one or more pieces of wood ? [26]

What appears to confirm this theory is the fact that in considerably later times the ægis ceased to be the attribute exclusively of the goddess Minerva. Some cameos and other antique gems show that it was borne by Alexander, and by the kings his successors ; and, later still, in imitation of them, by Roman Emperors and eminent warriors. Not that any of these princes or military chiefs actually wore an ægis upon their persons in war; but that they either kept them, for the purpose of display, as part of their state costume, or that they merely caused them to be introduced into the productions of the sculptor and the lapidary, in remembrance of an ancient tradition, and under the influence of eminently dignified associations. Fine examples of ancient works of art which illustrate these observations are the bust of Alexander the Great and the cameo of the apotheosis of Germanicus, both of them in the Imperial Library at Paris.

CHAPTER VI.

DEFENSIVE EQUIPMENT AND WEAPONS OF SAVAGE RACES.

ARMOUR AND ARMS OF THE FRANKS.

SECTION I.

Defensive Equipment and Weapons of Savage Races.

IT is a circumstance no less remarkable than true that certain characteristic features which distinguish successive epochs in history may be discovered having an independent, sustained, and sometimes almost a simultaneous existence in different regions of the earth. Thus, from a survey of the various savage races that at different periods, and having attained to varying degrees of civilisation, have spread themselves over the surface of the globe, we are enabled to identify the "Stone Period" with one particular people, while others we find to be severally the representatives of the "Bronze Period," and of the "Iron Period" in the earliest and simplest stages of its development. Certain races of Africa or of Eastern Asia have been found to exhibit a military condition corresponding with tolerable exactness with the state of the Gauls at the time of the Roman Conquest, or with that of the Germans in the first century of our era. Other races of Central America, who used weapons of bronze, have recalled to remembranc the Greeks of the Homeric age; and again, the aborigines of Australia and Oceania, with their implements and weapons formed exclusively of wood and

bone and stone, may be regarded as a curious revival of the
remote and comparatively obscure ages in which precisely the
same simple materials were in use for the very same purposes.
It is in consequence of facts such as these, that we now advert
to the military equipment and the weapons of savage races.

At the present time, it is true, the genuine savage armoury
is gradually becoming extinct. The vast extension of com-
mercial enterprise during recent years, coupled with the rapid
increase in all the means for intercommunication amongst
even the most distant races, have brought implements and
arms formed of iron almost universally into use. In this, as
in so many things, a prevailing uniformity is beginning to be
established throughout the human race.

The *bow*, the *lance* or *dart*, the *knife*, the *club* or *axe*
(which in its lighter forms represents the *sword*), and the
shield, compose the armoury that is common to almost all
savage races. Each race, also, is generally seen to have
had some weapon peculiarly its own ; and by some races some
one or other of the almost universal weapons that have just
been mentioned appears occasionally to have been unknown.
The bow, for example, until a very recent period, was unknown amongst the Australians ; but, for the absence of this
important weapon they found a compensation in the extraordinary skill and precision with which they threw their darts.

The lance, indeed, as we learn from travellers, is what may
be entitled the national weapon of the Australian aborigines.
It is about ten feet in length, very slender, made of cane or
reed, or of some light wood, and armed with a barbed point.
The lightness of this projectile, at first sight, would appear to
militate against its possessing any capacity for powerful projection. And such would be the fact if this dart had to be
thrown simply by the unaided action of the hand and arm—
as a light arrow, which carries with it immense force when
discharged from a bow, is almost powerless when merely

thrown by the hand.   The light Australian dart is propelled
by means of an instrument, devised for that purpose, called
the *Wummera ;* this is a piece of wood, straight and flat,
three feet in length, having at its extremity a tube of bone, or
a piece of tough skin, into which the end of the dart is placed.
The *wummera,* thus charged with the dart, is grasped in the
right hand, and the dart itself is held, and its direction determined by the thumb and forefinger of the left hand.   Before
the weapon is thrown, a vibratory movement is imparted to
it, under the impression that thus the aim may be taken with
greater precision.   When the dart is discharged, the *wummera,*
or throw-stick, of course remains in the warrior's hand.   This
simple process, which is highly creditable to savage ingenuity,
obtains for the weapon an extraordinary increase in both its
range and its striking force.

In addition to the interest excited by the *wummera* and
by some other rather singular weapons presently to be
noticed, visitors to museums are always forcibly impressed
with the prevailing lightness of every weapon (the clubs
only excepted) in the savage arsenal.   The lances and arrows,
many of them made of reed or bamboo, are indeed remarkable for their lightness; and this quality in these weapons has
enabled the makers of them to give them extraordinary
length.   Some of these lances are at least three times the
length of the weapon of the class now used by Lancers
in both France and England.   Some of the bows that may
be seen in the same collections, which are very light and yet
not deficient in strength, are not less than seven or eight feet
long.

In the second place, the astonishment of visitors and
students when examining collections of the weapons of savage
races is excited, and it is excited most worthily, by the complicated knots and ligatures, by which the heads of both
lances and arrows, and also of axes, are secured and held with

admirable firmness in the cleft extremities of these weapons. This mode of adjustment and fastening, to which reference has already been made (see page 6), is employed with equal success when the weapon's points are of iron, or of bone, stone, crystal, or some other hard substance used in its stead. What is still more astonishing, though no really adequate estimate can be formed on this point by means of visits to museums, is the dexterity shown by savages in the management and use of their weapons, and the efficiency which by their address and their muscular strength they are able to impart to them. With a dart propelled by a *wummera*, Captain Grey constantly saw the Australians strike down a pigeon at the distance of thirty yards. Cook also relates that, at the distance of fifty-five yards, savages, with the same weapon, discharged in the same manner, were more sure in their aim than European soldiers were with the musket and ball. One singular use that is made of the dart or lance is for fishing. One traveller assures us that he has seen Californians plunge into the Murray, lance in hand, and reappear with a fish transfixed on the point of the weapon. When used for such a purpose as this, the object would be struck with the lance held in the hand, and not by a blow from a javelin that had been thrown.[87] The Hottentots are also said to be almost as powerful and expert in javelin practice as the Australians. They can hit a hare on her form with their javelin, at the distance of thirty or forty yards. And with this weapon, called by them the *Rackumitick*, or with one resembling it, which, perhaps, is both longer and stronger, it is said that they venture to attack the elephant, the rhinoceros, and even the lion. We may suppose, however, that they assemble in considerable force for the chase of these large and formidable animals.[38]

So remarkable is both the skill of the American Indian, and his strength of hand, that he is well known to be able to drive his arrows quite through the bodies of horses, and

even of buffaloes. The traveller, Pubock, gives the following singular illustration of the skilful use of the bow and
arrow in savage hands. " The Indians of Brazil," he says,
" kill the turtle with an arrow. But, if they were to aim
directly at the animal, the arrow, striking it at an angle,
would glance off from its hard natural armour; they shoot
their arrow, therefore, into the air with such sure aim, that
it will certainly fall, point downwards, vertically upon the
shell of the turtle, and thus will pierce it through."

While treating of the use of the arrow by savage races,
it will be desirable to rectify an error which is somewhat prevalent. It is well known that all the savages of warm
climates are familiar with processes for the preparation of
virulent poisons, and that in these poisons they dip the tips of
their arrow-heads. The misconception that we would correct
is the supposition that these poisoned arrows are used indis-
criminately in war and for the chase. This is not really
the fact. The poisoned arrows are used in the chase almost
exclusively ; and, by the action, as it would seem, of a tacit
general understanding resembling the law of nations, the
warriors of savage races do not discharge poisoned arrows
against human adversaries.[39]

We proceed to describe certain singular weapons that are
peculiar to various races.

The *Boomerang* is peculiar to Australia. It is a piece
of wood, about three feet, or rather more, in length, which is
bent almost at a right angle. It is used, both in war and in
the chase, as follows. Held in the right hand at one extremity,
it is thrown, as a sickle might be thrown, either upwards into
the air, or in such a downward direction that it will strike the
ground at some distance from the thrower. In the former
case, when thrown into the air, the weapon first rises with a
rotatory motion, and then, changing its course, falls at the
precise spot to which the aim was directed, and there it strikes

either man or animal with the crushing effect of a heavy tile or similar weighty object. When it is delivered almost in a horizontal direction, but with such a downward inclination that it will strike the ground in the midst of its flight, it is in its rebound that the *boomerang* becomes true to the aim, and strikes the desired object. There remains one other method of using this most singular weapon yet to be considered. Having determined what object he desires to strike, the Australian carefully observes its exact position, and in his mind fixes its distance; then, having turned round, he throws the *boomerang* vertically. In consequence of the shape of the weapon, and of the manner in which it is thrown, after having traversed a certain distance the *boomerang* returns above the head of its master, and, rushing onwards, inflicts its blow upon the object towards which the back of the thrower had been turned. This may fairly claim to be considered the most remarkable of the many strange usages of savage warfare.[40]

The Malays, the savages of Borneo, and of the Valley of the Amazon, discharge their arrows and light darts through a long tube, which they apply to their lips, and then they give the necessary impulse by blowing with their breath. Thus, substituting for the bow (and also, in some sense, for the *wummera*), the *Sabarcane, Sumpitan*, or blow-tube, the Malays strike objects at great distances, with great force, and with astonishing precision of aim.[41]

The Patagonians of Southern South America have the *Bola*, and the *Lasso*. The *bola* is simply a long strong cord, or small rope, having a stone, or a ball of metal fixed at one end ; or, rather, it consists of two such cords, each provided with a stone or ball. The cords being secured by their other ends to the Patagonian, he whirls the two balls rapidly, and with great adroitness, about his head, and then discharging them at the object, strikes it as with a blow from a flexible club. A blow such as this, struck from the end of a long cord, takes effect with great violence; and the *bola*, having done its work in one instance, may be recovered and be in readiness for use on future occasions. The management of this *bola* requires long practice, and no ordinary skill. The *lasso* is a variety of the *bola*, which is used after a different fashion. Instead of having been whirled round the head to obtain a momentum, the stone or ball at the extremity of the *lasso* is discharged direct from the hand, propelled simply by the strength of the thrower's arm, and by his dexterity of movement; the cord flies with the missile to which it is attached at one end, and the other end is held by the thrower. Should the aim have been directed to the leg of a horse, either the limb is broken by the blow, if the ball strikes, or, if it only grazes and passes on one side, a jerk of the cord brings the ball back with a rotatory movement round the leg, or both the legs of the animal, and the cord thus is entwined around them. The Patagonian, by holding the cord tight, causes the horse to make a false step, or, in its sudden entanglement, he drags it at once to the ground. The *lasso* is also in general use throughout South America, and it is constantly constructed with a loop at its thrown extremity, instead of a stone or ball.[42]

SECTION II.

Armour and Arms of the Franks.

I.—THE FRANKS OF THE PERIOD OF CLOVIS, A.D. 481.

The Franks, those of the barbarian conquerors of Rome who have left to future ages the greatest name, for a twofold reason are specially interesting to the French of to-day, because they have both bequeathed to them their name, and have infused some admixture from their own German veins into the Gallic fountain-head of French blood. The

Franks also are better known than the other barbarian races —the Huns, Visigoths, Vandals, Ostrogoths, and others. If we were to attempt to give any description of the military equipments of any of the last named races, it would not be possible for us to offer more than a few general and vague statements, which would amount only to surmises or suggestions; whereas, in the matter of arms and armour, positive facts and exact details alone possess any interest or any value. We are content, consequently, to inquire into the military equipment of the Franks.

The Franks appear in history equipped—as might have been expected from the barbarism of their condition when they overran Gaul—in the simplest and most primitive manner. For defence, they were provided with shields alone; they had neither cuirass, nor mail-coat, nor even any helms. They went into action bare-headed, their bodies covered with a vestment of linen—a tunic, short in its skirt, and girded tightly to their persons. Tacitus says, it is true, that occasionally they were to be seen provided with cuirasses of Roman fashion; but, from his words it was evident he was alluding only to casual and exceptional examples; the results, we may be sure, of the spoiling of some dead Roman soldier, or of some other somewhat similar mode of acquisition.

Without any cuirass, then, and without helms, these wild warriors knew no other armour than *shields*, in form either circular or oval, constructed of wood, and provided in the centre with a large and boldly projecting *umbo*, or boss of metal. This boss, a kind of deep, circular pan made of iron, was fixed to the front of the shield, where it had a considerable projection, and was securely riveted over a hole in the centre; and thus the hollow under the face of the boss was open towards the reverse of the shield. Across this hollow, and consequently also across the central aperture in the shield, a plate of iron, having its sides somewhat concave, was well

secured; this plate was made to expand towards its extremities into three branches, or small bars, which were prolonged to the circumference of the shield, and imparted to it
a great strength and solidity. The central part of the bar,
under the raised hollow of the boss, afforded a convenient and
secure handle for holding the shield. The umbo, or boss, is
shown in Figures 17 and 18, which give a far more correct

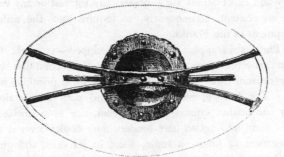

Fig. 17.—The Umbo, or Boss, of a Frank Shield, showing its under
surface.

Fig. 18.—The same in profile.

and much clearer idea of it than can be imparted by any
verbal description. In Fig. 17 the under side of the umbo is
shown, with the branched iron bar traversing its open hollow;
the outline of the oval shield itself is merely indicated by a
dotted line, to show that the wood of this shield has long
decayed, and left only the iron umbo. Fig. 18 shows the
upper side of the same umbo, with the projecting iron in
profile. When shield-bosses such as this were first discovered
in the graves of the Franks, it is easy to see how natural it

would be to suppose them to have been iron helms, and
particularly when the bar was wanting, and the umbo, or
hollow boss, was alone preserved.

The offensive arms are, first, the *Axe, Hatchet* or *Francisque*—the weapon generally in use among the Franks,
to which it is evident that they gave their own name. It
was certainly sometimes used by them as a weapon, as a
hatchet is used—that is, to strike blows, with the haft of the
axe held in the hand; but, the prevailing usage among the
Franks, and which was peculiar to themselves, was to hurl
this weapon at the head or at the shield of the enemy. An
axe-blow, thus delivered, would kill a man, and it would even
beat in a shield. And these blows, if once aimed, rarely, if
ever, failed to take effect; so great being the skill, and so
perfect the discipline of the Franks, that it was said of them
that they never missed their aim.

This *Francisque*, or battle-axe, was made under several
varieties of form. Some are found having a blade that is
long and narrow, slightly curved on its exterior face, and
deeply hollowed in the interior. Others, smaller in size, are
long in proportion to their size, and very slightly hollowed,
if at all. A third variety exhibits on one side of the haft a
blade such as those that have just been described, and on the
other side it is fitted with a kind of chisel, very like the blade
of a carpenter's plane.

Secondly, there is the *Lance* or *Framee*. The blade or
head of this weapon is found to have assumed a variety of
shapes. Researches and examinations have discovered some
that are long, others that are short, some triangular, some
elongated, and some leaf-shaped, others of a lozenge shape,
and others barbed. Some, again, have projecting hook-like
barbs at the base of the spear-head; but, in every instance the
entire head or blade is of one piece with the socket. Into
this socket the head of the shaft is inserted, where it is

secured by a rivet, which passes through it, and through two holes, pierced for its reception in the opposite sides of the socket itself.

The heads of the Frankish arrows, or rather of their *javelins* (for these weapons were thrown by them from the hand), are found in as many varieties of form and size as their lance blades. It has been supposed, and, apparently with good reason, that in such javelins as have broad barbs, the prototype of the famous *Angon* of the Franks may be discerned. This, however, is a subject of archæological research which is still open to discussion. Agathias has described the *Angon* with no little minuteness, in the following passage :— " The weapons of the Franks," he says, " are very rude. They have neither cuirass nor boots, and but a very few of them have helms . . . . They are without cavalry, but fight on foot with much gallantry, activity, and discipline. They use neither the bow, nor the arrow, nor the sling. On their left sides they carry shields, and their weapons are swords of the length of a man's thigh, axes having double edges, and darts. These darts, which are neither very long nor very short, can be used against the enemy either by holding them in the hand, or by throwing them. They are covered with (entirely formed of) iron, except the actual handle. At the head, and near the point, they have two curved pieces of iron, or blades (probably like small harpoon barbs), one projecting on each side. In battle they throw this dart against the enemy, and when it inflicts a wound, it becomes so fixed in the flesh by the small side blades, or hooks, near the point, that it can be extracted only with great difficulty, suffering, and danger, even should the blow not at once prove to be mortal. Again, should the enemy avert the blow so far as to receive the weapon in his shield, without any wound to his person, by the same hooks the dart remains fixed to the shield; and as it is tolerably long, and very heavy, while clinging to the pierced shield, it drags along the ground; being covered with iron, also, it cannot be cut through and so removed. At the moment of the embarrassment thus caused to his enemy, the Frank who has thrown the dart, bounds forward, places his foot on the end of his dart as it trails on the ground, and by this means compels his enemy either to lower his shield or altogether to abandon it; and then, when his enemy is thus uncovered, he rushes upon him, and with either his sword, his axe, or with another dart he kills him outright."[48]

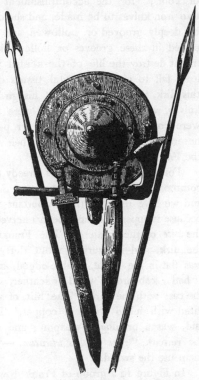

Fig 19.—ARMS AND SHIELD OF THE FRANKS.

Thirdly, the short sword, or dirk, called the *Scramasax*, which in reality was a large knife, at the most twenty inches long, and in its greatest width about two inches; its weight was about two pounds. This weapon was *caraxée*—hollowed, that is, so as to have two channels on each face, one of them being on each side of the central ridge of the blade; and these channels were filled with poison. It was with this murderous weapon that Fredegonde caused those deadly

H

blows to be struck, which have contributed, in no slight degree, to her evil reputation. When she had resolved to dispose
of Pretextat, Bishop of Rouen, "This queen,' says Gregory,
of Tours, "for the accomplishment of her purpose, caused
two iron knives to be made, and she ordered that they should
be deeply grooved or hollowed, and that poison should be
placed in these grooves or hollows, in order that the poison
might destroy the life of the sainted prelate, should the stab
itself fail to pierce the vital tissues of his frame." Besides
this dirk, the Frank carried at his girdle, one or more small
knives, which did not shut, but were worn in sheaths; they
were commonly used by him for peaceful purposes; but,
nevertheless, he also employed their services in war. Even
the Frank women carried them.[44]

Fourth, after the weapons already mentioned, which were
common to all the warriors, the true *Sword* claims our notice,
and we have reserved this important weapon until the last,
because it appears to have been reserved for the chiefs, and for
the *élite* of the soldiery. The Frankish sword, longer than
the dirk, and measuring about thirty or thirty-two inches,
was flat in the blade, double-edged, and sharp at the point.
It had a scabbard of wood or leather, which probably was not
the case with the dirk. The hilt, of wood, was often decorated with inlaid work in copper. This sword, as has been
said, was a privileged weapon; and so Tacitus himself has
the remark, "*rari gladiis utuntur*"—"a few only amongst
them use the sword."

In Figure 19 a group of Frankish weapons is represented,
of which each one speaks for itself.

II.—THE FRANKS OF THE PERIOD OF CHARLEMAGNE,
A.D. 768—814.

The period of the invasion of Gaul by the Franks, in the
reign of Charlemagne, is a blank which it is not possible to

fill. Written documents are very scarce, and figured monuments are altogether wanting. This is the less to be regretted, since it was an epoch in the history of arms and armour devoid of any distinctive characteristics, when the ancient styles were gradually degenerating, without any fresh modification that had attained to a perfection of its own.

Without any attempt to give a descriptive sketch of the wars of Charlemagne, it will be sufficient for us to set forth the names of the nations with whom he fought, and over whom he triumphed. These were the Lombards, the Aquitanians, and the Saxons. These last were doubtless armed at that time after the same manner as the Germans were when they conquered Gaul. It is probable that, in their military equipment, the Aquitanians and the Lombards in some respect adhered to old Roman usages, since they are so well known to have delighted to follow the traditions of Rome from age to age; as, indeed, in many things their descendants follow those traditions still. The Basques, who caused the illustrious emperor to undergo the celebrated defeat of Roncesvalles (in French, Roncesvaux, A.D. 778), do not appear so much to have entered into close combat with his soldiers and vassals, as to have engaged them with missile weapons—with the arrow, and the stone, either slung, or thrown by the hand.

The troops of Charlemagne himself now demand our attention. Those records of this period to which we are indebted for our information, bring before us two distinct classes of soldiers. The soldiers of one of these classes, the Franks, or great vassals of the crown (who were the true soldiers of their time, and by whom, for the most part, the ranks of the Emperor's army were filled), retained the same weapons that had been used by their predecessors, the Franks of the conquest of Gaul—the lance, that is, the javelin, the sword, both long and short, and doubtless also the axe, as we have just been contemplating them. In their defensive armour these later Franks differed from the soldiers of Clovis, by whom, as we have seen, the shield alone was in use. In addition to their shields, the military vassals of Charlemagne, who so far followed the customs of their forefathers that they went into battle bare-headed, or sometimes wearing a simple kind of leathern cap, were provided with the *Lorica* or *Brunia,* a true coat of mail. This *lorica,* a short and tight species of *paletot,* was padded, and also was more or less closely covered

with small pieces of metal sewn upon the fabric of which the piece of armour itself was composed. Another change, in a military point of view of the greatest importance, and which gave a fresh character to the troops of Charlemagne, was the introduction of a numerous cavalry. The earlier Franks had been exclusively infantry, and horses had been almost or absolutely unknown amongst them; but the Franks of the Emperor numbered in their ranks at least as many horsemen as foot soldiers. Thus, we are approaching towards the age in which cavalry,

Fig. 20.—SOLDIERS OF
CHARLEMAGNE.

soon to be entitled " chivalry," will form the strength of every army, and the infantry—the serfs and peasantry—will be esteemed as little in the camp as in the village.

The soldiers of the second class, who evidently formed a privileged body, and were looked upon somewhat in the capacity of an imperial guard, were altogether distinct from their comrades of the former class. In their equipment they bore a close resemblance to the Roman Prætorians; except that, instead of the true Roman globular helm, these Frankisn knights wore a helm of a triangular form, by no means prepossessing in its appearance, which, in place of a crest, was surmounted by a cluster of conventional foliage or scroll-work.

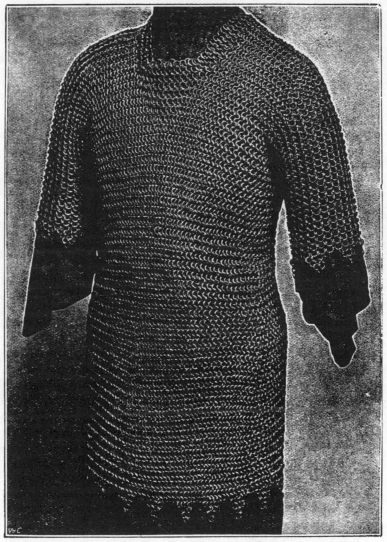

MAIL HAUBERK FROM SINIGALIA: 14th Century.
From Sir Noël Paton's Collection.

CHAPTER VII.

Arms and Armour of the Middle Ages.—Part I.

As an introduction to our researches into the history of the *Middle Ages*, and to our description of the *arms* and *armour* that were in use during the centuries which compose that great period, it appears to be desirable that, in a few words, we should set forth so much of the military system then prevalent, as will show upon what principles armies (French armies, at any rate) were levied, and recruited, and maintained in those days; so that, in the first instance, it may be possible to form a correct estimate of the troops by whom the armour was worn, and who wielded the arms.[45]

Throughout the entire period, distinguished and known as the "Gothic,"—from the 9th to the 16th centuries of our era, that is—the armed force which formed the army of France, was composed almost exclusively of the "*Gendarmerie*," or men-at-arms, a cavalry force, equipped in complete armour, and provided with the lance. These men-at-arms, or knights, were the lords (Seigneurs), possessors, or holders of fiefs, who, in consideration of these their fiefs, owed to their supreme suzerain, the KING, either directly or indirectly, a military service of a variable duration, but generally extending to about forty days. When the service required from them was longer than this, the King was supposed to give them a certain pay. The King, we say, was *supposed* to give this pay, because, in this matter, even in the case of their greatest and most

powerful vassals, the French sovereigns discharged their obli-
gations with extreme irregularity.   The act of calling together
the vassals in armed array, was entitled " convoking the *ban* "
—" *convoquer le ban*."

The infantry, at this period, was simply an assemblage
of serfs or dependents, who were led to the war by their
feudal lords.   We hear nothing of their having been formed
into bodies, resembling regiments and companies; and every
man appears to have armed himself in accordance with his
own taste, or as his means would permit.   This was the
common army—the *feudal army* of the period.

On extraordinary occasions, under Philip Augustus, temporary levies of a regular infantry were introduced, commanded
by chiefs, who were nobles.   This force was the " *Sergents
d'armes*," who fought with distinction (against the Germans)
at the Battle of Bovines (A.D. 1214), and who are to be carefully distinguished from the inferior foot-soldiers, little better
than an armed rabble, to whom, in France, during the middle
ages, the same title of " Sergeants " was commonly applied.
This institution speedily came to an end.

At two somewhat distant periods, in the 12th century, and
towards the close of the 14th, attempts were made, on a
grand scale, to establish the system of volunteers.   Certain
nobles, men well versed in the art of war, took upon themselves to collect recruits from amongst the most lawless classes
of men, such as brigands, robbers, bold serfs who had escaped
from serfdom, ruined nobles, and adventurous citizens.   These
men, all of them pre-eminently men of action, they formed
into regular companies; and then they tendered their services,
on certain terms, to the French monarch, or to other sovereign princes, as to the Count of Toulouse, for example, in the
12th century; and in the 15th century to the kings of England,
Spain, Portugal, and others.   For all fighting purposes, these
soldiers of fortune were excellent troops; but they had no

attachment, either to any cause or any country ; and, besides, they were men capable of any excess and crime, who were faithful only to the highest bidder, and always ready to transfer their mercenary services from one temporary master to another, as soon as an increase of pay or booty was offered to them. These free companies completely desolated whatever country was the scene of their operations, and their presence was the sure signal for ruin and devastation. But too well known is the terrible reputation of the " *Boutiers* " of the 12th century, which, in the 15th century, was even surpassed in atrocity by that of the " *Grandes Compagnies.*" It must be added, that these fierce and fickle mercenaries of the 15th century differed, in no unimportant degree, from their congenial predecessors in military organisation ; since they were masters of whatever military science was known in their times, and their ranks included men-at-arms (*gendarmes*), mounted archers, regular infantry, and every other arm then held in any esteem.

Charles VIII. (A.D. 1483—1498) abolished the feudal armies. He established a system by which the royal armies should be formed and recruited from armed bands of men, levied for the service of the king by officers commissioned for that purpose, and paid either directly from the royal treasury, or by means of taxes imposed for that express purpose on the provinces of the kingdom. From this time, the greater number of those gentlemen of France whose inclination led them to a military life, entered into the " *compagnies d'ordonnance* "—the regular royal army of the realm, either as officers or as private soldiers.

A similar system was adopted for the enlistment of a force of infantry. In each commune, a man skilful in handling the bow or the arblast was chosen, who was required to equip himself at his own cost, and in return was exempted from all payment of taxes. These men remained at home,

and were summoned to join their companies only in the time
of war; and then, also, they received pay. These archers
gained for the French infantry a truly deplorable reputation.

Some years later (about A.D. 1475) the French became
acquainted with the infantry of Switzerland. That was to
form an acquaintance with genuine soldiers—men thoroughly
in earnest, who came upon the scene sword and pike in hand.
The famous victories won by the Swiss at that time over
Charles the Bold, of Burgundy, secured for the mountaineer
soldiers the highest estimation amongst all classes in France.
This led to the abandonment of all hope of forming a native
French infantry, and to the establishment in its stead of hired
bodies of Swiss pikemen and halberdiers; and then it was
decided amongst military men in France, that the French
nobility alone were able to render any good service in war.

After the Swiss, the services of German mercenaries were
engaged by France. Francis I., however, in consequence of
the pressure of circumstances, when on the point of entering
on a war with Charles V., in the year 1534, was anxious again
to attempt the establishment of a national militia. He ordered
a levy of seven "legions," each to be composed of 6,000
infantry, "*after the manner of the Romans.*" Each legion was
to be composed of men chosen from the same province; and,
in like manner, the chiefs also were to be appointed to each
legion exclusively from the same province which had furnished
the men, in order that thus the courage and spirit of the
soldiery might be confirmed by local patriotism, and enhanced
by home associations and provincial emulation. This excellent
project was not carried into execution, but in its stead, the old
system of hiring foreign troops again was put into requisition.
These mercenaries, after their customary habit, proved a costly
resource; and they exacted the most arbitrary terms, which they
enforced peremptorily on the morning of any battle. Reliance,
however, was not permitted to rest exclusively upon these hired

A Basinet Transformed into a Pallad: 15th Century.
From Sir Noël Paton's Collection.

levies; but the system of "commissions" was made to extend
to the infantry. Officers expressly appointed were empowered,
under the authority of the king's patent, to recruit foot soldiers
from certain specified provinces, such as Gascony and
Dauphiny, which in a military point of view had a less unfavourable reputation than the rest of France. This plan for
forming companies and regiments from men who had voluntarily joined and had been regularly enrolled, and whom their
own future commanders had undertaken to obtain and to produce, continued in force for maintaining the greater part of
the French army until the year 1789. Foreign corps made
good any deficiency.

The Swiss and German troops who served in the French
armies were formed into bodies, that were equipped and
armed with a becoming uniformity. Thus the strange and
most inconsistent combination of dissimilar arms, and equally
incongruous military duties, which, early in the middle ages,
had been universal, had disappeared; each corps had its own
duties, and its own proper appointments, its own officers also,
and its suitable and uniform pay. On the field of battle troops
of various corps still appear to have been brought into very
close contact; but still each corps in reality was a distinct body,
halberdiers, pikemen, arquebusiers, and others, each class separate from every other, and having its own men connected
together in a correct military union. These troops, accordingly, formed the model upon which the main bodies of the
European armies were subsequently reconstructed. It will be
understood that at the first each body, uniform and complete
in itself, formed a *company*. The formation so well known
now under the title of *regiment* was not introduced until considerably later, nor does the origin of this term appear to be
clearly known.

In like manner, it was the influence of foreign hired troops,
which led to a complete remodelling of the cavalry of France.

Instead of the original men-at-arms, or knights, who alone had constituted the mounted forces of the French armies, the " *Estradiots*," Illyrian, or Dalmatian mercenary cavaliers armed with a *zagaie*, or javelin, pointed at both ends, and the German " *Reiters*," whose weapons were the pistol and sword, suggested the first idea of the various bodies of regular light cavalry, the mounted carabineers and others, that were established after the middle of the 16th century. At that time the lance began to give place, in the hands of mounted soldiers, to the arquebus and the pistol; but it was not until the middle of the " religious wars " (about A.D. 1575) that the original armour of the men-at-arms can be said to have fallen, in any decided degree, into disuse. Disorder and disorganisation then crept into every corps; the soldiers felt that their discipline had so far relaxed that each man might think and act in a great measure for himself; and hence, many of the soldiers, on their own authority, laid aside the cuirass and corslet, and in their stead assumed the simple buff-coat, or leathern tunic.

At this time, the ancient system of enlistment peculiar to feudal rule, the " Ban," had not become altogether obsolete; for in the 16th and 17th centuries, and even as late as the reign of Louis XIV. (A.D. 1643—1715), the French kings considered that, under certain contingencies, they might claim military service from all who held fiefs under the crown. This is not to be considered as implying that, in the 16th century, the feudal militia enjoyed a very high reputation, since on more than one memorable occasion these troops fled disgracefully from the field. Their misconduct, however, it is only fair to attribute to the true cause. The best men had been carried off to fill the ranks of the men-at-arms; and, consequently, the Ban, really strong only in numbers, but wretchedly deficient in all military efficiency, was composed only of those classes of people who had a decided distaste for a military life, many of whom were advanced in years, who invariably had no experience in the use of weapons, and were certain to be absolutely deficient in that grand military element, discipline. Such forces might have had their value in those early and rude times, when they would have been opposed to an enemy as unwarlike as themselves; but they proved to be even worse than useless in the face of comparatively modern discipline, order, and military science.

So unsatisfactory, and indeed so palpably calculated to lead to the most disastrous results, was the muster of the Ban when it had been summond to assemble by Louis XIV., that the king resolved never again to put into action that ancient national system for raising forces. And the " Ban " of France was never again convoked from that time.

Under the same sovereign, Louis XIV., the "*Conscription*," if not actually for the first time introduced, certainly was first brought seriously into operation. By the action of this system, men chosen by lot were formed into regiments, whose duties would be to guard the coasts, and to protect and maintain order in the cities and towns in time of war, without their having to take the field and to meet the enemy in open battle. The authorities had yet to learn that confidence might be reposed in the military instincts of the peasantry of France. The Revolution and the Empire have taught this lesson, and have shown the French to be a race, in their natural energy in no degree inferior to the Swiss and the Germans. It cannot be rightly objected to this opinion, that the French regiments of the period now under consideration were composed of soldiers who had been voluntarily enlisted; since a very decided distinction ought to be drawn and maintained between men who have offered themselves, of their own free choice, for military service, and who, in so doing, have proved both their inclination and their conviction that they possess the qualities suitable for the soldier's life and duties, and others who, without any other principle of selection than the chances of drawing

lots, have been taken by force to the barracks from their
workshop or their plough. These last are the questionable
soldiers, who were held to be incapable of ever being moulded
into the elements of effective armies. The opinion prevailed
throughout Europe that the conscripts, notwithstanding their
military equipment and training, would always retain that
faint heart which appeared to be common to all the peaceful
classes of their nation; and, indeed, to be a condition of their
nature. And at the commencement of the Revolution this
opinion was confirmed by the character and habits of the
French emigrants; it led other nations to enter with alacrity
into enterprises against France; and then it caused the first
great victories of the French to be regarded with such profound amazement.

The military organisation of the Middle Ages, as it would
seem, may be considered to have been already systematically
established at the end of the reign of Charles the Bold, of
France (A.D. 840 to 877), that is, about the commencement
of the reign of Alfred (A.D. 872—901) in England. The
only real soldier, the "Miles," or man-at-arms of that period,
was a man of wealth, and of noble, or at least knightly rank,
who went to the wars, mounted on a good war-horse, and
followed by an escort, more or less numerous in accordance
with his own rank and means, composed of vassals and serfs,
who were equipped with slings, bows and arrows, cutlasses,
and spears. When formed in order of battle these troops,
if troops they may be called, played but a poor and feeble
part. Without defensive armour, without such offensive
weapons also as were competent to meet and to check the
career of the horsemen, without tactics, too, and without
discipline, it was not possible that an infantry such as this
should withstand the shock of the mail-clad men-at-arms
with their long lances, their strong swords, and their
powerful horses. Hence the serious fighting in those

days took place between the mounted combatants—the men-at-arms.

For the earliest authentic contemporaneous examples of the equipment of this mediæval chivalry, we must refer to a work of the second half of the eleventh century, the Bayeux Tapestry, which illustrates the conquest of England by William of Normandy.

The more important circumstances connected with the Norman invasion and conquest are universally well known. Taking advantage of old promises made to him by Edward the Confessor (promises, however, which the Anglo-Saxon king revoked and cancelled when on his death-bed), and of an oath of allegiance which he had forcibly extorted from Harold (Edward's successor) while he was a prisoner, during Edward's life-time, in Normandy, William invaded England with an army of adventurers, who had been attracted to his standard by the hope of spoil, and who also might possibly have been in some degree influenced by a religious zeal in consequence of the declaration of the Pope against Harold, and in favour of William. Then followed (an event apparently without a parallel, and in most remarkable contrast to the experience of Cæsar so near the same scene of conflict), as the result of a single battle (Hastings, October 14, 1066), fought at the water's edge, the complete subjugation of England to Norman rule, and the establishment of an Anglo-Norman dynasty. We now will consider with what weapons (A.D. 1066) the battle of Hastings was fought, and with it England was lost and won.

In the Bayeux Tapestry we observe that some of the combatants, who are most actively engaged, are on horseback, while others are on foot; but it is apparent, at the first glance, that the arms and equipments of all these combatants are precisely the same. These men, then, who are fighting so vigorously on foot, we may confidently assume to have

I

been intended to represent, not infantry as distinguished from cavalry, but horsemen, who from some cause or other had been dismounted. The designer of this tapestry, we may suppose, did not condescend to give a place in so great a work to any but the "miles"—the noble or knightly soldier; and, so far as the tapestry was concerned, the peasant foot-soldier and the light-armed vassal had no existence. However that may be, the tapestry enables us to examine the arms and appointments of the soldiers of rank one by one.[46]

Fig. 21.—GROUP OF ARMS AND ARMOUR, FROM THE BAYEUX TAPESTRY.

Our attention is first attracted to the *head-pieces* of these warriors. They have the pyramidal form of a pointed cone (though possibly they may have had more than four sides). In front, these helms are elongated by a straight piece of iron, a short bar of rectangular section, which descends over the forehead and nose, and guards them against any horizontal blow : this is the *Nasal.* These conical helms appear to have been constructed of a strong iron framework, which was filled in and enclosed with either a thin metal plate or some woven material. They are not always provided at the back with neck-guards, evidently because the mail hauberk, which rose to the neck of the wearer and covered it, rendered such an appendage unnecessary. In Fig. 21, one of the rarer and more elaborate examples of the Bayeux tapestry helms is represented.

The body armour is a *shirt of mail* or *coat of mail*—a long, narrow, blouse-like garment, having short sleeves descending to the middle of the upper arm, which sometimes, perhaps, was formed of interwoven rings, or chain-work ; but more generally it was constructed of a stout woven fabric, upon which were sewn, or otherwise fixed, in either vertical, or horizontal, or oblique lines, rows of iron rings, or of small plates of the same metal in their form either circular, square, or triangular. [See Fig. 21.] This mail shirt, or *hauberk*, was fitted almost tightly to the person ; and at the bottom it was divided, so that the wearer when mounted might wrap one division of it round each thigh, or when on foot might have his limbs covered by the cleft extremities of his hauberk without any impediment to his free movements. The legs and feet appear to have been enveloped in simple bandages. or in fillets bound round them.

The defensive equipment is seen to have been completed by a *shield*, generally long in form, and rounded or oval at the top, the base being pointed, so that the shield resembles a kite : some examples, however, are circular All the shields are bordered ; some have certain rude dragon-like figures roughly depicted upon them ; but the more general decoration is a simple boss of slight projection, from which several bands radiate ; and studs also adorn both the borders and

the faces of these shields.   On the inner face, a hollowed
space appears quite at the top of these shields, which has been
supposed to have been designed to assist the wearer in carrying
his shield on his back when it was not in use in action.   Lower
down, about in the middle, two shorter hollow grooves, or
hollows, occur, parallel to each other ; and these, with two
slight bars, or two straps, form a double handle, by which
the warrior might adjust his shield to his arm, and wield
it with good effect for his protection.

The offensive weapons introduced into the tapestry are the
lance, sword, mace, axe, and the *bow* and *arrows*.[47]

The *lance* has a slender shaft, equal in circumference
throughout, and it is of moderate length, with a rather broad
iron head, both with and without barbs.   It is shown in use
both as a spear to thrust or charge, and as a javelin to be
thrown from the hand.   On the march the lance was supported
by resting on the stirrup.   The *sword,* the shape of which it
is not very easy to determine with minute exactness, is somewhat large, long, straight, broad in the blade, tapering from
the hilt to the point, and apparently double-edged ; when in
the scabbard, it was worn on the left side.   The *mace,* or
knotty club, very massive at the extremity, resembles the
similar weapon that is associated with our ideas of the Hercules
of classic antiquity.   It was generally made of wood hardened
in the fire, or sometimes of iron which had been modelled to
imitate the knots and inequalities of wood.   The *axe,* having
a single curved blade, presents almost exactly the appearance
of the modern hatchet, except that it has a very long shaft :
it evidently was a weapon that was held in high esteem.   The
bows and *arrows* do not present any peculiar features, nor
does it appear that the latter were used as missiles so frequently as javelins were.   [See Fig. 21.] One or two individuals
wear, with the sword, a long *dagger,* a weapon then rarely
used, but, at a later period, almost universal.   Spurs, con-

GOTHIC ARMOUR, probably Italian.
From Sir Noël Paton's Collection.

sisting of a straight sharp spike, the true "*pryck spurs*," occasionally are seen. The horse appointments are simple, and evidently well adapted to the uses required from them; the bridles have single reins; and the saddles which are provided with stirrups, are secured both under the bodies of the horses and round their chests.

It must be added, that in the Bayeux Tapestry the knightly and noble warriors in both the hostile armies have the same arms and appointments.

In the next place we proceed to consider the military equipment of the vassals and subjects of Louis the Young, Philip Augustus, and Saint Louis, of France, the warriors who conducted the first crusades, the most brilliant of all these remarkable enterprises. This will bring us from the era of the Norman conquest in the year 1066, to the close of the 12th century—that is to about the year 1200. At this period the arms and armour used in England evidently differed from those of France only in certain local peculiarities of minor importance; consequently, in the matter of arms and armour, the period which closes in England with the reign of Richard of the Lion's Heart, may be considered to be the counterpart in all important particulars of the contemporaneous period in France.[48]

The very long plated or mailed shirt with which the comrades and followers of William of Normandy were equipped, early in the 12th century was superseded by a defensive tunic, reaching about to the knees, and having short sleeves; sometimes, as before, it was covered with variously shaped plates of metal; but more generally it was formed of interwoven ring or chain mail, and this was sometimes single, at other times double, and occasionally, though but rarely, it was triple. Narrow and wrought throughout in one piece, this *hauberk* was adjusted to the figure by a belt about the waist; it had a hood or coif, of the same fabric with itself,

which might hang about the neck or be drawn up over the
head of the wearer, at his pleasure; and over this hood, as a
second defence for the head, the close-fitting iron helm was
worn. Under this hauberk the knight wore a tunic, or
camisia, of strong material, probably quilted. His sword
hung at his left side, supported by a broad belt, which was
carried over the right shoulder. This belt was decorated with
pieces of metal of various shapes.

Another change was introduced into the military equipment before the 13th century had far advanced. These
changes we may consider to have been the results of corresponding changes in the civil costume of those ages : and,
indeed, we have every reason to believe that all the early
changes in military equipment, arose simply from the desire
to follow and to conform to what was the prevailing fashion
of each period in the common costume of every-day life.[40]
The long mail tunic of the time of William the Conqueror,
with its skirt divided to cover the lower limbs, was a direct
imitation of the garment of the same description that then
was in constant use; and, in like manner, the coifed hauberk,
as it appeared in the beginning of the 12th century, was made
on the model of the ordinary *vestitus franciscus*—the ordinary
French habit of that period. And, as time advanced, one
change succeeded to another, first in the costume of peace,
and then, as a consequence, in that of war. Thus, early in
the 13th century, the sleeves of the hauberk were lengthened
until they covered the wrists, and the hauberk itself was made
to descend to the middle of the leg, thus following the fashion
which had substituted a long robe for the short tunic. Innovations began to be introduced into other parts of the knight's
equipment. He began to wear gauntlets or gloves of strong
leather, covered with mail or small pieces of metal; and
leggings (*chausses*) also, which were formed of mail, with
corresponding coverings for the feet (*champons*) came into use.

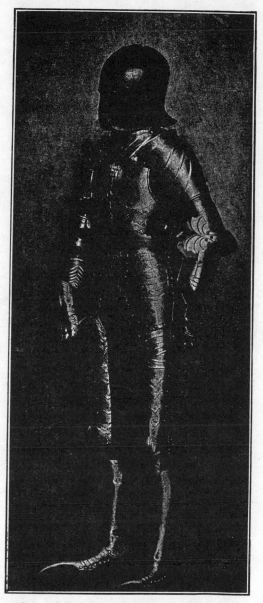

GOTHIC ARMOUR, said to be from the Church of Irene, Constantinople. At Parham.

The belt, too, changed its position. Instead of passing over the shoulder, it was adjusted about the waist, or even somewhat below the waist; and, being thus placed, it was permitted to drop down a little in front where the ends were united, and through the fastening was passed the sword, which hung obliquely from hilt to point, the point sloping away from the body on the left side. [See Note 69.]

A more important change, and one which was attended with no little inconvenience to the knights, took place in the time of Philip Augustus (A.D. 1180 to 1223, and therefore contemporary with our Henry II., Richard I., John, and Henry III). The small and tight-fitting head-piece was superseded by the more massive helm, or *heaume,* in the time of Philip Augustus; and in England the same change is exemplified, at the same period, in the great seal of Richard I. This helm is nearly cylindrical in form, flat at the top, sufficiently large to be put on easily over the mail coif, and of such height that it reached down almost, if not quite, far enough to rest on the shoulders. Two plates or bars of iron were fixed on the front, forming a cross; above the transverse bar, openings, called *vues* or *sights,* were pierced for vision, and holes were drilled lower down for breathing. This ponderous head-piece, which was carried suspended by a small chain from the saddle-bow (" where," says M. Lacombe, " it must have looked rather like a travelling kettle—*marmite de voyage* ") was assumed by the knight only when on the point of going into action. When he lost the battle of Mansourah, Saint Louis wore on his head a head-piece such as this.[50]

The use of this mighty *heaume,* introduced in the reign of Philip Augustus, was maintained until that of Philip IV., A.D. 1285—1314. An example is given in Fig. 22, which is a portrait of Saint Louis, as he is represented in the painted glass of the Cathedral of Chartres. Of the mail hauberk here the lowest part only, with the sleeves and the defence for the throat are shown. The rest of the figure is covered with the long, loose, flowing, sleeveless surcoat, which is secured about the waist by a narrow belt; the lower limbs are covered with chausses of mail, prolonged to cover the feet; the spurs are long, straight, and sharp. The heaume, or great helm, covers the head; the shield, which is very large, is charged with the ancient arms of France—the golden fleurs-de-lys, that is, are scattered over the whole surface of the azure field; and from the very long lance, the royal banner, charged with the same insignia, is displayed. No sword is visible, which, with other conditions of the design, shows that the composition has been *reversed*, so as to cause the right and left sides of the figures of both rider and horse to have the appearance of having changed places. The horse-furniture is very simple, and the charger is not encumbered with any bardings. The long surcoat, open in front, shown in Fig. 22,

Fig. 22. – SAINT LOUIS: 1226—1270.
(From Glass in Chartres Cathedral.)

became general at the time of Saint Louis, A.D. 1226—1270. Our small engraving does not show any visible tokens of the presence of the padded or quilted tunic, the *haqueton*, or *gambeson*, that was worn, doubtless, by the sainted king, as it was by other armed warriors of his era, beneath his mail, and which was generally as long, and often a little longer, than the hauberk itself.[51] The knightly equipment, as it is represented in this Fig. 22, must have been painfully oppressive to the wearer

from its weight and its thickness ; and, at a glance it must be
seen that a military costume such as this was singularly
ill qualified to be worn with either comfort or advantage
under the burning sun of Syria, or even in France. And
again, when he had been dismounted by any chance, it is
equally evident that a knight in this armour must have
entered upon the duties of a foot soldier under singular disadvantages.

But the armour of the middle ages had by no means
arrived at its greatest weight, or its most oppressive massive-
ness, in the days of Philip le Bel. About the middle of the
13th century, the injuries to which mail armour was liable
whenever it was exposed in any unusual manner, naturally
led to the introduction of additional defences for such parts of
a knight's person, as from experience he had learned to be
most in need of them. Small plates of iron, of various shapes,
were fixed, generally by straps and buckles, over the mail, in
order to give an increased security to the joints at the elbows
and knees. These secondary defences were severally entitled
coudières and *genouillières, elbow-guards,* that is, and *knee-
guards.* Another step in the same direction added *shoulder-
guards,* or *épaulières.* Then, as the 13th century passed into
the 14th, there succeeded hollow plates of metal which might
guard the outer or the most exposed surfaces of the limbs
themselves—plates to be buckled over the mail, and adjusted
to the outer surface of the upper arm, and to the front of the
lower arm, which bore the appropriate name of *gardes-bras,* or
arm-guards. Similar pieces of armour were fastened in the
same way also over the mail *cuisses* or *chausses,* to protect the
thigh and leg; these are *trumelières,* or *grevières.* A further
advance completed the additional defence of the limbs, by
carrying the plates round the limbs. This was effected simply
by having double plates, which would fit the limbs, fixed
together with hinges, and which might be secured by straps

and buckles. The hinges are almost always found to have been adjusted to the outside of the limbs.[52]

The thick quilted under-tunic—the *gambeson*, or *haqueton*, the mail hauberk, the additional defensive plates, and, over all, the helm and the surcoat, with the belts, and the shields, and the weapons, must have combined to form an equipment of such excessive weight that, when once he had fallen to the ground, the knight would find the act of rising to be attended with no little difficulty; and we may well believe that these carefully armed warriors not unfrequently lay prostrate and helpless, at the mercy of the meanest soldier who carried a knife, or liable to be trampled to death by any charge or retreat that might pass over them.

In this state of the military system it would soon become a necessity that a revolution in armour should be carried into effect; and there could be no uncertainty concerning the course that it would take. Recent changes would clearly presage the fresh change that was imminent. But before we enter upon any inquiries concerning the actual results that were effected by the revolution in armour to which we now refer, in order that we may be able to form a completely correct conception of the arms and armour of the 12th and 13th centuries, some details connected with our subject in those centuries must here be brought forward and described.

The knights of those centuries—that grand epoch in mediæval art—were so far from considering that their armour was sufficient for their protection, that they still retained the supplementary defence of the *shield*. It is indeed true, that their shields, which were flat or straight at the top, pointed at the base, and with the sides formed in graceful curves, were considerably smaller than those of earlier times, and that their dimensions continued to diminish as the 12th century came to its close. At first, these shields were generally "bowed" on their front face, that is, they generally presented

a convex external contour; but the smallest shields, which were almost "heater-shaped," were either quite flat or nearly so. Suspended from a *guige*, or shield-belt, which passed over the right shoulder, these shields, when the knights were dismounted, either were adjusted in such a manner as to cover the left hip, and with it the hilt and the upper part of the sword; or, at other times, they seem to have been fastened to the waist-belt by a clasp or very short strap.   When in the saddle, the knight would carry his shield—his *ecu*, as he called it at that period—over his shoulder, or,
perhaps, slung from his saddle-bow; but,
in the charge, and generally, as it would
appear, when in action, the shield was
carried in front of the knight's person, as
a breast-plate, hanging down from the
guige which was passed round his neck:
thus, while the right arm was free to wield
the lance, the mace, or the sword, the
left was equally at liberty to direct the
course of the charge.[53]

That the *sword* was worn on the left
side, has been already stated.   When on
foot the knight held it almost in a vertical
position, and he caused it to hang over
his left thigh obliquely when he was on
horseback.

Fig. 23.—EFFIGY OF A FRENCH PRINCE, about A.D. 1225: Abbey Church of St. Denis.

The noble personage who is represented in the accompanying engraving (Fig. 23) is some member, but it is not certain what member, of the old royal family of France, whose effigy is still preserved in the most interesting Abbey Church of St. Denis, near Paris. This figure, which in the engraving seems to have suffered a transposition of sides (probably the drawing on the wood for the engraver was *not* reversed, and

therefore the engraving itself *is* reversed) is thoroughly French
in all its details ; and, consequently, it must be regarded as an
example of the military equipment that was in use in France at
the commencement of the 13th century amongst personages of
high rank; but even in this local acceptation, the figure is in
some degree fanciful, and particularly in the introduction of an
embattled or mural crown instead of a regular head-piece.[54]

The cylindrical *helm* which was worn from
the times of Philip Augustus to those of Saint
Louis, under Philip IV, became more conical—
a change which cannot be considered to have improved the appearance of the head-piece, while it
failed to diminish its excessive weight.   In the

Fig. 24.—FRENCH
HELM : about
A.D. 1300.

monuments of this age, the helm, or " heaume,"
often appears in the form represented in Fig. 24.

At the same time, the socks of mail, which covered the
feet, show a tendency to become lengthened into a point.

Of the weapons in use at this same period, and which
were directed against the armour of mail with its covering
plates, the first and most important was the *lance*.   It varied
in its length ; but now it was made only to be wielded when
grasped in the hand, and not to be thrown under any circumstances as a javelin.   The shaft was strong and generally of
uniform thickness, and the head long, rather broad, and
without any barbs.   At first all the knights, without any
distinction, were considered to enjoy the same right and title
to display from their lances, immediately below the lance-
head, a *pennon,* or *gonfanon*—a small flag, which fluttered in
the wind.   After a while, however, this privilege was reserved
for rich and powerful knights, who came to the war attended
with a retinue of vassals and dependants.   Every knight of
this rank assumed the distinctive title of " Knight Banneret,"
a title derived from that variety of mediæval flag which was
distinguished as a " banner."   In England all knights dis-

played the pointed or swallow-tailed " pennon," charged with
their badge ; and, instead of pennons, the nobles and men of
greater wealth and importance, who bore the title of " Ban-
nerets," from their lances displayed square (or rectangular
elongated) "banners," upon which their armorial insignia were
blazoned in full.[65]

Until the 14th century the *sword* varied but little from
the form in which it is depicted in the Bayeux Tapestry.
The hilt, with the guard, produces a cruciform figure ; the
blade is long, straight, tapering slightly towards the point,
double-edged, and having its two edges separated by a central
ridge.[66]

Of the remaining weapon, the *mace*, hammer, or *martel-
de-fer*, it is unnecessary for us to give any description, since
the representation of a mace in the engraving, Fig. 27, No. 3,
is able to speak all that can be desired on its own behalf. In
England the same mace was used, and also a regular *hammer*,
of which a remarkable example exists in the effigy in mail
armour preserved at Great Malvern.

At present we have been treating only of the arming and
the equipment of soldiers, at the lowest of knightly rank, all
of whom, as a matter of course, were horsemen. The foot-
soldier of the same period, whose presence is scarcely to be
discerned in the imagery of the middle ages—at that period
of the middle ages, at any rate, now under consideration—
cannot be described with certain accuracy. It may be assumed,
however, that he wore for defence a strongly quilted garment,
with a simple yet strong head-piece ; and that of his weapons
the sling was the most common, and the most dangerous the
French or the Turkish bow, the former of moderate size, and
the latter smaller, but both of them made of goats' horns
which had been brought from the East after the first Crusade.
These foot-soldiers also used the cross-bow, which was not
the powerful weapon that it afterwards became. K

From this slight and unfinished sketch it is evident that the infantry of France in the 12th, 13th, and 14th centuries, which was composed of the vassals and feudal dependants of the nobles and knights, as a military force was altogether distinct from the contemporary arm of the same class and rank in England. Of the English yeomen of those days, those famous archers, it certainly cannot be justly said that in the warlike imagery of the middle ages they could claim no place.

When the barons and knights of the West went to Syria under the banner of Richard Cœur de Lion (A.D. 1189 to 1199), and under that of Louis IX. (A.D. 1226 to 1270) to Egypt, in those regions which were so different from their own native lands they had to encounter warriors, whose armour and arms and system of warfare were alike strange and new to them. It will not be devoid of interest for us to compare these renowned combatants, and to observe in wha' more prominent and important particulars they differed from one another in their military appointments. This difference may be concisely summed up in the two words "heavy" and "light." The Crusaders were heavy cavalry, the Saracens were light cavalry. The soldiers of the West formed in a solid line for the charge; and they were well prepared to deliver terrible thrusts with stout lances, and to strike crushing blows with ponderous and strong maces and swords. The soldiers of the East were equipped for active and swift movement, and for rapid manœuvres; they were masters of fence with the light keen-edged scimitar, and were well skilled in handling the bow and arrow, and in darting with sure aim the sharp *jerrid* or slender javelin.

The Saracen chiefs wore armour of ring or chain mail, admirably wrought, strong, and capable of great resistance, yet light and flexible, and in every respect very greatly superior to the more massive and cumbersome personal equipment

SUIT OF MAXIMILIAN ARMOUR: 16th Century.
Belonging to Mr. Percy Macquoid.

which the Crusaders carried with them to the first Crusade.[57] This oriental mail also was richly and delicately adorned with gilding, but had no additional defences of plates attached to it. The head-piece, in like manner, was light, and afforded a remarkable contrast to the Western heaume; it was gilt and damascened with gold, with a far higher art than was then known amongst the armourers of the West. This casque, which was made of iron, was globular in form, or somewhat pointed at the crown; it was provided with a nasal, which was prolonged until it rose above the crown of the head-piece, where it expanded to receive a plume. The shield was small in size, round, boldly convex, and with an umbo, or boss, which projected and ended in a point. The offensive weapons were the dart, the scimitar, the dagger, the bow and arrows; and, after the first Crusade, to them the lance was added. The inferior soldiers of the Saracens were, for the most part. archers.

The knights of the West, well padded as they were, armed in mail and plate, and fastened to their saddles by the weight of their helms and of their double and triple armour, armed with long and strong lances, and mounted on immense Norman and Flemish horses, when formed in their long, well-dressed and serried line, brought to bear upon their opponents a weight and a pressure that at the first proved to be irresistible. Thus, in the earliest engagements, the Saracens were almost invariably broken and discomfited. But, when they had acquired some experience of their invaders, the Saracens were not long in recovering all the advantages which, for a while, had been in abeyance. It was not possible for them to be unconscious of the fact that in their climate theirs was the superior equipment, and the more advantageous system of warfare. So they returned, undismayed, to a conflict which for the moment had appeared to be almost hopeless. Lighter and more alert than the Crusaders, they rushed now on one

flank of their massive battalions, and now on the other; as
their opponents stood firm, yet almost powerless, they would
sweep round them like a whirlwind; or, if at any point they
met with even a severe repulse, they returned speedily to the
attack, with fresh vigour and in increased numbers. And
they were brave warriors, those dexterous and indefatigable
horsemen. They would beat down the levelled lances with
their scimitars; and, while the knights, compelled to use their
swords, were with difficulty bringing those weapons into play,
the quick-eyed Saracens sought and found weak points where
they might drive home their finely-tempered blades.

And, again, comparatively trifling obstacles, such as might
naturally arise from the nature of the ground whereon they
fought, would check, and perhaps completely paralyse, the
otherwise resistless charge of the heavy cavalry (it was the
old story of the phalanx repeating itself), and would expose
them to be sifted by the Saracens with showers of arrows,
and with the tremendous *Greek fire*. This Greek fire was
the terror of the Crusaders. " Every time," says Joinville,
" that the good king (the French Crusader Prince) heard
them projecting this fire, which when in the air was attended
with a loud roar, he would throw himself prostrate on the
ground, and with uplifted hands, and his face turned towards
heaven, he would vehemently implore for himself and his
army the Divine protection against so tremendous an engine
of destruction."

Now, concerning the armour which has just been described,
perhaps at too great length and with excessive minuteness of
detail, it may be inquired whether, massive and cumbersome
as it was, it afforded, at any rate, a complete and perfect
defence. The hauberk, supported by the quilted under-tunic,
and strengthened by the additional plates, very generally
offered an effectual resistance to both blows and thrusts of the
sword, and to arrow-shots. By the thrust or stroke of the

lance this armour was not unfrequently broken through or torn; and, even when the mail held firm, the man was not always much the less injured by blows such as these. He, indeed, was so far in safety that he had not received the lance-point in his body; but, nevertheless, he might be very seriously injured by the bruising effect of the blow. Against the mace the hauberk was even less effective for securing the wearer, than against the lance. It is true that the mace, or battle-axe, was chiefly used for blows struck upon the head of an enemy, and, consequently, it had to do for the most part with the helm. Massive as were the helms, or " heaumes," that we of late have been examining, they were often crushed beneath the mace-blows that fell upon them; or, if they remained entire, these helms were necessarily powerless to save the wearer from being stunned, and consequently from losing his equilibrium in his saddle—a most serious, and in all probability, as we have seen, a fatal mischance. And, besides, since they constantly rested on the shoulders, these helms, under the force of a strong blow, sometimes would cause a fracture of the collar-bone. When once on the ground, however he might have been unhorsed and brought down there, the knight was at the mercy of the foot-soldiers; that is, he was in their power, and, unless they supposed that he might produce an important ransom, he was certain to find no mercy at their hands. One chance, indeed, the knight had, even when on the ground and prostrate, and for this he was indebted to the strength of his armour. It was just possible that repeated blows from either spear, or dagger, or club, might be necessary before his armour could be beaten through; and meanwhile his assailants might be assaulted in their turn, and before they had found time to complete their work and to kill him, they might themselves have fallen.

The French historians, who have written concerning the times now under our consideration, are unanimous in their warm commendation of the strong and almost impenetrable armour, which then had been recently invented and brought generally into use. They evidently take delight in recording that when armed in their favourite armour, the knight was in safety until his war-horse had been killed under him. They admit that when once he had been dismounted and thrown on the ground, it would not be possible for him to rise again without assistance; and, therefore, in such a case they are aware that the knight's armour would be to him of but little avail. And it is a consequence of such a condition of things, these chroniclers add, that in battles the loss in killed had become so much less than it had almost invariably been in earlier and ruder times.[58] All this certainly was evidence of progress; but still it is somewhat remarkable that the progress thus achieved, and that all these complicated devices for the protection of the person of the combatant should belong to the period which is called the " Age of Chivalry," and that this term " chivalry " should always be considered to imply the existence of the most undaunted personal courage, coupled with an almost culpable disregard of life and safety.

" For myself," adds M. Lacombe, " in my estimation the little[59] modern foot-soldier, in the cloth tunic of his simple uniform, who stands firm and steady in the face of both rifled cannon and rifles, approaches nearer to the realisation of the military ideal, and is a more truthful impersonation of the chivalrous than the great baron of the olden time, covered from head to foot with an iron sheathing of mail and plate. They certainly had the name—chivalry—in those days; but whether they possessed the thing itself—the chivalrous—is questionable."

Whatever sentiments he may entertain towards the warriors of antiquity, the sympathies of M. Lacombe evidently are not with the armour-clad barons and knights of the middle ages. Between them and our own soldiers and the French and other European soldiers of to-day, it is scarcely possible to draw a faithful parallel.   Each group belongs to its own age, and is surrounded and associated with its own distinct and characteristic accessories.   We know, and we hope that we are able to appreciate, the true genuine pure chivalrous spirit that lives in the hearts of living soldiers, their birthright at once and their inheritance from their comrades who have gone before them.   May we not also concede the spirit of chivalry, in its truth and purity, to those more remote men-at-arms, in whom the genius of their own times is reflected with such vivid fidelity?   If science was in its early childhood when they wore their armour and laid their lances in rest, art then had attained to a vigorous and noble maturity.   The men of the days of chivalry flourished amidst chivalrous surroundings; and, surely, it is scarcely consistent to assume, because of the excellence of their armour, that they were not chivalrous themselves." [60]

CHAPTER VIII.

Arms and Armour of the Middle Ages.—Part II.

In the reign of Philip VI., of Valois (A.D. 1328 to 1350), in France, and when in England Edward III. was king, the terrible and most unhappy hundred years' war between those countries had its commencement.[61] Then there appeared on the scene of the great historic drama the *Grandes Compagnies* —armies, that is, composed of mixed bands of mercenary soldiers who, having made a military life their profession, were always ready to enter into any service which would secure to them the highest pay, accompanied with the most attractive promise of plunder. These men, who included the natives of many countries in their ranks, knew no other interest than their personal advantages, and owed no allegiance except to themselves. In the war between England and France, they sometimes were French and sometimes English, their standard having been determined by their paymaster. During intervals of truce, these bands carried on war, and most atrocious and cruel was their system of warfare, on their own account with the peasantry, and with such citizens as might be exposed to their attacks. They included in their numbers cavalry and infantry, men-at-arms and archers, and miscellaneous bands. Men of noble birth and high rank rode amongst them side by side with peasants, or with serfs who had escaped from vassalage. Alike in their passions, their morals, their pursuits, and their military aspect, it may easily be supposed that but slight distinction amongst them grew out of any differences there might be in their birth, their education, or their original rank.

To these men, brigands as they were, belongs the merit of having brought about that revolution in arms and armour, to which reference was made in the last chapter, and which the equipment of the more honourable troops of Louis IX. had rendered both necessary and inevitable.[62]

The civil costume had just undergone a thorough change. The long double robe, the coat and surcoat (*cotte* and *surcot*) which had been worn in France since the time of Philip Augustus, had given place to the *pourpoint*, a kind of paletot, fitting tight to the figure, buttoned from top to bottom in front, without any collar, provided with half-sleeves, padded and quilted, and swelling over the chest. As we see in the monuments of the period, under this pourpoint the coat, or *cotte*, was still worn; but now it had become a narrow and short blouse, in comparison with its earlier form and proportions, although still its sleeves might be longer than those of the pourpoint, and it might descend lower than that garment. Instead of the coat (*cotte*) in its new form, the men-at-arms adopted as their under-garment the quilted pourpoint, which they wore without sleeves; and over this, for defence, they placed a shirt or tunic of fine mail, a little longer than their pourpoint, and having sleeves; this they called the *haubergeon*, or diminished hauberk, and it was soon worn by all ranks, and the original long hauberk was altogether abandoned. In England, however, the shortened mail tunic generally retained the old name, and was called either hauberk or haubergeon. Whatever additional guards had been affixed to the mail of the hauberk in earlier times, to protect the shoulders, elbows, and knees, and also the more exposed surfaces of the limbs, were retained; and at this time the limb-guards were made to enclose the limbs within back and front pieces, hinged and buckled together; and the lower arm and the leg received habitually the same defences of plate-armour, which before, while almost always given to the upper arm and the thigh, in their case were rather exceptional than general. These defences for the lower arm and the leg were severally named *avant-bras* and *grevières, lower arm-guards,* and *leg-pieces.*

The *garde-bras,* or upper arm-guard, had its form somewhat modified at each extremity, both towards the shoulder and the bend of the arm, where it was finished in three or four circular overlapping plates, which gave more liberty to the limb. At the shoulders also, and at the openings in the arm-guards at the elbow-joint, and in like manner at the similar opening in the leg-pieces at the joints of the limb, where the mail would be visible, shields of very small dimensions were fixed, which more or less resembled convex discs. In England, at this time, the cuisses and chausses, or leg-coverings of mail, were not worn beneath the plate, nor had the shortened hauberk sleeves, except quite early in the new period. The openings, however, in the plate, at all the joints of the limbs, and on the instep, were filled with small pieces of mail fixed within the plates. The feet were covered, not with mail, but with *sollerets,* formed of articulated plates, and the *spurs* were always of the *rouelle* form. The new armour for the foot, following the civil fashion (or leading it), eventually, in the 15th century, ended in extravagantly long points; and then the spurs were also scarcely less extravagant in their projection from beyond the heels. It will be observed that the plate sollerets were pointed, from the time of their first introduction, throughout the 14th century, and until some little time before the close of the 15th century.

The happiest innovation of all was the abolition of the heaume, or great helm, and the substitution in its stead of the *basinet,* a smaller and lighter head-piece, which was somewhat globular in form, but was raised a little above the head, and terminated above in a point. The basinet, while always conforming to the general characteristics of its proper type, admitted many modifications in its form and contour. As it decidedly differed from the heaume, in being only a true head-piece without descending over the head and resting on the shoulders, notwithstanding the circumstance that it was often made in such a prolonged shape at the back and sides as to cover the neck of the wearer, the basinet was considered to be incomplete without having appended to it, and depending from it, a mail defence for the neck and shoulders, called the *camail*. This is the lower part of a mail coif, a hood, or a tippet of mail, which was fixed to the basinet, and hung gracefully over the shoulders, covering the upper part of the body-armour, but leaving the face bare. The defensive action of the basinet was completed by the further addition of an efficient protection for the face, which was accomplished by means of a piece that would completely close-in the open front of the basinet itself. This piece, called the *mesail*, or *mursail* (from the kind

Fig. 25.—FRENCH BASINET WITH CLOSED VENTAILE.

of resemblance it necessarily bore to the muzzle of an animal), but more generally known in England as the *ven-*
.üle, or visor, was pierced for both sight and breathing, and was adjusted in such a manner that it could be raised or lowered, or could be altogether removed, at the pleasure of the wearer; and, as a matter of course, this visor was not lowered and secured in front of the face except when the combat was imminent. In England the basinet was constantly worn with the camail, but without any ventaile; and in this case the great helm was retained, and in action was worn over the basinet, and, as of old, resting on the shoulders. A plate for additional defence sometimes was screwed upon a basinet.

In England the camailed basinet ceased to be worn when the
15th century was only two or three years old; but the basinet
itself continued in use, having, in place of the camail, a gorget
of steel plate, encircling and protecting the throat. In Fig. 25
a representation is given of a French basinet, without any
camail, but having the acutely-peaked visor or mesail lowered
and closed.[63]

The men-at-arms still used the old weapons of the earlier
knights with some comparatively trifling modifications. Their
lances, longer and heavier than before, instead of following the
earlier usage of having the shaft plain and even from end to
end, had their shaft increasing in circumference near the end
furthest from the point; and, also at the handle the shaft
passed through a small circular shield, or hand-guard (called a
vamplate), which was fixed to the shaft of the lance, and was
found to be of great use in giving firmness and stability to the
grasp, as well as for protecting the hand.

The *sword* is also seen to differ in a very decided manner
from the corresponding weapon of the earlier ages, when,
having been made to be used both for striking blows with the
edge and thrusting with the point, it could scarcely be considered really efficient for either purpose. Now, the sword,
designed to be used only for delivering a thrust with the
point becomes a *rapier*, long and slight and sharply pointed,
and thoroughly efficient for the use assigned to it. This
description, which is applicable to French swords, does not
extend to the contemporaneous English weapons. In England, the earlier swords, even if they were not very perfectly
adapted for thrusting, were perfect in the hands that then
wielded them for striking blows; and, later, the English
swords of the fourteenth century and of the early part of the
fifteenth century, while well qualified to inflict wounds with
the point, were second to none in their efficiency for the
delivery of genuine hard English blows with their edge. The

rapier belongs to another—a later and a perfectly distinct period—in the history of English weapons. In France the *mace*, the hammer amongst weapons, came into more general use when the rapier form of sword began to prevail.

The infantry,[61] in the fourteenth century, began to arise from out of its nothingness, and to assume on the field of battle that importance which from thenceforth was destined continually to increase. The power of this arm was first shown by the foot-soldiers and the archers of England, and this was done by them in a manner that was felt very severely by the French. At Crécy (August 26, 1346), the first lesson was given, and it was a very harsh one. On that day, however, the French army had in its ranks an infantry force which ought to have been able to have decided the victory. This was the corps of Genoese crossbow-men, in the pay of France, which in the first instance was opposed to the English archers. Unhappily, the crossbow-men had to open the discharge of their bolts while their bow-strings were still wet from a heavy shower, and so the missiles would not fly with their proper force. On the other hand, the archers of England had succeeded in keeping their bow-strings dry. When the Genoese desired to retire (and they had a good reason for such a desire), King Philip, who with his knights and men-at-arms was in the rear of the Genoese, would not suffer them to fall back, and, in his violent indignation, as a true (?) warrior of the knightly class, he exclaimed—" Forward, and strike down this useless rabble, who thus are blocking up the way in our front!" And with his squadrons of cavaliers the king charged the army of England, trampling under foot the dead bodies of his own Genoese crossbow-men.

This was far from being the first occasion on which such an incident had taken place; nor was Crécy by any means the first mediæval battle that commenced with the destruction of the foot soldiers by the cavalry of their own army.

When we consider the utter contempt in which the knights held the unfortunate peasantry whom they dragged with them to battle, it certainly does not appear very easy to assign any satisfactory reason for their encumbering themselves with such auxiliaries. Armed as they were, the French foot-soldiers could not possibly oppose any effectual resistance to a charge of mounted men-at-arms : and the estimation in which they were held by their noble and knightly comrades is shown but too significantly by their readiness to crush and destroy them, at any moment, on the very field of battle. The presence of these troops, then, if troops they may be called, in the armies of France, can be explained apparently only by the fact, that it was customary to begin a battle with such an attack as the foot-soldiers might be able to make. It is certain that battles then opened with an advance of the French infantry; and it would seem to have been the motive of the commanders in ordering such a movement, to place their own inferior troops in a position where they might cause some little annoyance to the hostile chivalry, and might take off the edge of their fresh energy ; but the discomfiture and the destruction also of the infantry, while discharging the duty assigned to them, were regarded as matters of course ; so much so, in fact, that if they fought too well, and accordingly were not routed with sufficient speed to satisfy the impatience of their own knights, those valiant warriors took upon themselves to complete the overthrow of their hapless fellow-countrymen, and, like King Philip at Crécy, delivered their own charge through (or, more probably, over) the shattered ranks in their front.

At Crécy, the Genoese were not quite so easily crushed as the royal chivalry doubtless had expected; indeed, so far were they from submitting with good humour to the charge of their mounted allies, that they actually resisted it. Thereupon a strange, yet disastrous confusion ensued; and thus were the French knights for a considerable time entangled amongst the Genoese, while the English archers with a sure aim poured upon them their deadly arrows in flights thick as hail. At last, having disposed of the Genoese with no little difficulty, in grievously diminished numbers the French knights fell upon the English archers, and they succeeded in breaking their lines, but not without fresh and very serious loss. Then they closed with the knights of England, and were driven back by them. Such a result was inevitable. Once more, in retreating, the French knights were exposed to the terrible discharge of the English archers; by whom, without any such deliberate intention on their part, the fate of the Genoese was fearfully avenged. So the victory that day was with England.

But there yet remains to be noticed another event that took place at Crécy, which was calculated to enhance most powerfully the importance of infantry, and to secure for that arm a very different reputation with the highest military authorities. At that battle, setting an example altogether new and without precedent, the Prince of Wales (the Black Prince) caused his men-at-arms to dismount; and with the butts of their lances resting on the ground, acting as infantry —infantry with knightly armour and weapons—in obedience to his command, they received and repulsed the charge of the French knights. The complete success of this manœuvre caused it to be imitated for at least two centuries. The French made an experiment, in imitation of the tactics of the Black Prince, at Poitiers (September 19, 1356). Unfortunately for themselves, they applied the excellent example of the Prince in a manner which reversed both his motive and his course of action. The English army had been formed in order of battle on rising ground, difficult of access, and to which indeed there was a practicable approach for an attacking force only by a single defile. By this pass the French men-at-

arms were led, dismounted and in their full armour, to attack
the English position, and, if possible, to carry it by storm.
This was an enterprise of a very different character from the
calm and steady formation of his dismounted knights by the
Black Prince, for the reception of an impetuous and somewhat disorderly attack.   The English archers at Poitiers, well
covered by thickets, lined the pass, and with their arrows drove
the toiling men-at-arms of France before them in terrible
disorder and with frightful loss.   Two of the three French
divisions broke into hopeless confusion, and fled, without
having effected much more than an advance within sight of
the enemy.   The third division, led by King John (A.D. 1350
to 1363), made an effort to rally and to save the day; but
they were assailed, first by the same formidable archers who
had routed their comrades, and then by the English knights,
who remounted for their charge.   Escape for them, consequently, was impossible, and they were either killed or cap-
tured almost to a man.

At Cocherel, and at Auray, some time later (May 16, and
September 29, 1364), we discover a novel application of the
same principles.   The men-at-arms dismounted and charged
on foot; and in order that they might be able to manage their
lances more effectually under such unusual conditions, before
they went into action they reduced their length from the customary twelve feet to about five feet.   At Auray the English
archers showed that they possessed other military qualities, in
addition to their well-known ability to shoot with a sure aim
and great power from a long distance.   Intermixed with the
dismounted men-at-arms of their own army, with their swords
and cutlasses they fought hand to hand against the lances of
the enemy.

It is necessary that we should here explain the unquestionable fact, that at the period under our notice the English
foot-soldier, in addition to the superiority of his military

equipment, was superior to the French soldier of the same
order in the great and vital qualities of courage and energy.
This arose, we may assert with confidence, from the treatment
(so different from that which was experienced by the French
foot-soldier) shown to the foot-soldier of England by the
nobles and knights of his own nation. By them he was
treated with consideration and respect and confidence, as
a good soldier and a brave man; and whenever an occasion
served, he received practical proofs of the high estimation in
which he was held. In battle some English barons and
distinguished knights always joined the bands of their archers,
and fought side by side with them in their own ranks.

The French naturally desired to have archers of ther own;
and they soon succeeded in organising a force of bowmen
who, in the estimation of Juvenal des Ursins, an historian who
wrote a little later, were as good, and indeed even superior to
'he archers of England. " In a short time," says this chronicler,
' the French archers became so expert in their use of the
bow, that they were able to discharge their arrows with a
more sure aim than the English; and, indeed, if these archers
had formed a close confederacy amongst themselves, they
might have become a more powerful body than the princes
and nobles of France; and, accordingly, it was the apprehension of such a result as this which caused the French king to
suppress the archer force in his army." Possibly the French
writer may have been slightly prepossessed in favour of his own
countrymen; and when he found that the French archers
were considered to be capable of surpassing nobles and knights
in military prowess, he might naturally suppose them to be
the most perfect archers in the world. At any rate, their
own sovereign considered them to be even too perfect; and
so he did not give to the bowmen of England an opportunity
for bringing this question of national superiority to a practical
test. Without a doubt, the archers of England would have

candidly admitted their own comparative inferiority, when
once they had felt a proof of being inferior.   A very decided
and decisive proof would certainly have been required, since,
even in those days, we may suppose that there existed some
presentiment of that later evidence of insular obtuseness, which
is said now to render English soldiers unable to understand
when they are beaten.   In the days of Crécy they were not
beaten; and Juvenal des Ursins has told us that, some little
time after Crécy, the French archers were too good to be
permitted to attempt to beat their English contemporaries.
Certain English writers, on the contrary, are disposed to suspect it to have been just as well for those skilled archers of
France that they never were able to make the trial.

It is a singular fact that an early French historian should
not only have described the powerful impression produced in
his own times upon the popular mind in France by a body of
soldiers formed from the humbler classes, but also should
have shown that this most important force troubled the
mighty ones of the earth with an implied threat of a revolution, distant, indeed, but in due time certain to take place.

We may now consider the military equipment of archers
in their palmy days.

Their proper weapon, the *bow*, to which they owed their
reputation, by right first claims our attention.   Amongst the
archers of England it was exclusively the great bow, five feet
in length, and formed of yew, which at a range of at least
240 yards discharged a strong arrow, sharp and barbed.   The
shafts of these arrows were provided, near their base, with
feathers, or with strips of leather.   They were carried, not in
such a quiver as appears in antique statues of Apollo or Diana,
but bound together in a sheaf, and so suspended from the
waist-belt.   When in the act of commencing battle, the
archer shook out his sheaf of arrows and placed them under
his left foot, their points outwards; and thus he had only

to stoop down in order to take them one by one in his hand as they were required. " A first-rate English archer," says Prince Louis Napoleon, " who in a single minute was unable to draw and discharge his bow twelve times with a range of 240 yards, and who in these twelve shots once missed his man, was very lightly esteemed." It is doubtful whether, at so great a distance, an arrow could have struck its mark with sufficient force to penetrate a knight's surcoat and hauberk of mail ; but it would kill his horse, which was not yet provided with defensive armour, and this was the very circumstance which caused that change in tactics which has been mentioned.[65]

At all periods in the history of warfare it always has been a matter of great difficulty for infantry to resist and repel the shock of a cavalry charge. In some ages, as for example in the 12th century, this was a military problem for which it was held to be hopeless to seek for any solution ; while at other periods, as in antiquity, this same problem was considered to be difficult, though by no means impossible, to be solved. It does not appear from Homer that the war-chariots, which then took the place of cavalry properly so called, were particularly formidable to the combatants who fought on foot. It is evident that they served simply to carry the warriors here and there, on the field of battle, with greater rapidity than they could have moved without them. The warriors voluntarily, and, indeed, systematically, dismounted from their chariots when they were about to engage in actual combat, and they fought on foot ; which, assuredly, they would not have done, had their chariots offered to them those advantages in action which afterwards they acquired when mounted on horseback. Thus we never hear of any such thing as a charge by the Homeric war-chariots.[66] The Greek phalanx, again, had no great dread of cavalry—a fact easy to be understood, since to break into that massive and serried formation a body of horse would have been required, far more numerous, and infinitely better provided and trained than the Greeks or their enemies were able to bring into the field. In like manner, the Roman legion did not consider it necessary to bestow much attention on hostile cavalry. The precautions, however, that were adopted at the battle of Zama, by Scipio, against the Numidian cavalry, a body of horsemen of a peculiarly formidable character, have been observed and recorded. He formed his lines in such a manner that unusually wide spaces were left between the companies into which his legions were divided. Scipio knew that horses, when they are caused to charge men in line, and especially when they feel the points of weapons, only attempt to glide along the length of the obstacle and to escape by the flanks; and, consequently, he desired to oppose to the Numidians a formation of his infantry with a front as little extended as possible. The plans of that illustrious general were attended with the full measure of the success that he anticipated from them. And, in general also, the legion which fought in its customary open formation, divided into sections of companies, was in an excellent condition to resist cavalry with good effect. In the middle ages, on the other hand, either the foot soldiers were very inferior in military qualities (which was really the fact) or (which also in some degree was probable) the art of training horses had made a great advance, or from some other causes, for a long period it appeared to be altogether hopeless for any infantry to attempt to encounter the career of the Western mounted men-at-arms. The revival of the military art dates from the very day upon which this opinion ceased to prevail.

The charge of cavalry is checked by two forms of resistance, which, though really distinct, are generally applied in combination. First, that is, by presenting a line of pikes or bayonets, which is too strong to be broken; and secondly, while the charge is yet being made, by striking down by means of missiles, either arrows or bullets, so many of the horses that the advancing column is necessarily shaken, or, perhaps, actually thrown into disorder.

Whenever any improvement is made in arrows and other missiles, cavalry sinks in importance—for a time, that is to say —and until fresh and more effectual means are discovered for repelling the new or improved missiles. What has just now been described took place at Crécy. The English archers on that day shot down the horses of the French knights in considerable numbers; and their arrows wounded many others, which, through their violence and terror, contributed in a great degree to break up the cavalry and destroy its efficiency. Indeed, the French knights at Crécy were unable to accomplish more than to reach the position of their enemies, when they melted away, so to speak, and were either dispersed or destroyed. Foot soldiers, who stood firm and in good order, under such circumstances, had every advantage. And this it was which, when once clearly understood, led the knights to dismount and to form on foot in rear of the archers, where they might receive a charge of cavalry without injury to themselves, and repel it to the utter discomfiture of the cavaliers.

After a while (early in the 15th century), an innovation was introduced, which, in some slight degree, affected the practice of the archers. This was the introduction of a large shield, called a *pavise*, or *pavas* (also called a *mantlet*), a kind of movable breastwork, which, resting on the ground, covered almost entirely the person of the soldier.[67] Not only when on the march, but also in battle, and above all at sieges, the knight had his pavise carried before him by a page or valet. Square in outline, and convex in form, this pavise was sufficiently large to shelter both the page and his master; the latter it must be added, still continued to carry his regular shield. It is curious to enumerate the defences which thus the warrior of that age interposed between his person and the

weapons of the enemy—his haqueton, hauberk, a breastplate
(or *plaston*) probably, surcoat, with iron outer-guards for the
limbs and joints, then the shield, and, last of all, the great
pavise. Bodies of *pavisiers* were formed on each side, in
action; and, doubtless, these strong defences were opposed,
as much as possible, to the hostile archers. All this shows
how terrible the bows and arrows had become.

We now return to the equipment of the infantry. When
not provided with a long-bow, the foot soldier carried a *cross-
bow*, or *arblast*. In its elementary form, this is a weapon
composed of a short bow adjusted to a staff, called the *arbrier*,
or *stock*, and fixed at right angles to it, close to one extremity.
For a while, during the 12th century, as the long-bow in the
14th, the cross-bow had the reputation of being a weapon
terrible beyond all others. At that time, probably, it was
a novelty. It does not appear at all in the Bayeux tapestry,
nor in any other monument of the 11th century. It is
remarkable, also, that when the cross-bow was first introduced
it was forbidden to be employed by Christians in warfare with
one another, as being too murderous a weapon; this was at
the second Council of Lateran, held in the year 1139; and
it was only new inventions, or early ones revived, that were
interdicted in such a manner as the cross-bow was at that
time. If it has not hitherto been mentioned amongst the
weapons of the 12th and 13th centuries, it has been omitted
because, notwithstanding its reputation, the cross-bow at that
period was but little used, so that even in the Crusades (when
its use was allowed) this weapon performed only a very subordinate part. The reasons for this will soon be apparent.
In the 14th century, the cross-bow was much more generally
used; thus, as we have seen, the French army at Crécy
included in its ranks 6,000 Genoese cross-bowmen.

The cross-bow, simply formed from a bow and a stock,
may be used with more precision than the long-bow; but,

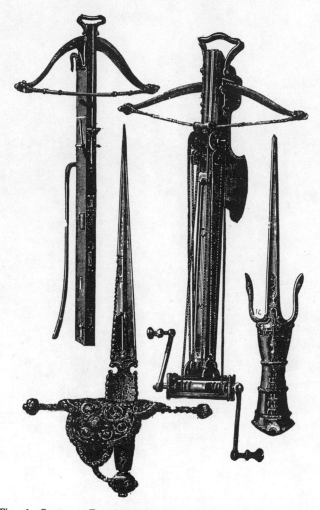

Fig. 26.—Group of Two Arblasts or Cross-bows, and Two Daggers.

1. Hand Cross-bow.   2. Rolling-purchase Cross-bow.   3. Left-hand Dagger.
4. Moorish three-point Dagger.

at the same time, it is both inconvenient when in use, and heavier to carry. Again, it can be protected from the very injurious action of rain only with great difficulty ; and, finally, it has a considerably shorter range than the long-bow. Should it be desired to give it an equally long range, it would be necessary to add greatly to the strength of the cross-bow; and this, in its turn, would require some mechanical apparatus to draw the bow-string, which implies a further addition to both weight and inconvenience. At the end of the 13th century, and at the commencement of the 14th, all the cross-bows that were in use had their bow-strings drawn by means of machinery ; and of these cross-bows, or arblasts, there were three varieties, severally named—the *hind's foot*, the *lever*, and the *rolling purchase*—*arbalétes à pied de biche, à cric,* and *à tour.*

A few words may be said by way of description of each of these varieties of this weapon. The distinctions, it will be observed, between these varieties of the cross-bow consist exclusively in the varied means that are employed for bending the bow and drawing up the bow-string.

1. The *hind's foot* (called also the *goat's foot*) *cross-bow* (*à pied de biche,* or *à pied de chevre*). The apparatus employed to bend this cross-bow is a lever composed of two articulated pieces. The smaller piece, or the small arm of the lever, is divided into two branches, each of which is provided with a kind of fork. When the bow is to be bent, the bowstring is grasped by one of these branches; and then the other branch, by means of its long fork, rests on points placed on the two sides of the stock. The archer, having taken a firm hold of the larger piece or arm of the lever, draws it back; the small fork, with the bowstring in its grasp, follows this movemen ; the bowstring is brought up to a notch, in which it is caught, and remains fixed ; and thus this bow is drawn up and ready to act.

2. The *lever cross-bow* (*à cric*).   A stout and strong cord
secures to the bow-stock a *pignon,* that is, a toothed wheel,
enclosed within a circular iron case.   This wheel is in gear
with a rod, which is straight, but has a hook at its further
extremity.   When the wheel is turned by means of a handle,
the rod is advanced until the hook at its extremity is made to
grasp the bowstring; then by the reversed action of the wheel
the rod is drawn back, and the bowstring follows with it to
its own proper place.   See Fig. 27, No. 2.

3. The *rolling-purchase cross-bow* (*à tour,* or *de passot*).
The stock of this bow is furnished at its extremity with a
kind of iron stirrup, into which the archer inserted his foot,
that he might be enabled to bend his bow with a greater
purchase.   At the opposite extremity is fixed a compound
tackle, or system of pulleys, over which strong cords are led;
and these cords being set in motion over their pulleys by
means of a small windlass, and the pulleys themselves at one
end of the tackle having been hooked to the bowstring, the
bow is thus bent.   The string is then lodged on a nut, the
tackle is removed and suspended from the archer's belt, the
arrow, or bolt, is laid in its proper place, and the weapon is ready
for the aim.   In Fig. 26, No. 2, a cross-bow of this class is
represented; and in No. 1 of the same figure is shown a
simple cross-bow, which is drawn up by the action of the
left foot and the right hand.

The *sword* of the foot soldier differed from the corresponding weapon worn and used by the knight, in having its blade
much narrower.   Besides such a sword as this, when he was
provided with neither long-bow nor cross-bow, the foot soldier
carried either a pike or a *vouge,* a strong staff, having at its
extremity a long point also very strong, which, in fact was a
kind of spear; or sometimes he was armed with the *guisarme,*
a lance having a small axe fixed at the foot of its blade or
lance-head on one side, and generally a spike projecting on

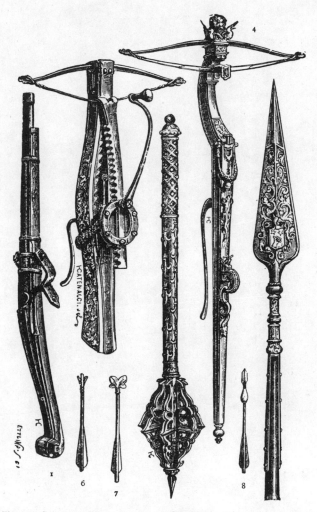

Fig. 27.—GROUP OF TWO ARBLASTS OR CROSS-BOWS, THREE ARBLAST-BOLTS,
A MACE, A PIKE, AND AN EARLY MUSKET.

1. Early Musket.   2. Lever Cross-bow.   3. Mace.   4. Decorated Cross-bow of
Catherine de Medicis.   5. Decorated Pike.   6, 7, 8. Cross-bow Bolts.

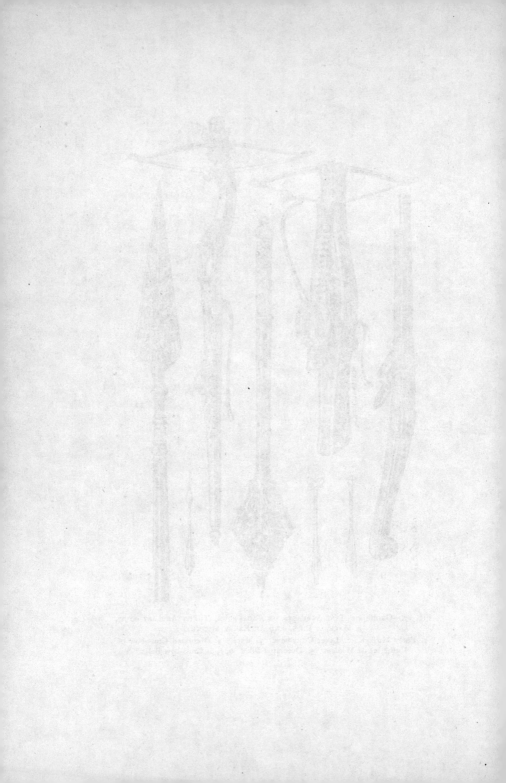

the other side. (See Fig. 68, Nos. 12 and 13.) This weapon, after having been suffered to fall into disuse in the 14th century, again became popular in the 16th under various appellations. The terms *partizan, halberde,* and *guisarme,* denote the same class cf weapon, which admitted various modifications. (See Fig. 68, Nos. 10, 11, 12, and 13.) It will be observed that in all these examples a lance-head and ,an axe are present. In the 16th century both the lance-head and the axe are made to cut in various ways, and they present to the eye strange and often fantastic modifications of form. At this time, also, the guisarme often gives place to the *fauchard,* a weapon of a truly formidable character in close fight, and rightly considered almost too cruel to be used in Christian warfare ; it resembles a very large razor-blade fixed to the end of a staff, and it is represented in Fig. 68, No. 4.

We may now direct our attention to the defensive equipment of the foot soldier. The common soldier, as has already been stated, who would be a serf, or peasant escaped from serfdom, figures but little, if at all, in the military imagery of the middle ages previous to the 14th century. If by any chance we meet with him at an earlier period, we find that his costume in war externally differs scarcely at all from what it had been when he was at work in the fields ; still, imbued as he naturally would be with that sentiment of his age, which would suggest to him to regard armour as the only true military uniform, he appears always to have worn beneath his customary clothing whatever pieces, or fragments of pieces, of armour he might have obtained, either from the wreck of a field of battle, or from any other source ; he also gladly assumed any quilted garment that he might be able to add to his scanty armoury. In the 14th century, on the contrary, the foot soldier may almost be said to have a definite and characteristic military costume of his own. On his person at this time he wears a *jaque,* or *jack,* which is a pourpoint, or quilted tunic, made of leather, and well padded; or a *brigandine*, also a pourpoint, but which is covered over with small iron plates of various forms, and may be called a studded tunic. For the legs and arms he has half-armour; that is, instead of having his limbs encased in armour, he has defences for the more exposed parts of them, which, accordingly, may be distinguished as *demi-gardes-bras*, *demi-grevières*, &c. On his head he wears a *chapel-de-fer*, or iron cap, furnished with a broad and slightly curved rim; or the *salade*, a head-piece having large projecting defences for the back of the neck, and square plates to cover and protect the ears.

The armour of the knight we left when in a condition of semi-transformation; now we proceed to trace out the completion of the change from the defensive equipment of mail to the suit of plate armour, the full panoply of chivalry.[68] It is the civil costume which, undergoing a fresh change in fashion, furnishes as usual the motive for a corresponding change in armour. Under Charles VI. of France (A.D. 1380 to 1422), contemporary with Richard II., Henry IV., and Henry V. of England, instead of the true pourpoint or surcoat, a short vest was worn, slightly padded, fitting tight to the figure, and having long narrow sleeves; and the chausses (breeches), which covered the rest of the body, being also tight (or elastic so as to cling to the figure), the men at a little distance appeared to be altogether destitute of all clothing, so that it was said of them that they resembled skinned rabbits—a pleasantry that was by no means inconsistent.

However this may be, the new substitutes for the quilted surcoat were found to leave the lower part of the body and thighs much less protected than was satisfactory. The new covering for the armour might be the fashion, but certainly it was not safe. It would be necessary to discover a remedy for this; nor would such a discovery be attended with any difficulty. A corslet of iron, formed of two pieces, was soon introduced, which enclosed and protected the body, front and back, above the waist, and as low down as the hips ; this may be called a *demi-cuirass*. It was worn over the haubergeon, and formed a very efficient defence as far as it went. In order to complete the defence, to the lower part of this demi-cuirass there was attached a system of articulated *lames*, or narrow plates, in their contour adapted to cover the figure, and so arranged that each one would slightly overlap the one below it ; thus was formed a species of kilt of armour, or iron petticoat, called *faudes* (and in England known as *taces*). Over the flanks, on each side of the figure, to the faudes or taces was appended a plate, or small shield, or *garde-faude* (in England called a *tuille*), which would cover the front of the thigh, and, being secured by only straps and buckles, would allow free movement to the limb. These plates (tuilles) appear in almost every variety of form—square, hexagonal, lozenge-shaped,

Fig. 28.—FRENCH KNIGHT DIS-MOUNTED, *temp*. CHARLES VI. OF FRANCE, A.D. 1380-1422.

serrated, &c. In front, and also behind, the haubergeon was shown uncovered.

Such was the armour worn by the brothers of Charles VI., the " Sires des fleurs de lis," when they went to war. Such also was the armour of the famous Duke of Burgundy, John the Fearless, who caused the Duke of Orleans to be assassinated ; and the same armour was worn by the nobles of Armagnac and of Burgundy, who, in the 15th century, desolated France with such ferocious rapacity.

M

Under Charles VII. of France (A.D. 1422 to 1461), the half cuirass became the complete cuirass, which enclosed the whole body from the throat downwards. This important piece of armour, however, was not like the modern cuirass, simply a sleeveless tunic, or vest of plate ; nor did it resemble its own predecessor, the demi-cuirass, in being formed of two pieces for breast and back ; but the cuirass of this period was considerably sloped away, on each side, at the shoulders ; and there was fixed, to meet the slopes, a system of articulated plates, curved in half-circles, and projecting considerably, after the manner of a thick and large epaulette ; this part of the cuirass was called the *epaulière*.

Now that we have before us plate-armour in its most perfect development, as it appears in Fig. 29, we may enumerate the several pieces of which the suit is composed :—

1. The *cuirass*, covering the whole figure, breast and back.

2. The *epaulières*, guards for the shoulders.

3. The *brassarts*, or arm-guards.

4. The *coudières*, elbow-guards, and coverings for the inside of the elbow-joints.

5. The *avant-bras*, guards for the lower arms.

6. The *faudes*, or *taces*, with the *tuilles*, which have just been described.

7. The *haubergeon*, or defence for the body worn under the cuirass.

8. The *cuissarts*, thigh-pieces.

9. The *genouillières*, knee-guards.

10. The *grevières*, leg-pieces.

11. The *sollerets*, or *soulières* (with the *spurs*), laminated coverings for the feet ; and

12. The *gauntlets*, pieces of armour that have not yet been described, and which in the time of Charles VII. were recent inventions (in France) ; they were composed of pieces of iron sewn on gloves of strong leather, for the protection of

Fig. 29.—SUIT OF ARMOUR OF CHARLES THE BOLD.

the hands and wrists. The only protection (in France) to the hands, in earlier times, was the leather glove.[60]

No mention is made by M. Lacombe of the additional plates that, towards the close of the 15th century (at any rate in England), were screwed upon the cuirass, and that were added, after the shield had generally been laid aside, to the primary defences of the left arm. Nor are the belts noticed; nor do the heraldic accessories of the noble and knightly panoply, in themselves, at the era under consideration, matters of no slight importance, appear to have attracted M. Lacombe's attention. In like manner, the horse-furniture of the period has been passed over without any description or remark. (See Chapter XI.)

The celebrated warriors of France, who flourished in the 15th century, continues M. Lacombe, are universally well known. To awaken the remembrance of a thousand acts of bravery, intermingled also, unhappily, with as many of violence and rapacity, it is enough to mention the names of La Hire, Xaintrailles, D'Alençon, and Richmond; but, for the honour of the period, never let it be forgotten that the armed image of Joan of Arc (A.D. 1431) shines pure and radiant, high above them all.

In order to complete the recapitulation of the innovations in arms and armour that were effected in the 15th century, the head-piece and the sword must be added to the body-armour. The head and the neck, as has been shown, were covered and guarded by the *basinet* and *camail*—the latter pendant from the former. About the middle of the century, the basinet gave place to the *armet*, or *helmet*, a head-piece consisting of a globular iron cap, which spreads out with a large hollowed projection over the back of the neck, and in front has a piece formed like part of a bowl, so as to cover the mouth and chin. This piece, called the *bavière* (*beavor*, or *mentonière*), is pierced with holes for respiration.

In order to fill in and to defend the space left open before the face of the knight, between the front rim of the helm itself and the upper part of the *bavière*, a movable plate, pierced with narrow openings for sight, was added; this is the *visière*, or *visor*.   Finally, at the bottom of the helm, and below the bavière, instead of the mail camail, the *gorgerin*, or *gorget*, completes this head-piece.   It is formed of a series of circular pieces of plate, jointed and carefully connected together to cover the throat, and (after the manner of an iron cravat) to connect the helm with the body-armour.[70]

In the case of the *sword*, the changes which it underwent during this century produced a weapon that, instead of being long and narrow, was somewhat shorter, broader at the head of the blade, and gradually tapering towards the point—a weapon, in fact, that in many respects closely resembles the sword that was in general use in the 12th century.

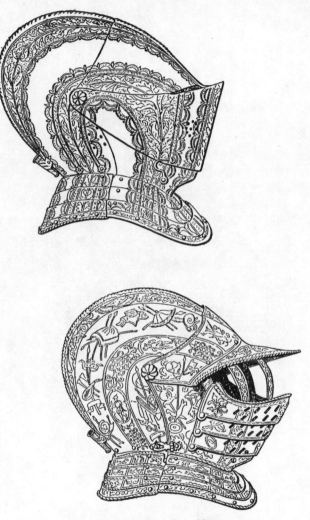

HELMETS: 16th Century. From MEYRICK.

CHAPTER IX.

ARMS AND ARMOUR DURING THE TRANSITION PERIOD OF THE 16TH AND 17TH CENTURIES.

In the case of arms and armour, as also with reference to so many other things, the 16th century is an era which leads the way, not to a *renaissance* of earlier forms and usages, but to the introduction of such as are altogether novel. We now are about to observe in what manner, and by what gradual processes the arms and armour of the middle ages, instead of aspiring towards the attainment of any higher degrees of perfection, for the most part fell into disuse, and finally disappeared. We shall find that this great change was accomplished little by little; that first one weapon and one piece of armour was laid aside, and then another, until at last the triumph of the modern arms was complete. The cannon and the gun, it will be remembered, had been invented long before they came into general use; and their general character had been understood during many years, while yet they remained in so rude a condition that they were considered to offer few if any advantages over the ancient arms, or over the armour with which those ancient arms were associated.

We shall find it to be a curious, and also an interesting subject for inquiry, to examine in their last forms, and to follow through the successive degrees of their decadence, each weapon and every piece of armour that we have already seen to have been employed in the warfare of the Gothic era.

Armour claims the precedence. The final disappearance of defensive armour was an event that was altogether unex-

pected when fire-arms first took their place amongst weapons
of offence.   It is worthy of remark, however, that throughout
the last age of armour the attention both of armourers and of
their patrons should have been devoted, not to any important
improvements in the defensive qualities and capacities of the
panoply, but almost exclusively to its adornment and decoration.   All that rich and fanciful fertility of invention, which
distinguishes the artists of the 16th and 17th centuries, was
lavished upon the enrichment and ornamentation of armour;
and, on the other hand, the nobles were profuse in their
expenditure in the purchase of such armour as would be
remarkable, as well for rarity as for richness and beauty.
There prevailed, indeed, a warm rivalry amongst the possessors of luxurious and costly armour; until, during the
Renaissance, this taste was carried to a ruinous excess.

So numerous are the important works of the armourers of this period, and so rich also is the apparently
inexhaustible variety of their truly splendid decorative treatment, that it would be a hopeless task to attempt even to
enumerate all the finest examples that may be found preserved in the numerous collections and museums that are in
existence in Europe.   Much less would it be possible to
describe them all ; so that we shall be content to give descriptions of a few exceptionally fine suits and pieces of armour in
the subsequent chapter on " Decorated Arms and Armour."
In this present chapter it will be our plan to trace out and
to describe the minor changes and modifications in defensive armour, which marked its decadence, and immediately
preceded its disuse and abandonment.

At the end of the 15th century, and at the beginning of
the 16th, at the moment in which we now resume our
inquiries and remarks, the *breastplate* (*plastron*) is globular,
or has a swelling contour.   The last plate of the *epaulière*, or
shoulder-guard, becomes flatter and more upright (and on the

SUIT OF ARMOUR OF HENRI II. OF FRANCE: A.D. 1547—1559.
In the Museum of the Sovereigns, at the Louvre, Paris.

left shoulder more so than on the right), and forms about the throat a kind of iron collar, having its edge irregular and serrated, which was designed to receive and avert any blows from lance or sword that might be delivered againt that part of the knight's person.[71] These *passe-gardes*, or *garde-collets*, which sometimes are greatly elevated, distinguish the armour of the reigns of Charles VIII., Louis XII., and Francis I., of France (severally, A.D. 1483 to 1496; 1496 to 1515; and 1515 to 1547). The *garde-faudes*, or *tassettes* (*tuilles*), which before were formed of a single piece, generally having the form of a tile or being cut deeply to a point, become rounded, and are composed of several distinct pieces. The *soleret*, also, which had been extended to an extravagant length, and was acutely pointed, is shortened to the length of the foot, and at the front it is cut off square, in common with all the foot-coverings of the period.

The civil costume, as has already been observed more than once, always influences the military equipment. As a fresh proof in support of this theory, armour is now found to have been systematically modelled in accordance with the costume in fashion at the time; and to have been fluted and slashed precisely after the prevalent treatment of garments made of rich textile materials, such as velvet, silk, and satin, and also of cloth.[72]

A feature that would soon be exaggerated, begins to make its appearance under Francis I. This is a ridge (in England called the *tapul*) which divides the breast-plate and cuirass into two compartments, and is carried out to a point, in accordance with the taste of the armourer, over the middle of the body. Under Henry II. (A.D. 1547 to 1559), and more particularly under Henry III. (A.D. 1574 to 1589), in imitation of those fantastic garments which are first seen in the pictures of the time, the ridge of the cuirass is wrought to an edge, and this edge is prolonged so as to descend towards

the waist, and at the same time it is finished in a more prominent and sharper point.

Then there succeds another change of peculiar significance.
The *grevières* and *solerets* (defences for the legs and feet) begin
to be laid aside altogether.   Here is the first decided step
toward the final disuse of all defensive armour.   It is probable
that, as the armour was strengthened about the body, in order
to render the breast-plate proof against fire-arms, this increase
of weight made it necessary to obtain a corresponding lighten-
ing in some other direction, and accordingly the pieces which
have been mentioned were sacrificed.   The next step was the
disappearance of the *braconnière*, or the *faudes* (the *taces* of
English armour), and the *tassettes* also; but these were
replaced by large and deep *cuissarts*, or thigh-pieces, which
(since they perform a two-fold office) may be called large
tassettes; they extend from the hips to the knees, and are
divided in the middle.   (See Fig. 29.)   The *passe-gardes*
(elevated shoulder-pieces) take their departure at the same
time; the *epaulières* (true shoulder-guards) again become
simple and compact; and the *grevières* at last are replaced by
buff leather boots which reach to the knees.

Armour, modified by changes such as these, is found to
have remained long in use.   The portrait of Philip of Cham-
pagne, in the gallery of the Louvre, shows that this armour
was worn as late as the time of Louis XIII. (A.D. 1610 to
1643).   It must be borne in remembrance, however, that in
portraits, armour was not unfrequently represented as a dignified and honourable costume, after it had ceased to be worn
for defence.   Some minor intermediate (between Henri II.
and Louis XIII.) changes are worthy of notice.   Under
Henri IV. and Louis XIII. the *cuissarts* (thigh-pieces) are
made of much lighter metal plates, and in order to make them
conform more perfectly to the civil costume, their dimensions
are enlarged.   The breast-plate, on the other hand, is again

shortened, and it is drawn to a much less advanced and decided point.

Whilst in France, in the matter of armour, the fashions and usages of earlier ages were abandoned only by slowly progressive degrees, important events took place more in the north of Europe which were destined to hasten onward the revolution in military equipment. A man of thoroughly original genius, Gustavus Adolphus, effected a complete change in strategy and military tactics. It is not for us, indeed, here to investigate and consider these strategical innovations in detail, or with any direct reference to themselves; but they do concern us so far as they exercised a powerful influence upon arms and armour, and the use of them in warfare. In this comparatively limited field—in dealing, that is, with arms and armour—as in all other matters, Gustavus Adolphus showed himself a man of modern times; and, as such, he was the enemy of the old defensive equipment which deprived the soldier of freedom of movement, and seriously affected his spirits; and all this to no purpose, since his armour did not secure the soldier against musket-balls, nor even against balls projected from the then recently improved arquebus. But, in order that we may understand the condition of things to which we now refer, it is necessary for us to retrace our steps somewhat, and to look back to a rather earlier period.

We have already seen that greaves and solerets had been abandoned for some time. The illustrious captains of the 16th century, and notably Saulx-Tavannes and Lanoue, in their theories were considerably in advance of their contemporaries. These men of singular discernment condemned armour altogether; they had no greater affection for the breast-plate than for the rest of the suit. For reasons of their own, the soldiers eagerly desired the abolition of armour. It was not a very easy matter to enforce their wearing the

regulation armour.   In the first place, they—the soldiers—had
to pay for it (and it was always costly enough); or, which
amounted to the same thing, the cost of their armour was
deducted from their pay.   In the next place, the fatigue
occasioned by wearing their armour was intolerable.   And
then they began to be impressed with the conviction that, if
their armour did afford to them a more than questionable
protection against hostile blows, it certainly produced (as if
to balance the account) some maladies that were incidental
to the use of it.   Lanoue has affirmed that he has seen many
soldiers at thirty years of age, who already had become partially deformed, or in a great measure deprived of their natural
physical strength, solely in consequence of having habitually
worn their armour.   The sentiments of the French soldiers
upon this subject were confirmed by the German troopers,
who, in their first campaigns in France, appeared equipped in
buff leather coats instead of armour.   So the French soldiers
fell into the habit of arming themselves only at the moment
of battle ; or they would consider surprise, or anxious haste
to appear in their proper positions, to be a sufficient pretext
for not assuming their armour at all.   On some occasions also,
the *tabard* (a kind of blouse), that was worn by the men-at-
arms over their armour, was put on without the armour, the
absence of which, consequently, could not thus easily be
detected ; and thus they preferred to go into action *armed* in
their tabards only.   The repugnance to armour, accordingly,
was generally prevalent ; and the modern spirit already pro-
tested against what it held to be the obsolete traditions of the
middle ages.   Nevertheless, kings and princes generally continued to maintain the necessity of armour, as an essential
condition of sound discipline ; and, therefore, they interposed
their authority, and prevented for a while that complete abandonment of armour, which they saw to be both desired and
threatened.   Louis XIII. in particular, and Richelieu himself

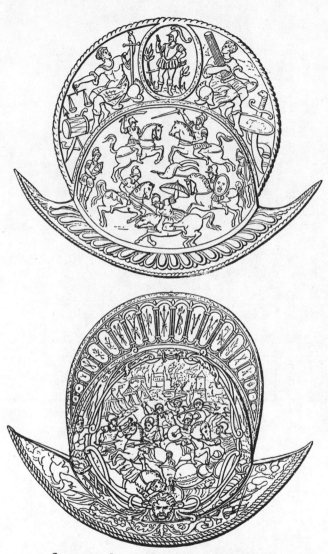

SPANISH AND ITALIAN MORIONS, 1560. From MEYRICK.

N

also, took active parts in the controversy, and were zealous defenders of the old system. They even attached the penalty of degradation to every man-at-arms who might appear without his armour in the presence of the enemy.

The principles of Gustavus Adolphus (A.D. 1612 to 1633) were directly opposed to sentiments such as these. He took away from his soldiers—at any rate from the greater number of them—both their *cuissarts* and their *brassarts* (all their limb armour) and left them only a light cuirass. Thus reduced, the armour, which was virtually useless against fire-arms, against bayonets and swords was still effectual for defence, and it caused very slight inconvenience to the soldier, nor did it impede the dexterity of his movements. Commanding officers, even though they might be imbued with the modern spirit, with some appearance of reason might regret that the reformation in military equipment did not stop at the point to which it had been brought by Gustavus Adolphus, and where he left it.

In France the movement was less rapid. At the accession of Louis XIV. (A.D. 1643 to 1715), armour was still worn. About the year 1660, or rather later, all defences for the limbs ceased to be retained in use, and the cuirass alone remained— the last relic of the old complete panoply. The cuirass then was worn either over or under the uniform tunic. Twenty years later the cuirass itself was laid aside. The last foot soldiers who wore it in France were pikemen ; and that arm was abolished in 1675. After them, that ancient usage of war which equipped the soldier in armour, was retained in the French armies only by the *gendarmes*, of whom each regiment included in its ranks one troop or company. The deviation from a decided uniformity in each regiment which was occasioned by the presence of this small body of men-at-arms, led to the formation of a single regiment of *cuirassiers*, who enacted a prominent part in the wars of Louis XIV. In connection with the usages of this period, it must be mentioned that officers and gentlemen, after they had altogether ceased to wear the cuirass in the field, still retained it when it was their pleasure to sit to artists for their portraits.

In siege operations, and in the trenches, the case was altogether different. There the men who were engaged still wore complete armour—breast-plate, leg-guards, metal solerets, and so forth. Armour such as this is very heavy. The helm, too, which accompanies it, is remarkable for its weight; and, indeed, it resembles the head-piece of Philip Augustus, the

massive *heaume*. It was called the *pot-de-fer*. The chronicles of that time tell us how Louis XIV., like all other soldiers, went into the trenches in full armour and wearing the *pot-de-fer*.

This leads us naturally to some further consideration of French military head-gear. The helmet, or *armet* remained in use for the cavalry throughout the 16th century, and until the middle of the 17th. It was worn at the battle of Rocroy (A.D. 1643), and in a contemporaneous representation of

Fig. 30.—FRENCH ARMOUR OF THE 17TH CENTURY.

that conflict, it is represented with a grated visor, worn by the gentlemen who surround the Prince de Condé. The Prince himself, however, appears wearing a hat, that began to be fashionable, and which in the course of the reign of Louis XIV. rose to higher favour than the helmet. In Fig. 30, the helmet, or *armet*, with its visor, is represented. The hat (*chapeau*) that has just been noticed, was made of felt, with a wide brim, and was surmounted by a plume of feathers ; in the inside it was fitted with a steel cap, that was either perforated or plain.

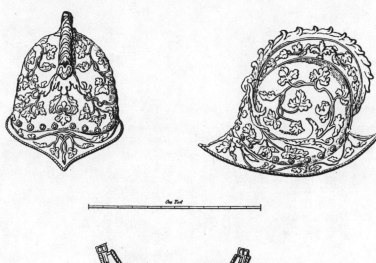

One Foot

A BREAST PLATE AND MORION, 1595. FROM MEYRICK.

This hat, which in pictures appears like a simple hat of felt, in its turn, disappeared ; it did not long retain its place in the favourable estimation of men of rank and distinction, but by the soldiery, both horse and foot, it was generally worn for some time. Certain corps, such as the Cuirassiers and the Guards of the King's Household, had iron hats (*chapeaux en fer*) without any external covering of felt, but broad-brimmed and provided with a nasal. In a short time the iron cap, which was worn as a lining to some other head-gear, was replaced by an *armature,* or circlet of the same metal, or simply by two iron bands curved and placed cross-wise. At last iron disappeared altogether ; and so the gradual change in the head-piece, that had been in progress during such a long period, at length was consummated.

What has just been stated refers only to the cavalry of France. With reference to the French infantry, in the 16th century each corps had a head-piece peculiar to itself; or one, at any rate, which each corps was generally in the habit of wearing. The *burgonette,* shown in Fig. 32, No. 2. the head-piece of the pikemen, consists of a cap, a neck-piece, and two ear-pieces (*calotte, couvre-nuque,* and *oreillères*). The *morion,* worn by the arquebusiers, is a pointed oval helmet, surmounted by an

Fig. 31.—FRENCH MORION OF THE 16TH CENTURY.

elongated crest ; its rim, which is bent down over the ears, is formed in a curve that causes it to have somewhat the appearance of a boat that has been overturned. In Fig. 31 is represented a *morion* of the 16th century, which is enriched with most elaborate ornamentation. Helmets of this kind were frequently the subjects of similar artistic adornment. The *cabasset*, or common infantry head-piece, is simply a light morion, or iron cap, with a wide brim that is much lowered. The *morion* and the *cabasset* were in use only in the 16th century. The *burgonette* with a nasal was commonly worn by foot soldiers in the time of Louis XIII. (A.D. 1610 —1643).[73]

The *halberd* and the *pike*, from the time of Louis XI. to that of Francis I. (A.D. 1515—1547), enjoyed a reputation which speaks very highly for the skill and gallantry of the Swiss foot soldiers, who used these weapons almost exclusively. After the defeat of Charles the Bold, Duke of Burgundy, by the forces of the Swiss Cantons, for a while no sovereign felt confident of victory without having in his army some of the redoubtable mountaineers. Upon the same principle, the Swiss weapons, the halberd and the pike were supposed to be the only arms which in the hands of foot soldiers were competent to resist the charge of mounted men-at-arms. It must be admitted, indeed, that with these weapons, and more especially with the pike eighteen feet in length, the Swiss had brought about almost a complete revolution in military tactics.

We have seen how the power of infantry, as a distinct and thoroughly effective arm in warfare, began to be understood and recognised in the 15th century. Before that time, infantry on a field of battle in the middle ages were scarcely, if at all, taken into consideration. In the 15th century, the method adopted for the purpose of successfully resisting the charge of mounted men-at-arms in armour of proof, consisted in opposing to the cavaliers, in the front, the archers or crossbowmen, whose duty it was to break the first rush of the hostile charge by killing as many as possible of the horses; and then in the second line, in rear of the bowmen, the men-at-arms were formed in close order, dismounted, but in their full armour, and with their lances advanced. The Swiss, who had no horses and but little armour, when they were called by Charles the Bold to occupy a prominent position in the world's stage, were content to oppose themselves to the Burgundian chivalry, formed in deep and compact battalions, in which each man, firmly grasping his long pike, stood as close as possible to his next comrades. Thus it was that they literally revived the ancient Macedonian phalanx. And, not only did this order of battle serve them well for a victorious defence, but it also proved equally effective for offensive action. On more than one occasion, without awaiting the shock of the cavalry, the Swiss threw themselves with resistless force upon the columns in their mid career, maintaining all the while the even closeness of their own ranks.[74]

The successes of the Swiss modified the prevalent existing ideas on military tactics, and suggested the various discussions and disputes concerning the art of war, which engrossed so much of the general attention throughout the whole of the 16th century. It then was admitted, in direct contravention of the earlier universal belief, that infantry formed in heavy battalions, and consisting of pikemen, halberdiers, and arquebusiers, in suitable proportions, constituted, at least in an equal degree with cavalry, the nerve and strength of an army. As a general rule, the arquebusiers, as marksmen, were placed in the front of the battalion. When the hostile charge was delivered, these men took shelter under the long pikes of their comrades, who were formed immediately in their rear. The halberdiers, again, still more in the rear, were to repulse the horsemen, should they succeed in breaking the lines of the pikemen. The halberd, being shorter and more easily handled than the pike, was admirably adapted for hand-to-hand conflict with the knight.

The battle of Marignan (near Milan, September 13, 1515), in which the Swiss suffered a severe defeat by French cavalry, in some degree affected the prestige of the soldiers of the Confederate Cantons; and, during the Italian wars which followed, the German infantry were admitted to be the equals of the Swiss in the solidity and power of their formation. But nothing took place which in any way or degree led to the slightest modification of the prevailing general opinion concerning the strength and importance of infantry in an army.

Another relic of earlier mediæval equipment, thanks to the Swiss, fell into disfavour at this same time. This was the *shield*. The Swiss found shields to oppose serious impediments to the formation of their compact columns and close lines; and, consequently, they boldly abandoned them; and in their stead they were content to place in the front line those among them who possessed any armour. Following this example, the men-at-arms next gave up their shields. The fine bas-reliefs of the tomb of Francis I., at St. Denis, show how rare the shield had become at the time of the battle of Marignan (A.D. 1515). When it does appear at that period, it is generally circular, made of wood covered with leather or *cuir bouilli* (boiled leather); but sometimes these shields are constructed of chased metal. It was called the *rondelle*, or *rondache* (*target*). After the time of Francis I. (after about A.D. 1550), whenever a shield makes its appearance it is an exception to the otherwise universal usage. The commanders of the infantry, indeed, had shields which were carried for them by attendants; but they were regarded rather as relics of ancient usage, than as means of defence on which they themselves placed any reliance. In siege operations, during the rounds of night patrols, and when making reconnaisances, shields continued to be used (as exceptional arms on exceptional occasions) as late as near the end of the 17th century. It is also well known that the Scots auxiliary troops, who took a part with the French forces at the battle of Fontenoy (A.D. 1745), appeared with shields or targets.[75]

The *lance* continued in use, and maintained in some degree its ancient reputation, throughout the 16th century; but in the year 1605, when he reorganised the French ordnance companies, it was abolished in France by Henry IV. During the advance of the 16th century, indeed both the old knightly weapon and the heavily armed cavaliers themselves gradually lost something of their earlier importance. Many cavalry corps, who were more or less light, were formed in France after the model of the Germans, who first established the cavalry arm upon a modern system, as the Swiss had been the first to effect the same thing with infantry. The most celebrated corps, who gave their model to the French, were the "German Troopers." Their appointments were black throughout, and they were armed with swords and pistols. These *cottes noir* (black-coats), mercenary troops, who were to be seen serving in the ranks of both parties, the Roman Catholics and the Protestants, in the religious wars, desolated the countries in which they were employed, and overwhelmed the humbler classes of the populations with their depredations and their cruelties. "I have seen the Black Trooper," says D'Aubigné, "as a thunderbolt sweeping through France."

The *pike*, which we have just been observing in its proudest days, with the arquebus and the musket, was the principal weapon of the French infantry until about the year 1640. As this period drew nearer, the fire-arms continually acquired fresh importance, and the men who used them became comparatively more numerous; and, in like manner, the pike-men were reduced in due proportion in their numbers, and their weapon was found to be less effective than in times past. Towards the middle of the 17th century also, upon the northern frontier, there appeared in the French armies a new weapon, which was destined to suppress the pike altogether. It was a slender sword-blade that was fixed to a small round wooden handle; and this handle, in its turn,

was inserted into the muzzle of a gun-barrel, and so converted
the gun itself into a halberd. The new weapon was the
bayonet, of which the origin is still a subject of discussion
amongst archæologists. It would seem that, in the primitive
form that has now been described, this weapon was invariably
used in connection with guns against the larger and fiercer
animals of the chase ; and, certainly, if this be the case, sooner
or later, it would inevitably be suggested that the same weapon,
so valuable in the hunting-field, might be made signally
effective in actual warfare.

Notwithstanding the original inconvenience arising from
its preventing the proper use of the fire-arm while it was fixed
in its muzzle, the bayonet was at once preferred to the pike.
Accordingly, when small fire-arms were given to grenadiers
and artillerymen, who previously had been exclusively occupied
with either their grenades or their cannon, their guns were
provided with bayonets.[76]

The first great improvement in this new weapon consisted
in making it concave in its contour, as it still is, in place of
flat—its original form. Then succeeded the idea, which led
to the addition of such a socket to the bayonet-blade as would
admit of its being fixed to the end of the gun-barrel, without
in any way interfering with the loading and firing the piece.
It was in the year 1703, and by the advice of Vauban,
that the guns of the French infantry were provided with
bayonets. Early examples are represented in Fig. 50, Nos.
1, 3, and 5.

M. Lacombe here introduces a passage from an old French
work, which, as he says, may claim to be considered as both
curious in itself, and worthy of attentive consideration, as well
from what it contains concerning the early period in the
history of the bayonet, as from its observations on the use of
the pike, and also on the system of military tactics which was
transmitted to the 17th century from the 16th.

"The author of the *Art Militaire*, a work attributed to M. de Langée, in the time of Francis I., Machiavel, and the Seigneur de la Noüe, in their political and military essays, and other writers also who, both in their times and subsequently, have treated of military matters, have all been unanimous in holding the opinion that at least one-third of the infantry force of an army ought to be pikemen, and that it is a matter of the gravest importance that these pikemen should be posted when in action in front of each division. The strongest and most powerful men were chosen to fill the ranks of the pikemen, and they received rather higher pay than the arquebusiers and musketeers.

"The Swiss and Germans were pre-eminently skilful in handling the pike; and for this reason the foot soldiers of those nations, for a considerable length of time, were esteemed to be the best in Europe.[77] M. de la Noüe frequently complains that the French were not able to accommodate themselves to the use of this weapon, and that they were in the habit of adducing their own incapacity in this respect, as the one sole reason for their failing to be superior to the Swiss and German infantry; whereas, the truth was that in the wars in which in those days the French armies were engaged, and more especially in their Italian wars, the defeats that were sustained by the arms of France were generally brought about by the caprices and misconduct of their Swiss and German auxiliaries. Experience has since shown the strict justice of those remarks of that famous captain.

"The necessity of having a body of pikemen in every battalion of infantry has been invariably maintained until recent times, when a change of opinion was brought about in the minds of military men in the manner following.

"In the year 1715, a short time before his death, the late Baron d'Asfeld related to me how, in 1689, on his return from Hungary, he commanded a corps of 2,000 men that had been

sent by the King of Sweden to assist the Emperor against the
Turks. M. de Louvois questioned him, he added, at considerable length concerning the manner in which military
enterprises were carried on in that country. And, in reply,
on that occasion he said to M. de Louvois, amongst other
things, that the Emperor had removed the pikes from all his
infantry, and in place of them had provided the men with
muskets ; that the Emperor had been induced to make this
very decided change in weapons in consequence of the superiority of the Turks over the Christians as swordsmen ; and
particularly, because the Turks both used their sabres with
special success against pikes, and they were in great dread of
fire ; that, after mature reflection upon these facts, the
Emperor had arrived at the determination to abolish the pikes,
and to increase in a proportionate degree the number of the
musketeers—that is, to increase in his army the power of
firing upon the enemy ; also that, for these same reasons, they
formed their battalions and squadrons in closer order than
formerly, and so left to the Turks on the field of battle less
favourable opportunities for taking them in flank when an
engagement at close quarters had become general.

 " He added, in his conversation with me, that M. de
Louvois had deliberately weighed all these considerations in
connection with some other practical arguments against the
use of the pike ; that the minister had laid the whole question before the King ; that the King, while he confessed
himself to be powerfully impressed by what he had heard,
could not resolve to introduce so great a change ; and that
the minister dared not to urge the matter any further, being
unwilling to charge himself with such a responsibility as must
ensue, should the result of the proposed change be proved by
the course of events to be unfavourable. Then, an incident
which took place at the battle of Fleurus, in 1690, revived
the consideration of the relative importance of the pike and

PARTISAN OF THE GUARD OF THE DUKE OF PARMA:
16th Century. From MEYRICK.

the musket. This incident was the comparative ease with
which in this battle certain battalions of Dutch pikemen were
disposed of, while some German infantry without any pikes,
but able to maintain a heavy fire, offered a much more formidable resistance.

" Such then, for the time, was the position of this important question. And now I proceed to state what I have yet
to add on this subject. When carrying the war into the
Barbet Alps, Marshal de Catinat took their pikes away from
his soldiers, on the plea that they were of but little avail for
mountain combats, and he substituted muskets in consequence
of the much greater advantages to be obtained from the use of
fire-arms. Then this same change was maintained in the wars
in Italy, because there the country is much broken, and does
not admit of free action for large armies on widely extended
plains. The final issue was that the King, after having taken
counsel with many generals, who held various opinions, and
after he had most carefully compared whatever arguments
and facts had been adduced on either side, accepted the views
of Marshal de Vauban, who advocated the abolition of pikes,
in opposition to those of M. d'Artagnan, afterwards Marshal
of France, under the name of Montesquiou, and then Captain
of the French Guard. The consequence was that, in 1703,
the King of France (Louis XIV.) issued an *ordonnance* by
which all pikes were abolished in the infantry, and guns were
substituted in their stead. This, then, is the epoch of this
comprehensive change—one of the most important that for
very many years had been introduced into the military system
of France."—[Daniel, *Milice Franç*, t. ii., p. 390.]

Two points here are specially observable. In the first
place, in the time of which this author treats, as in the middle
ages, the grand consideration that first claimed attention from
military men was the discovery of such means as would render
infantry invincible when opposed to cavalry; and this still

o

continues to be the fundamental problem of military science. Secondly, we see the fire-arm constantly advancing and rising higher in reputation and esteem. Since the close of the 16th century, the merits of the gun were gradually better under stood, and the consequent estimation in which that weapon was held steadily though slowly made progress. In order to encounter cavalry with a good hope of success, in the 16th century, reliance was placed upon a mixed infantry force composed of pikemen and arquebusiers, the pikemen generally being considered the more important arm. With the succeeding century came the change in favour of fire-arms, which led eventually to the suppression of the pike altogether. Gustavus Adolphus, to whom the mind naturally reverts whenever the early development of the system of modern warfare is the subject of consideration, was the very first who had a glimpse of the true state of things. He ventured to form in line, against cavalry, infantry composed almost exclusively of arquebusiers. He merely said to them, "Fire at fifteen paces! "

It is remarkable in these discussions on the relative merits of the pike and the gun, that there should have been no allusion to the bayonet.

The *sword*, in the 16th century, in its blade presents several varieties of form ; and the arrangement and details of its hilt generally are complicated in their character. In order to be enabled clearly to understand descriptions of the swords of this century, it will be necessary first clearly to define certain technical terms that have been used to distinguish different parts of this weapon.[78]

The *blade* (*lame*) comprises the following subdivisions :— The *tongue* (*soie*) is the spike which usually forms a prolongation of the blade, and which is fixed into the hilt in order to join the hilt and the blade together ; the *heel* (*talon*), the uppermost part of the blade itself, is next to the hilt, and it is

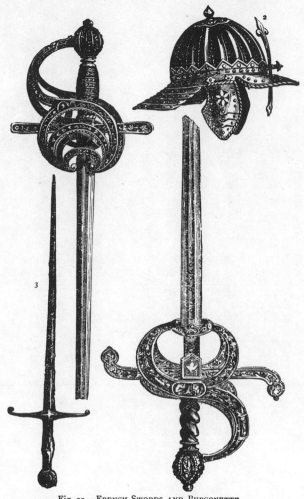

Fig. 32.—French Swords and Burgonette.

1 and 4 Swords of the 16th Century.   3. Sword of the 13th Century.
2. Burgonette.

almost always somewhat larger and more massive than the rest of the blade; then succeeds the *body of the blade* (*corps de la lame*); and finally there is the *point* (*pointe*).

The simplest variety of *hilt*, again, which we have seen to have been in use in the middle ages, has its distinct parts; these are—the *pommel* (*pommeau*), the ball or cube of metal which generally forms the uppermost finish of the hilt; the *barrel* (*fusée*), which is the hilt itself, adapted to be grasped by the hand; and the *cross-guard* (*quillons*), the transverse bar that forms a cross with the blade and the barrel, at their point of junction.

To these, the primary parts of the hilt of the sword, must now be added those other pieces which distinguished the hilts of sixteenth century swords. It will be kept in remembrance that all these additional pieces are rarely, if ever, to be found united in the hilt of any one single weapon; still, for the sake of both brevity and clearness, it appears to be desirable to describe some single typical weapon that may be supposed to possess every one of the additional hilt-pieces. In addition to those primaries (so to speak) of the hilt, the pommel, barrel, and cross-guard, our model sword in its hilt has also a *guard* and a *counter-guard* (*garde* and *contre-garde*)—that is, it has on each side of the barrel, or fusée, and perpendicular to its axis, a plate of metal, flat or concave, plain or in open-work; from these guards curved *branches* proceed, either directly or obliquely, to the pommel; then there is a species of *basket-hilt* (*pas-d'âne*), or a series of rings that issue from the cross-guard, and are curved back upon the blade itself and in the same plane with it; and, finally, there is the *second guard* (*seconde garde*), between the two extremities of the rings of the *pas-d'âne*. Such, in its most complicated form, is the sword-hilt of the 16th century. In Fig. 32, Nos. 1 and 4, two examples of swords of this era are represented. They may be compared with good effect with No. 3 in the same group—a simple, thoroughly soldier-like weapon of the 13th century.

The sword that was used by the soldiery (*gens d'armes*) is much more simple. Of the pieces that have just been enumerated, the hilt of this weapon, in addition to the three primary pieces, seldom has more than the " guards." The civic sword (*l'épée de ville*), on the other hand, at least has the " branches," if it has not the " guards " also with them. It is this last sword, indeed, that most commonly possesses some one of the complicated hilts that have been described. These hilts, in the first instance, were devised with a good motive, in order to receive and turn aside an adversary's weapon; but, in many instances, they degenerated into mere vehicles for elaboration of ornamentation.

A classification of the swords of the 16th century, based upon the varieties of their hilts, would be far less accurate and satisfactory than one that would be determined by the form of that most essential part of the weapon, its blade. Accordingly we proceed to describe certain swords of different types, all of this century, to which distinctive names have been given. From these varieties all the other kinds of swords may be derived more or less directly.

The *estoc,* Fig. 33, No. 3, a large sword with a rigid blade, which is hollowed out, or grooved, throughout its length. The mounted man-at-arms carried the *estoc* suspended from his right saddle-bow. At the same time he was careful to have in its proper place on his left side his true sword (*l'épée*). This last weapon. differed from the former only in being shorter.

The *two-handed sword* (*épée à deux mains*), Fig. 33, No. 4, was the distinctive weapon of the German *lansquenets,* or mercenary foot soldiers who, with the " reîtres," or troopers of the same class and of the same country, played such a distinguished part in the French religious wars. This enormous

Fig. 33.—Swords and Culverin.

1. Culverin.   2. German Sword.   3. Estoc.   4. Two-handed Sword.
5. Italian Malchus.

weapon, with its straight expanding blade of portentous size, double edged and sharp in the point, with its long hilt also and its massive cross-guard, and with the threatening spikes that usually give a species of grim decoration to the base of the blade, presents an alarming figure in our armouries and museums. It appears, however, from the reports of military historians, that this gigantic variety of the sword in reality was by far less formidable than might have been expected from its appearance. The blade of this sword not uncommonly affected a wavy or flaming (*flamboyante*) outline. The "lansquenets," who were provided with this great sword [for it was not by any means in universal use amongst them], were generally posted in the front line; and it required both a special training and no ordinary skill to enable them to use their weapon effectively against their enemies, without at the same time seriously damaging either their comrades or themselves. On the march this sword was carried, after the manner of a guitar, on the back, where it was suspended from a broad leather belt, which crossed the figure diagonally.[70]

The *braquemard*, or *cutlass*, a comparatively short weapon, holding a place midway between a sword and a dagger, has a straight flat wide blade, that is pointed and very sharp at either edge. It generally has on the hilt only a cross-guard that curves on both sides towards the point of the weapon. A variety of this class of sword, which is remarkable for the width of its flat blade, is called a *malchus*. Fig. 33, No. 5, shows an Italian example of the *malchus*, with a blade of unusual length, and also a distinct variety of hilt.

The *épée de ville*, or *civic sword*, that has been already mentioned, has a great variety of blades. A sword of this class, with a long straight and narrow blade, has been distinguished by the title of *verdun*. Examples of these swords may be seen in the Artillery Museum, at Paris, in extraordinary numbers; when placed erect, they would reach from the heel to the middle of the chest of a man of ordinary height; and it is evident that the examples in question have been worn only when the wearers were in their saddles.

With its long and slender blade very sharp near the point, the *rapier* (*rapière*), above all others, has always been the favourite sword for single combat. For its guard, this weapon generally has a kind of small basket or *shell* (*coquille*), pierced with a multitude of minute perforations, designed to entangle and break off the adversary's point. Straight and long— sometimes very long—cross-guards project on either side of these shells. This kind of hilt gives ample opportunity for ornamentation; and, in fact, rapier-hilts are very generally seen to have been chased and pierced with astonishing lightness and delicacy. In this case the perforations that have been mentioned are superseded by the details of the decorative designs, by the sunk spaces amidst the foliage, by the flowers in relief, or by geometrical figures that take a part in the composition.

It can be scarcely necessary to state, and yet it is only simple justice to record here, that the most renowned sword-blades were forged in Spain, and particularly at Toledo, from whence they were eagerly sought by princes, nobles, and knights throughout Christendom.[80]

Throughout the whole of the 16th century, the sword was worn suspended from a belt; and when the hand of the wearer was not resting on the pommel, the blade of the weapon crossed the calves of the legs on the slope.

Under Louis XIII. (A.D. 1610—1643), the blade of the military sword has no particular characteristics. The hilt has its cross-guard bent with a contrary curvature, so that on one side the curve sweeps up towards the pommel, and on the other side it falls towards the blade. The habit of wearing the sword behind the person commenced in this reign. This adjustment was effected by attaching the weapon to a shoulder-

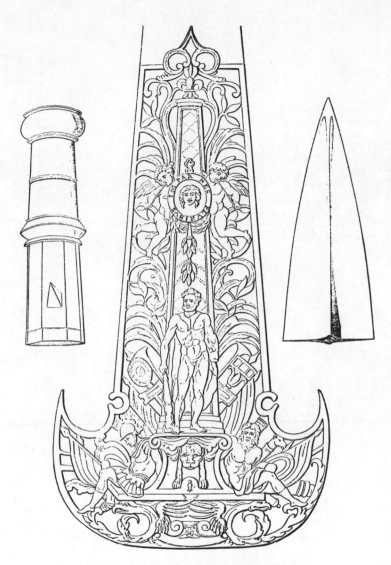

PARTISAN OF THE GUARD OF LOUIS XIV.: 17th Century.
From MEYRICK.

belt, or *baudric* (*baudrier*), which crossed the figure like a scarf; this belt was very short, and consequently the hilt of the sword struck the back.

During the long and brilliant reign of Louis XIV. (A.D. 1643—1715), in place of the cross-guard to the hilt, the sword had a single guard on one side, and on the other side a branch which was connected with the pommel. The baudric or shoulder-belt increased in both length and width, so as to offer more surface for luxurious embroidery, and the weapon hung obliquely on the hip. At the end of the reign, however, the use of the early sword-belt that was worn under the tunic was revived. At this same time also a new variety of sword was in great favour for duelling; it is the *colichemarde*, a corruption of the word *Kœnigsmark*, the name of the inventor. The peculiarity of this weapon is, that from the hilt the blade for some length is tolerably broad, then suddenly by a rectangular step on each side it becomes narrow, and terminates in a very sharp point. This conformation of the blade has the advantage of placing the centre of gravity in the hilt, and consequently the weapon is remarkable for its lightness and convenience in the hand.

As early as the 14th century, and sometimes even still earlier, a very short sword is represented in monuments, attached to the right side of military belts, corresponding with the position of the regular sword on the left side. This weapon is the *miséricorde*, or *dagger of mercy*, so called because it was habitually used to stab the fallen and vanquished foe, when in such extremity either that mercy or quarter would be sought, or that it would be a merciful deed to put an end to the sufferer's agonies.[81] A dagger, sometimes so short that it is really a poignard, was certainly in use before the 14th century, and at that period it no less certainly was exclusively used by men who fought on foot. Somewhat later, as appears from the certain authority of contemporary monuments, the

dagger gradually became more generally adopted ; nor was it
restricted then to foot soldiers ; but on the contrary, gentlemen
and men-at-arms, and even nobles and knights themselves, are
shown to have added the *miséricorde*, or dagger, to their other
weapons.   At the end of the 15th century, and also in the
16th, the dagger is always put in the belt, but it falls more on
the loins than by the side.   Certain soldiers, such as the " lansquenets," for example, have a dagger, the sheath of which
expands so as to form a wide case, that holds a single knife,
or more commonly is filled with several knives of various
forms.[62]

The weapon that in the 16th century was called a *main
gauche* (a *left-hander*), was a dagger especially used in duels.
It has a very characteristic form.   On one side of the hilt it
has a guard which is curved and carried up to the pommel in
the form of a half-shell ; from the *talon*, or heel of the blade,
on the opposite side, is a hollow indent, intended to hold the
thumb.   The weapon was held in the left hand, with the
thumb above and the guard below ; and it was used, whilst
making an attack with the sword held in the right hand,
to ward off the blows or thrusts that the adversary might make
with his sword.   Such was the practice of fence at that time.
The elaborate enrichment that was introduced into the guards
of these weapons is exemplified in Fig. 26, No. 3.   The use
of the dagger, it must be added, as a military weapon, was
not retained in France long after the 16th century.

The *sabre* differs essentially from the sword, not indeed in
the circumstance that its blade is generally more or less curved
(for, at the present time in France, a straight sabre, the *latte*,
is used by the cuirassiers), but because it has a single edge
only, and the thickness of the blade is greatest at the back,
and from the back to the edge it gradually becomes thinner.
Swords are thickest in the middle of the width of the blade,
and have two edges—a structure which causes them to be

MAIN GAUCHE WITH STEEL HILT: 16th Century.
Belonging to Mr. Percy Macquoid.

inferior to sabres for striking heavy blows. The sabre, in fact, is a large knife; and between it and the sword there is exactly the difference that there is between the knife and the poignard.

The sabre is an oriental weapon—oriental in its origin and general use. Not, indeed, that sabres were absolutely excluded from the armouries of the west; for, in the monuments both of antiquity and of the middle ages, here and there the figure of a sabre may be discerned; there are exceptions, however, to the prevailing rule, and that rule is the sword. The Poles and Hungarians, whose weapons are so decidedly impressed with an oriental character, are the European nations that introduced the sabre amongst the French. Towards the close of the reign of Louis XIV. (about A.D. 1710), the sabre was generally in use in French cavalry corps. The Hungarian hussars, who figured amongst the soldiers of the empire, and with whom the soldiers of France first formed an acquaintance in the year 1690 in a manner disastrous enough for the hussars, having subsequently by some means become the fashion, appear to have taken a part in bringing about the change in the cavalry weapon. The Marshal de Luxembourg, having taken some squadrons of hussars into the pay of France, " employed them in his service; and, so greatly did their conduct redound to his credit that he wrote in highly favourable terms concerning them to Louis XIV. The hussar troopers who carried the marshal's despatch to Fontainebleau produced there an excitement that rose to a veritable infatuation. It was instantly determined that a regiment of French hussars should be formed forthwith.

" The first French hussars (the ' hussars of the Marshal de Luxembourg ') were habited and equipped in the Turkish fashion. An enormous moustache drooped over the chest; but, with the exception of a long tuft on the crown, their heads were closely shaven. On their heads they wore a fur cap, surmounted by a cock's-tail plume. Their uniform

P

consisted of a scanty tight-fitting tunic,with breeches that were very large at the top, and tight below the knee, where their boots were drawn over them.   This was their complete costume, and it was worn without any kind of under-garment whatever.   For protection against the inclemency of the weather they were provided with tiger (or panther) skins, which they wore suspended about their necks (prototypes of more recent hussar pelisses with their fur lining) ; and these they adjusted in such a manner as would best oppose them to that quarter from which the wind might be blowing upon them.   They were but inferior shots ; but with the curved sabre they exhibited a dexterity that was truly wonderful.   In common with the cavaliers of the East, they were masters of that scientific art, which empowered them to strike off the head of an enemy at a single blow."—[Quicherat, in the *Magasin pittoresque*, vol. 28, p. 388.][83]

In our own times the sabre takes rank before the sword, since it is the weapon of all cavalry corps, and also it is much used by infantry.

The *scimetar*, or very light sabre, with a blade curved like a crescent, still continues to be the favourite weapon that is used with such extraordinary dexterity by the active and expert swordsmen of the East.

Fig. 34.—ITALIAN GROTESQUE DOLPHIN-HEAD HELM : IN THE
RUSSIAN MUSEUM.

DEMI-SUIT OF THE EARL OF ESSEX, WITH CLOSED HELMET, MAGNIFICENTLY
ENGRAVED AND GILT.
From the Guard-Chamber at Windsor Castle.

CHAPTER X.

ARMS AND ARMOUR IN ENGLAND.

IN the " Notes " appended to the text of this volume I have endeavoured in some degree to compensate for the general absence from the text itself of such notices of English Arms and Armour, as would naturally be expected by English readers in a work which had appeared in their own language. But the necessary requirements of " notes " prevented their conveying anything resembling a definite sketch, complete as far as it professed to go, of any one department or division of the general subject; and consequently, in this present chapter I have proposed to add to the contents of M. Lacombe's treatise, a concise sketch of the leading characteristic features of Arms and Armour in England.   I desire it to be distinctly understood that this sketch does not profess to be more than a sketch—a concise and a slight sketch ; and also that it will be found not to have attempted to accomplish more than what, in the first instance, it professed to undertake. Accordingly, I have desired here to direct attention only to what are strictly typical examples ; and all minute descriptions of details, together with notices of the various modifications of the more decided types which were simultaneously in existence, I have considered to be excluded from my present purpose.

The authorities upon which, in addition to actual pieces of armour and original weapons, I have relied, and to which I have referred the reader, for the most part are monumental effigies, and the armed figures that are represented on early seals.   These are at least comparatively easy of access ; and

they possess several qualities of peculiar importance. For
example, they are *contemporary works,* and represent what
was well known to the artists by whom they were executed.
They also give faithful representations both of *details,* and
of *complete suits of armour,* as such suits were actually worn
by certain historical personages at certain fixed periods ; and,
therefore, they determine the periods to which all the component parts of suits of armour are to be assigned, and so they
enable us to avoid grouping together pieces of armour which
in reality belong to several periods. And, again, the armour
represented in these works is invariably free from extravagances and fanciful peculiarities ; and, accordingly, it may
readily be accepted as giving a faithful portraiture of the true
typical style and fashion of armour, as in reality it was generally produced and worn at successive periods.

As a matter of course, the representations of armed figures
and groups of figures in early illuminations possess also a very
high value. Nor are they the less valuable from the circumstance that, in addition to their corroboration of the testimony
of effigies and seals, they abound in examples of almost every
conceivable modification of the more decidedly pronounced
types. The illuminations, moreover, retain the important
element of colour, of which only a few traces that yet linger
here and there are still to be discerned in monumental effigies.

It is to be understood that in all cases, as a general rule,
effigies, seals, and illuminations alike represent the arms and
armour that were *in use at the time in which each one of those
works was executed.* Their arms and armour are the arms
and armour of the year in which the sculptor, the engraver,
or the illuminator severally worked ; so that then only do we
possess in effigies, seals, and illuminations, veritable portraits
of arms and armour when those works are contemporaneous
with the personages whom they represent. It must be added
that, with very rare exceptions (exceptions from many causes

easy to be detected) effigies were certainly executed either during the life-time of the personages represented, or immediately after their decease; and, in the case of any man of high rank, it may be assumed as certain that the armour represented in his effigy was carefully studied and faithfully modelled from the suit—in all probability the favourite suit, that he had habitually worn. The use of any seal by the person whose portraiture it bears, proves its authenticity; unless, indeed, it can be shown (as in a few instances of seals of great importance it may be shown) that some particular seal was made for one personage and was used by another. This is the case with the Great Seal of Edward II., which was made for his father; but this is one of the exceptional instances which serve to establish contrary rules. An appeal must be made to various concurrent circumstances in order to arrive with certainty, not at the date of the events represented in any work of early art, but at the date of the production of such work, whatever it may be, whether illumination, or picture, or coloured glass, or ivory carving, or architectural accessory, or any other work.

In like manner, the descriptions of arms and armour given by early writers must be accepted and treated as descriptions of the arms and armour *of their own times.* It is Froissart armour, of which the famous chronicler has bequeathed to us his vivid word-paintings; had he undertaken to give a minute description either of the battle of Hastings or of the siege of Carlaverock, we may be confident that he would have armed both William of Normandy and the first of the Plantagenet Edwards after the very same fashion, and in both that he would have reproduced the armour which the Black Prince wore at Crécy.

Veritable specimens of early armour are at once rare, and of considerable value; such relics, consequently, as do exist are to be found only in a few great collections, except in the case of a comparatively small number of suits, generally of the close of the 15th century or of a still later period, which are in the possession of private collectors, together with certain scattered solitary portions of some good knight's harness of proof. All represented armour, and whatever relics of the early armourer's skill and art may still be in existence, mutually illustrate each other. For the most part, it is the sculptured effigy, or the engraven seal, or the graphic illumination, which determines the era of the original helm, or of the hauberk or plate for the defence of breast or limb; and, on the other hand, in the highly-prized treasures of armouries, and museums, and collections, are found the evidences which attest the accurate and exact fidelity of the mediæval sculptors and draughtsmen.

Examples of original weapons, and particularly swords, exist in considerable numbers in England; and very many of the finest and most interesting of these remains are in private collections; all mediæval weapons of early date, however, are comparatively rare.

When entering upon any inquiries concerning the varieties and the characteristics of early arms and armour, it is always necessary that the relative influences which the offensive weapons and the defensive equipments exercised upon one another should be taken into consideration. The very aim and purpose of armour imply the existence and the certain operation of such influences as these. As soon as the armour was found to be an effectual defence against such arms as were in use, attention was immediately bestowed upon the improvement of the existing arms; and the introduction of new and more destructive weapons was certain to follow. This would lead to corresponding efforts to strengthen the armour, and to consolidate its protecting capacities. And thus there would be maintained, as indeed there always has been maintained, a struggle for supremacy between arms and armour. As is well known, the question that was so long at issue in the middle ages, was finally solved, so far as the wearing of armour by knights and soldiers was concerned, by the introduction of gunpowder and the use of fire-arms; but yet, this same question, modified in conditions and circumstances, has revived in our own times. The armour now covers, not "hearts of oak," but ships framed of massive beams; and the crushing and crashing penetration of enormous shot and shell has succeeded to lance thrusts, and to blows of swords and maces, and to the sharp hail of "clothyard" arrows. Now, also, we add inch to inch in the thickness of our armour-plates, and ton to ton in the weight of our guns, until it may fairly be expected that this new strife between arms and armour will end, as it ended before, in the ship-armour becoming too heavy for the ships, and the guns too ponderous for the gunners. What may be the next phase in the rivalry between arms and armour must be purely a matter of speculation; so far, however, the final issue may be anticipated, as to assume that the universal supremacy of arms over armour must at last be completely established. There are limits beyond which no armour can be improved and strengthened; but the possible power of weapons (or at any rate of implements of destruction) appears altogether to defy limitation.

In this chapter I have not attempted to treat of any weapons that may have been in use, or of any defensive equipment that may have been worn in Britain, until after the establishment of the Norman dynasty in this island. M. Lacombe has noticed the arms and armour of the primitive races, and also those of both the Anglo-Saxons and their Norman conquerors; and in my Notes 4, 6, 12, 13, 15, 33, 43, 44, and 46, I have endeavoured to apply his remarks to our own remote predecessors. and to the races which succeeded to them.

The ARMOUR that has been worn in England since the

Norman conquest may be divided into four great groups, each of them associated with its own historical period.

1. First—MAIL ARMOUR: The period of its use ending about A.D. 1300.

2. Second—MIXED MAIL AND PLATE ARMOUR: From about 1300 to about 1410.

3 Third—PLATE ARMOUR From about 1410 to about 1600.

4. And Fourth—HALF-ARMOUR: The period of the partial use of armour, extending to the commencement of the 18th century.

In each of these great primary groups the armour may be subdivided, so as to form a small series of secondary groups.

The ARMS that have been worn and used by Englishmen may be grouped with the Armour; and they also may be classified according to their several special characteristics, as —1. *Shafted Weapons:* such as lances, &c. 2. *Shaftless Weapons:* such as swords, &c. 3. *Bows and Arrows.* 4. *Firearms.*

I. MAIL ARMOUR.—(1) The period of pure mail armour, without any other secondary or additional defences over the mail, except the *heaume* or great helm worn over the mail coif, may be considered to have closed about the year 1350. (2) From about the middle of the 12th century to about the year 1300 mail armour continued to be worn without any departure from the earlier usage, with the exception of the occasional addition of small elbow-guards, and the more general adoption of knee-pieces over the mail.

Great uncertainty still exists, notwithstanding the most careful investigation of the subject, with reference to the defensive equipment in use during the first centuries of the middle ages, and which constituted the transition from the armour worn by the warriors of antiquity to the true mail of the early mediæval knights. It is certain, however, that in those early times stout quilted garments were worn for defence. Rings also, and studs and scales of metal were added, which were either sewn, riveted, or otherwise fixed to the surface of those quilted garments, for the purpose of giving such additional protection as might be obtained without any serious drawback from the flexible character of the armour. True mail armour of interlaced rings may be considered to have been adopted generally in Western Europe after the Crusades.

The examples of effigies to which I shall refer I have selected for the most part from the noble series that have been engraved with such admirable fidelity and true feeling in " Stothard's Monumental Effigies ; " for thus I have been enabled to facilitate references to engraved representations of the examples. It will be understood, accordingly, that, unless a reference be made to some other work, all the examples of effigies are engraved in Stothard's volume.

In the 13th century there prevailed no recognised uniform military equipment. The *hauberk of mail*, with a *coif* to cover the head, and sleeves for the arms, reached to the knees ; and it was covered with a long, loose, flowing surcoat, sleeveless, girded with a narrow belt about the waist, and open in front below the belt. Beneath the hauberk was worn a quilted tunic, called a *haketon*, or *gambeson ;* sometimes an iron plate, or *plastron-de-fer*, covered the breast, and a steel or iron cap, or *chapel-de-fer*, either rounded or flat at the top, covered the head, both of them beneath the mail. The hauberk sleeves were prolonged to form mittens, which covered the hands. The lower limbs were covered with *chausons*, or trews, above the knee, and below the knee with *chausses* of mail that were extended to cover the feet. Over the mail coif a massive *heaume*, or *helm*, was also worn, either with or without a *nasal*, and sometimes with a movable *ventaille*, or visor, and occasionally made with a wide rim. The sword was long, straight, and ponderous; with it the lance, the mace, the guisarme, the halberd, the bill, and the military flail were in use.

As the century advanced, various additions to the armour were gradually introduced, together with certain modifications. Plates, or pieces of *cuir bouilli*, were placed over the elbows and knees; elbow-guards, or *coudières*, however, were rarely adopted till after the year 1300, but the *pouleyns, genouillières*, or knee-pieces became general before the close of the 13th century. The hauberk after a time was shortened; and about the middle of the century a sleeved surcoat was sometimes worn; studs and scalework were introduced; the mail mittens sometimes were divided into fingers; about 1270 the helm was made rounded at the top; about 1280, *ailettes*, or small shield-like appendages to the shoulders, were attached to the mail; and at the close of the century, *greaves*, or *jambarts*, appeared to be worn over the mail for the additional protection of the front of the lower limbs, below the knees. The spurs, having a single spike, are known as *pryck-spurs*. The sword-belt, which was very broad, was loosely buckled over the hips. His helm was sometimes secured to the person of the knight by a chain.

Examples: Sculptured effigies in the Temple Church, London; the effigy of Earl William Longespée, half-brother of Richard I., in Salisbury Cathedral, A.D. 1226; effigy at Great Malvern, and another at Gosberton, in Lincolnshire; the effigies of Sir Robert de Vere, at Hatfield Broadoak, in Essex; of De Montfort, at Hitchendon, in Buckinghamshire; of the younger Longespée, at Salisbury; and of Edmond, first Earl of Lancaster, A.D. 1296, in Westminster Abbey. Also, the brasses to Sir John d'Aubernoun, A.D. 1277, at Stoke d'Abernon, in Surrey; to Sir Roger de Trumpingdon, 1289, at Trumpington, near Cambridge; to Sir Robert de Bures, 1302, at Acton, in Suffolk; and to Sir Robert de Setvans, 1306, at Chartham, Kent; all engraved in my own "Monu-

mental Brasses and Slabs." The great seals from the Conquest
to Edward II., with many other seals of the same period, give
admirable examples of the knightly appointments of the time.
The comparatively small seal of Sir Alexander de Balliol,
A.D. 1292 (Fig. 35), exemplifies, in a characteristic manner,

Fig. 35.—SEAL OF ALEXANDER DE BALLIOL, A.D. 1292.

the practice of the early possessors and users of seals to have
their own figures, armed and mounted, represented drawn
from life in those very important and truly interesting works
of art.

II. MIXED MAIL AND PLATE ARMOUR: About 1300 to
about 1410.—The addition of secondary defences to the mail
armour, which had been introduced as the 13th century was

drawing towards its close, in the 14th century was carried on from step to step and subjected to various changes and modifications, until at length the complete panoply of plate armour made its appearance.

1. FIRST PERIOD, TO ABOUT 1325.—Additional plates, in the first instance, were placed over the mail, without any other decided change in the general character of the armour; the surcoat, however, about 1320, was sometimes shortened. The fresh additions were *demi-brassarts* and *vambraces*, severally for the protection of the back of the upper arms from the shoulder to the elbow, and of the front of the lower arms from the elbow to the wrist; circular plates or roundles were fixed in front of both the shoulders and the elbows to guard the joints, and they were respectively entitled *épaulières* and *coudières*, or *coutes; ailettes* began to fall into disuse. The *pouleyns*, or knee-guards, were elaborately enriched; and the *jambarts*, which covered the front of the leg from the knee downwards, were continued in laminated work over the feet. The shield became somewhat smaller, and sometimes was flat. Gauntlets were introduced.

Examples: The sculptured effigy of Earl Aymer de Valence, 1323, in Westminster Abbey; brasses, Gorleston, in Suffolk, and to a Fitz Ralph, at Pebmarsh, in Essex, both about 1320, and engraved in " Brasses and Slabs."

The great value of the *Inventories of Armour and Arms* that were made in early times, and which occasionally have been preserved, I may here consistently notice, since the most important information relative to the period now under consideration is conveyed by the inventory of Piers Gaveston, drawn up in 1313, and printed in the *New Fœdera*, vol. ii., p. 203. Another equally valuable document of the class, the inventory of Earl Humphery de Bohun, 1322, is printed in the *Archæological Journal*, vol. ii., p. 349.

2. SECOND PERIOD, TO ABOUT 1335.—About 1325 the

HELM OF SIR JOHN GOSTWICK, died 1541, believed
to have been worn at the Field of the Cloth of
Gold, 1520, and now hanging over his tomb in
Willington Church, Bedfordshire.

long and flowing surcoat, open in front, appears to have been superseded by an extraordinary garment called the *cyclas*, which was laced at the sides, and reached a little below the knee behind, while in front it was cut very short and displayed the escalloped and fringed border of a second padded and quilted garment, or *haketon,* that was worn between itself and the mail haubeik. The secondary defences of the knees, legs, and feet remained the same ; but the sleeves of the hauberk sometimes were cut short about the middle of the lower arm, and the arms from the elbow to the wrists were encased in plate *vambraces* beneath the mail ; and the roundles at the elbows and shoulders sometimes assumed the form of lion's faces. *Ailettes* ceased to be worn. The comparatively light and close-fitting helm, the *basinet,* also, which some years earlier had been introduced, was worn without any mail coif beneath it ; and, for the protection of the neck a kind of tippet or curtain of mail, known as the *camail,* was attached to the basinet by a lace drawn through small staples (*veryelles*), and it hung down over the shoulders and the upper parts of the breast and back. The shield assumed the " heater " form. The long straight sword was suspended from a simple belt by swivels attached to the scabbard. Spurs with *rouelles* were sometimes worn.

Examples : The sculptured effigies of a De Bohun, about 1325, at Hereford (engraved by Hollis, but not by Stothard) ; of Sir John de Ifield, about the same date, at Ifield, Sussex ; and of Prince John of Eltham, 1334, in Westminster Abbey : also the brasses to Sir John de Crewe, about 1325, at Westley, in Cambridgeshire ; and to Sir John d'Aubernoun the younger, 1327, in the same church which contains the brass to his father (all engraved in " Brasses and Slabs.")

3. THIRD PERIOD, TO ABOUT 1360.—Splinted armour, sometimes showing the metal, and sometimes having it covered, but showing studs on the covering, together with

Q

studded *pourpointerie*, began to prevail about the middle of the century. The surcoat was shortened so as not to fall lower than the knees, and it was worn with a loose skirt below the waist, open in front; it displayed the armorial insignia of the wearer blazoned only above the belt, where it

Fig. 36.—SEAL OF SIR THOMAS DE BEAUCHAMP, K.G., A.D. 1344.

fitted close to the figure. Occasionally, however, the surcoat had no skirt, and was cut short like the *jupon* of the succeeding period. It is certain, from the evidence of unquestionable authorities, that until late in this period the early mail defences for the limbs were occasionally retained in use without any additional plates or other secondary guards. A collar or *gorget* of mail, and sometimes, either over it or in its stead, a gorget of plate at times was worn about the neck. The basinet, when not worn under the great helm, was commonly fitted with a ventaille; also a close-fitting head-piece was in use, having a broad and flat projecting brim. The sword was sometimes shorter, and the adjustment of the belt simple; the sword itself also was secured to the person of the warrior by a chain from the pommel.

Examples: The sculptured effigies of Sir Roger de Ker-deston, 1337, at Reepham, in Norfolk; of Sir Oliver de Ingham, 1343, and of Sir Roger de Bois, about the same date,

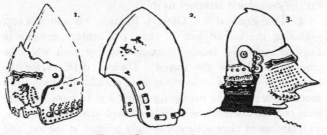

Fig. 37.—BASINETS AT PARHAM.

both at Ingham, in the same county; and an unknown effigy of great interest in Tewkesbury Abbey Church, the date about 1360: also the remarkable brass to Sir Hugh Hastings, A.D. 1347, at Elsing, in Norfolk, in which are introduced no less than nine armed figures, one of them mounted (engraved in the "Norfolk Archæologia," and in Cotman's "Brasses," and in part in my "Heraldry," "Brasses and Slabs," and "Brasses of England.") The Great Seals of Edward III., again, to-gether with the seals of various important personages of his era, exemplify, in a characteristic manner, the style of their armour and the changes that were introduced into it. In Fig. 36, the seal of Thomas de Beauchamp, third Earl of

Warwick, A.D. 1344, is represented; it shows the earl fully armed and mounted on his charger. The reader will observe all the details of the equipment of both man and horse in this excellent example. The arms of Beauchamp (a bar and six crosses of gold on red) are repeated on the surcoat and shield of the earl, and on the ample *bardings* of his charger. (The inscription on this seal is completed on the counter seal.)

The examples of basinets here engraved are in the armoury of the Hon. Robert Curzon, at Parham. Fig. 37, No. 1, shows the visored basinet in its earliest form, and is as early as 1310; No. 2, about A.D. 1330, shows the staples for the lace of the camail; and the visored basinet, No. 3, about A.D. 1365, has the camail still attached to it.

4. THE FOURTH OR CAMAIL PERIOD, TO ABOUT 1405, —During the second half of the 14th century, armour in England assumed a decided character, so that for a while the progress of change was stayed. Studded defences for the limbs, with others of scale-work, were occasionally used until about 1380; but the prevailing usage was to have both the arms and the lower limbs entirely encased in armour of plate, with laminated plate sollerets, acutely pointed at the toe, and rouelle-spurs. The body was covered with a short hauberk, reaching to about the middle of the thigh, and, after about 1380, apparently sleeveless. The roundles at the shoulders and elbows disappeared; and in their places were introduced laminated *épaulières*, and elbow-guards, that in some degree conformed to the structure of the joint. Under the hauberk a globular breast plate was generally placed; and over the hauberk was worn the *jupon*, a species of surcoat without sleeves, which fitted tight to the shape, and was somewhat shorter than the skirt of the hauberk; it was made of some rich material, almost invariably blazoned with the armorial ensigns of the wearer, and at the bottom it was escalloped, or cut into some rich open-work pattern; it was laced at the

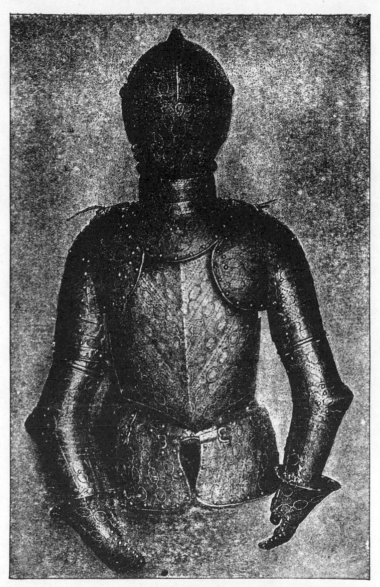

ITALIAN SUIT OF BLUED AND GILDED STEEL COVERED WITH APPLIQUES OF GOLD.
In the Guard-Chamber of Windsor Castle. 17th Century.

sides, and in some cases quilted. The belt at this period was remarkable both for its splendour and for the singular method by which it was adjusted about the hips, so that it appeared immediately above the escalloped edge of the jupon, which, in its turn, was a little higher than the bottom of the hauberk. This belt was fastened either with a rich clasp in front, or by a buckle, in which case the end of the belt was adjusted in the same manner as prevails in the adjustment of the Garter of the Order. From the hip-belt was suspended, on the left side, the long sword, with cross-guard, rich hilt, generally octagonal pommel, and decorated scabbard; while, on the left side, attached to the belt by a cord or strap, hung the *misericorde*, or dagger. (See Note 81.) Before about 1380 the basinet was very tall; but afterwards, though still acutely pointed, it was reduced in height. The basinet was worn both with and without any *ventaille* or visor, but the *camail* was universal, and, until about 1390, the lace by which it was usually attached to the basinet was without covering, and therefore visible; later in the century, and until the camail itself ceased to be worn, the camail-lace or other mode of attachment was covered by a plate, generally enriched, which formed a part of the basinet. *Goussets* of mail were worn at the joints, where the plates were necessarily open to allow for the movement of the limbs. Shields are no longer represented with armed figures. The great helm continued to be worn, but only when actual combat was imminent either in the field or the lists, over the basinet; the basinet, in this case, would be without any ventaille, since that protection for the face would have been adjusted to the helm itself; and, in order to carry the protective power of the helm to the greatest possible perfection (weight, apparently, in those times being regarded with indifference), a strong secondary reinforcing plate (*pièce de renfort*) was firmly fixed to one side of it—that side which the wearer would take care to oppose to hostile thrusts and blows,

while he endeavoured to look about him, as he best might,
through the uncovered narrow cross-clefts in his helm. A fine
example of such a helm, with the *pièce de renfort* fixed on the
left side, is represented, from the original in the Parham
armoury, in Fig. 38.

Heraldic crests began to be worn a little before the first
half of the 14th century had been completed ; and as the
second half of the century advanced they gradually were
adopted by all warriors of high rank, and also somewhat later
by all men of knightly degree. A fan-like decoration, both

Fig. 39.
CRESTED HELM OF SIR
HUGH HASTINGS,
A.D. 1347.

Fig. 40.
CRESTED HELM OF
RICHARD II.

Fig. 41.
CRESTED HELM OF
EARL EDMUND
DE MORTIMER.

for the knightly helm and for the head of the knight's war-
horse, had been introduced at an earlier period, as appears
from the seal of Alexander de Balliol, Fig. 35. A flowing
scarf or *contoise* was worn, with the earliest crests, attached
to the helm ; but this gave way to the *mantling*, a very small
mantle of some rich material, attached with the crest to the
helm or basinet, which was worn hanging down behind upon
the shoulders ; it generally ended in tassels, and had its edges
jagged or escalloped. Fig. 39, the helm of Sir H. Hastings,
1347, represented on his brass, to which I have already referred,
is an early example with both crest and mantling ; and another
example of both crest and mantling, the crest rising from out

Fig. 38.—Helm of the 14th Century, with pièce de
renfort: Parham Armoury.

of a coronet, three years earlier, has been given in Fig. 36.
The crested helm of King Richard II., Fig. 40, has been
drawn from one of the fine sculptures in Westminster Hall.
In this example the lion-crest stands upon a " cap of dignity,"
and on either side of the helm there is an ostrich feather erect.
In Fig. 41, from the seal of Earl Edmund de Mortimer,
1400, is shown, rising above the helm from a coronet, a peculiar style of crest formed of several rows of feathers set erect,
and clustered closely together; it was called a *panache*, and
was held in very high estimation.

Examples: The sculptured effigies cf Sir Walter Arden,
A.D. 1380, at Aston, in Warwickshire; of Sir John Calveley,
about 1390, at Banbury, in Cheshire; and of John, Lord
Montacute, 1389, in Salisbury Cathedral. Also brasses to several
members of the De Cobham family, at Cobham, in Kent;
to Sir John de Paletoot, 1361, at Watton, in Herts; to Sir
John Argentine, about 1375, at Horseheath, in Cambridgeshire; to Nicholas, Lord Burnell, 1382, at Acton Burnell, in
Shropshire; to Sir Thomas Burton, 1382, at Little Casterton,
in Rutland; to John Cray, Esquire, of the same date, at
Chinnor, in Berkshire; to Thomas, Lord Berkeley, 1392, at
Wotton-under-Edge, in Gloucestershire—in these brasses the
laces of the camails are shown on the basinets, but in the
examples that follow the camail-laces are covered. Brasses
to Sir Robert Swynborne, 1391, at Little Horkesley, in Essex;
to Sir William de Bryenne, 1395, at Seal, in Kent; to Sir
John de Saint Quintin, 1397, at Brandsburton, in Yorkshire
(this figure is remarkable for the richness of the hip-belt); to
Sir G. de Felbrigge, 1400, at Playford, in Suffolk; to Sir
Nicholas Dagworth, 1400, at Blickling, in Norfolk; to
Thomas de Beauchamp, Earl of Warwick, 1401, at Warwick;
and to a knight unknown, about 1405, at Laughton, in Lincolnshire. Seals also continue their faithful illustration of
armour and weapons.

The sculptured effigy of the Black Prince, who died in 1376, which rests upon his monument in Canterbury Cathedral, may be added to the foregoing examples as the typical armed representative of the camail period of armour in England. (See Note 69 for some notice of the gauntlets of the effigy of the Black Prince.) Above the monument at Canterbury there hangs a shield and jupon, with a helm, the scabbard of a sword, and a pair of gauntlets, all of them traditionally assigned to the age of the Black Prince, and indeed considered to have been worn by the Prince himself; the shield and jupon, however, display the arms of Edward III., and not those of his illustrious eldest son. This noble effigy has been engraved by Stothard; and all the brasses that have been specified in this section are engraved in one or other of my volumes.

5. THE FIFTH, OR TRANSITION PERIOD, TO 1410.— As it would naturally have been expected, before its final disuse, the camail was occasionally retained for a few years after the prevalent adoption of unmixed armour of plate. Accordingly, I must here refer to a small group of transitional examples which exhibit plate armour in its earliest character, with the exception of the camailed basinet. It is probable that the hauberk may have been habitually worn at this time, and, indeed, till about 1420, or even later, under the plate. In the examples that now follow (engraved in my " Brasses ") the hip-belt of the last period is represented.

Examples: Brasses to Sir Thomas Braunstone, 1401, at Wisbeach, in Cambridgeshire; to Sir Reginald de Cobham, 1403, at Lingfield, in Surrey; and to Sir J. Wylcotes, 1410, at Great Tew, in Oxfordshire—in the last example a plate gorget is worn over the camail.

III. PLATE ARMOUR.—1. FIRST PERIOD, TO ABOUT 1430.—The armour has now become a complete panoply of plate. The jupon has disappeared, and the polished breast

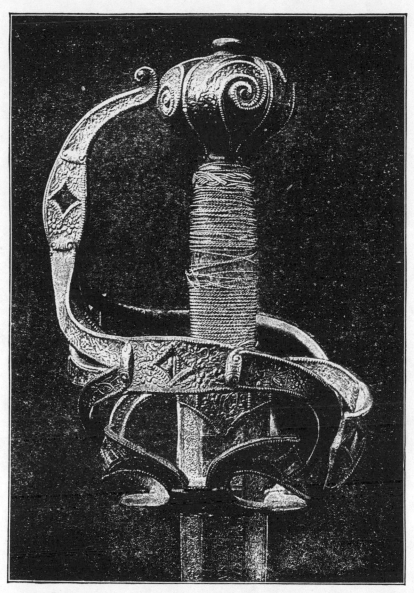

SWORD, PROBABLY OF JAMES I., WITH BASKET HILT, ENTIRELY COVERED WITH
RAISED GOLD DAMASCENING. Preserved at Windsor Castle.

and back-plates were worn without any textile covering. Roundles, or in their stead palettes somewhat resembling small shields, have been added in front to the upper part of the breast-plate, for the protection of the shoulder-joints; and the elbow-joints were generally guarded with plates that resemble expanded fans. The basinet, though still pointed at its apex, was more globular than at earlier periods; and it was connected with a gorget of plate. The helm was retained as before. Below the waist, and there connected with the bottom of the breast-plate, the body was protected by a series of narrow overlapping plates, attached to a lining of leather or pourpoint, and denominated *taces*. The fingers of the gauntlets were commonly made to represent the human hand, by having the finger-nails engraved upon them. The sword-belt was narrow, and worn diagonally over the taces; in some few instances, however, the hip-belt appears worn over the taces; and occasionally the two belts are both represented as worn together. The sword preserves its general character without much modification; but the cross-guard is usually quite straight and plain, and of considerable length; and the pommel has the general contour of a pear. The misericorde is worn on the right side.

Examples: The sculptured effigies of Michael de la Pole, Earl of Suffolk, 1415, at Wingfield, in Suffolk; and of Sir Edmund de Thorpe, 1418 (he wears his plate armour over a mail hauberk), at Ashwell-Thorpe, in Norfolk. Brasses to Sir Ivo Fitz-Waryn, 1414 (with hip-belt), at Wantage, in Berkshire; to Sir John Peryent, 1415 (with hip-belt), at Digswell, in Hertfordshire; to Sir Thomas Swynborne, 1412 (with diagonal belt), at Little Horkesley, in Essex; to Sir Symon de Felbrigge, K.G., 1413 (he has the royal banner of Richard II.), at Felbrigg, in Norfolk; to Sir John Lysle, about 1420, at Thruxton, in Hampshire; to Thomas, Lord Camoys, K.G., 1424, at Trotton, in Sussex; and to Sir

Thomas Brounflet, 1430, at Wymington, in Bedfordshire (all engraved in " Brasses," or " Brasses and Slabs ").

The two effigies of Sir R. and Sir T. Swynborne, father and son, admirably drawn and engraved in their brass at Little Horkesley, and in perfect preservation, as they lie side by side beneath their elaborately splendid canopies, exemplify, in significant contrast, the distinct styles of the camail and the pure plate periods of armour.

2. SECOND PERIOD, TO ABOUT 1450.—Again, as at the commencement of the 14th century, the system of adding secondary defences, or reinforcing, appears in active operation. The taces were frequently escalloped; small plates of various forms, named *tuilles*, were suspended by straps from the lowermost tace, one or two on each side to cover and protect the thigh in addition to the *cuissarts* of plate; the sollerets became of extravagant length; shell-like plates were added to the gauntlets, to cover the backs of the hands; additional plates of various forms and sizes were fixed at the elbows and shoulders upon the ordinary armour, and a remarkable diversity is seen to have existed between the corresponding reinforces or additional defences of the right and left sides of the same figure; the right arm being so accoutred as to be as well as possible adapted for offensive action, while the left was carefully protected by the elaborate defensive armour. The plates that were fixed to the elbow-pieces were entitled *gardes-de-bras*; those that were placed in front of the shoulders were *placates*; but when the shoulders were covered by the reinforce-plates, they were distinguished as *pauldrons*. The sword and its belt continued without much change, the guard of the weapon now generally bending downwards at its extremities, and the pommel as commonly was globular but pointed above. The helm, somewhat modified in form, was still worn with its splendid heraldic accessories. Over the armour, a new variety of short (sometimes very short) surcoat, styled a *tabard*, was worn; it

ARMET OF SIR GEORGE BROOKE, K.G.,
8TH LORD COBHAM.

From his tomb at Cobham Church, Kent.
1480—1500.

ENGLISH ARMET.

From the Collection of Seymour Lucas, A.R.A
Date about 1500.

R

had short sleeves, and (with the exception of one or two very early examples) the arms of the wearer were emblazoned as well on each sleeve as on the body of the garment. The example, Fig. 42, is from the brass to William Fynderne, A.D. 1444, at Childrey, in Berkshire.

Examples : Brasses (all engraved in my volumes) to John Leventhorpe, Esquire, 1433, at Saw bridgeworth, Herts ; to Roger Elme- brigge, Esquire, 1435, at Bedington, in Surrey ; to Sir Richard Dyxton, 1438, at Cirencester ; to John Daun- delyon, Esquire, 1445, at Margate ; to a De Cuttes, about the same date, at Arkesden, Herts ; to Walter Green, 1450, at Hayes, Middlesex ; to John Gaynestord, 1450, at Crowhurst, in Surrey ; also, with an early tabard, to John Wantele, 1424, at Amberley, in Sussex.

Fig. 42.—TABARD OF
WILLIAM FYNDERNE.

The typical example of the period is the truly noble bronze effigy of Richard Beauchamp, K.G., Earl of Warwick, in the Beauchamp Chapel, at Warwick. The earl died in 1439, and the effigy, finely engraved by Stothard, was executed about 1454. The head, resting on the crested helm, is bare ; the breast-plate is reinforced, as well as the shoulder-guards ; the pauldrons have low upright neck defences, or *passe-gardes ;* the coudières are large, and of the same form and size on both arms ; there are five taces, showing a skirt of mail beneath them ; and, besides two large tuilles, there are two smaller ones or *tuillettes.*

For some notices of the archers of England, with a repre- sentation of a small group of them in action under the standard of Earl Richard de Beauchamp, see Note 64.

3. THIRD PERIOD, TO ABOUT 1500.—Throughout this

second half of the 15th century, various new and supplementary pieces of armour were introduced, designed to reinforce the body armour, the head-piece, and the defences of the limbs; and, at the same time, the primary pieces underwent various modifications, all of them tending towards increasing extravagances of form, dimensions, and adornment. At this period a *lance-rest* was fixed to the upper part of the breast-plate on the right side.

Examples: The sculptured effigies of John, Earl of Shrewsbury, 1453, at Whitchurch, in Shropshire; of Robert, Lord Hungerford, 1455, in Salisbury Cathedral; and of Sir John Crosby, 1475, in the church of St. Helen, in the City of London. Brasses (with tabards, all engraved by Waller) to Sir John de Say, 1473, at Broxbourne, Herts; to John Feld, Esquire, 1477, at Standon, also in Herts; and to Piers Gerard, Esquire, 1492, at Winwick, in Lancashire. Also brasses (without tabards) to Henry Parice, Esquire, 1465, at Hildersham, Cambridgeshire; to Sir William Vernon, 1467, at Tong, Salop; to Henry Bourchier, K.G., Earl of Essex, 1483, at Little Easton, in Essex (all engraved by Waller); to Richard Quatremayns, Esquire, and his son, about 1475, at Thame, in Oxfordshire; to Sir Anthony Grey, 1480, in St. Alban's Abbey Church (engraved in " Brasses," and " Brasses and Slabs "); to Sir Thomas de Shernbourne, 1459, at Shernborne, and to Sir Henry Grey, 1492, at Ketteringham, both in Norfolk (and both engraved by Cotman); also, to Sir Thomas Peyton, 1484, at Islesham, in Cambridgeshire.

4. FOURTH PERIOD, TO ABOUT 1525.—At the commencement of the 16th century, the pointed sollerets were succeeded by broad *sabbatons*, cut off square or rounded at the toes. Skirts of mail at this time again came into use. The armour generally became more massive, and the fashion began to prevail for adorning it with elaborate enrichments. Plumes of flowing feathers were attached to helms.

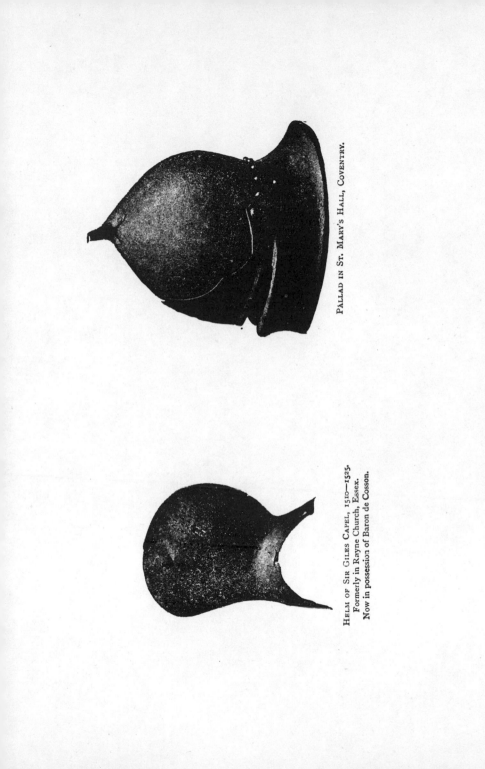

PALLAD IN ST. MARY'S HALL, COVENTRY.

HELM OF SIR GILES CAPEL, 1510—1525.
Formerly in Rayne Church, Essex.
Now in possession of Baron de Cosson.

Examples: Effigy of Sir Giles Daubeney, K.G., 1507, in Westminster Abbey. Brasses to Sir Humphrey Stanley, 1505, in Westminster Abbey ("Brasses and Slabs"); to William, Viscount Beaumont, 1507, at Wivenhoe, in Essex (Waller); and to Sir Roger L'Estrange, 1506, at Hunstanton, Norfolk (Cotman).

5. FIFTH PERIOD, TILL THE CLOSE OF THE 16TH CENTURY. — Throughout this period, the armour of princes, nobles, and men of wealth, continually increased in splendour of decoration, while at the same time as true armour its character continued to degenerate. The fashion which assimilated the armour to the general form and adornment of the costume of the time obtained favour (see Note 72), and fluted, laminated, and puffed suits were made,

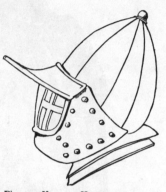

Fig. 43.—VISORED HEAD-PIECE, ABOUT 1580: TOWER ARMOURY.

and were elaborately enriched with various surface ornamentation. Very large pauldrons were worn; and laminated skirts of small overlapping steel plates, called *lamboys*, took the places of both the taces and the tuilles of somewhat earlier times. To the thoughtful observer it will be evident that the successive changes which at this period took place in armour, tended towards that gradual disuse of all armour which its insufficiency as a guard against fire-arms was very decidedly bringing on.

Examples: The figures in armour represented in the Tournament Roll of Henry VIII., preserved in the Heralds' College; the suit of armour of Henry VIII., in the Tower

Armoury.   Effigies of Sir William Pickering, 1574, Great St.
Helen's Church, London; of Sir William Thynne, 1584, and
of Lord Norris and his six sons, 1601, all in Westminster
Abbey (not engraved).   Brasses to Sir Robert Clere, 1529,
Ormesby, Norfolk; to Sir William Molineux, 1548, at

Fig. 44.—BREAST AND BACK-PLATES, ABOUT 1580.

Sefton, in Lancashire (Waller); to Sir John and Sir Edward
Greville, 1546 and 1559, at Weston, in Warwickshire; to
Humphrey Brewster, Esquire, 1593, at Wrentham, Suffolk
("Brasses and Slabs"); and to John Clippesby, Esquire,
1594, at Clippesby, in Norfolk (Cotman).

The great seals, and the seals of nobles and other impor-

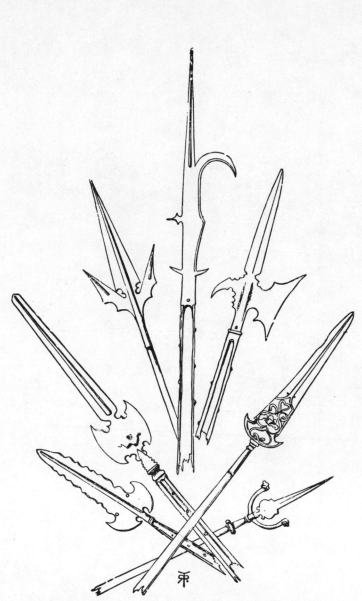

Fig. 45.—GROUP OF ENGLISH HALBERDS, BILLS, AND PARTISANS.

tant personages, continued to exemplify armour and swords during the 15th and 16th centuries.

The *salade,* a light open helm, which in its simplest form was little more than a close-fitting cap, extended so as to cover the sides of the face and the back of the neck, was very generally worn in the 16th century. It had been introduced as early as about A.D. 1400, and it was constantly enriched with varied ornamentation. The *morion* was a variety of the salade.

In Figs. 43 and 44 are shown characterist.c specimens of the helms that were in general use in the last quarter of the 16th century, and of the breast and back-plates that were characteristic of the same period.

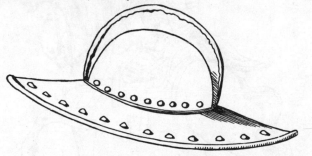

Fig. 46.—HEAD-PIECE, ABOUT 1645.

IV. HALF ARMOUR.—From the end of the 16th century till the commencement of the 18th, armour was worn almost as much for display as for real service. At any rate, it was laid aside piece by piece, except on occasions of ceremonial; the more important pieces, the helmet and the breast and back-plates were considered sufficient; and equipments of buff leather were held to be preferable to such as were made of iron, until at length armour, properly so called, ceased altogether to be regarded as a necessary or even as an appropriate defence for a soldier.

In this sketch I do not propose to follow the course of the

decline of armour, or to trace out the progressive stages which eventually led to its being abandoned. Neither is it my purpose here to add to what may be found in the Notes on the subject of Fire-arms. I bring this chapter to a close with an example (Fig. 46) of such a simple head-piece as was com-

Fig. 47.—ENGLISH CUIRASSIER OF THE TIME OF CHARLES I.

monly worn by pikemen about the year 1625; and I add a group of such bills, partisans, and halberds (Fig. 45) as were in use in England, drawn from originals in the armoury in the Rotunda at Woolwich; and also (Fig. 47) a portrait of such a cuirassier, armed with a wheel-lock carbine, as might have mounted guard at Whitehall in the year that Charles II. was born.

SILVER ARMOUR OF PRINCE CHARLES, AFTERWARDS CHARLES II.
Tower of London.

CHAPTER XI.

MODERN ARMS.

PART I.—ARTILLERY.

THE word " Artillery,' in its primary and true acceptation, has been used to denote every variety of engine that has been in use on the field of battle, and more particularly in the operations of sieges. We now propose to pass in review and briefly to describe the principal machines that were employed on such occasions, before the discovery of cannon.

We have already seen how the ancient Assyrians, in their sieges, made use of an enormous spear to breach walls ; and how their soldiers were sheltered under strong timber-work sheds, while by sheer strength, or aided by some simple machinery, they thrust forward their battering spears. The same machine, or, at any rate, one that is analogous to it, is found amongst the Romans under the name of *Terebra.* The *catapults,* and the *beliers,* or *battering-rams,* which are mentioned in the most ancient histories of all nations, are also met with amongst the Romans, and subsequently they appear in France, where Roman traditions were long preserved. In our endeavour to trace the history of these engines from age to age, we shall not fail to find that our inquiries are over-shadowed with a certain degree of obscurity.

The *belier,* or *battering-ram* was a long and strong beam of wood, armed with an iron head, representing more or less correctly the head of a ram (adopted, doubtless, in conse-quence of the natural habit of the animal to *butt* with its head and horns), and sheltered under a kind of pent-house, from the roof of which it was suspended by ropes. This battering-ram, having been brought up close to the hostile wall, was driven against it by the strength of men's arms. Preparation was made for the approach and use of the ram, by means of the *terebra* (auger, or boring implement) which has just now been mentioned. The *terebra* was a long and strong spear, placed on a kind of pin or axis, so that it might be worked in a groove by some machinery which has never yet been clearly understood. (See *Histoire de la Milice Française*, par le P. Daniel, t. 1er., planche 10.) What is well known is,

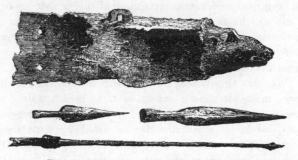

Fig. 48.—Assyrian Battering-Ram and Spears.

that the auger was caused to advance against the walls by men who worked some kind of capstan and cables. The work that the auger had to accomplish was to break up the first stone, and thus to make the commencement of a breach ; and then the ram would be brought up to enlarge the opening by beating away the adjoining stones. In Fig. 48 an Assyrian battering-ram and some spears are shown.

The *catapult* discharged great darts armed with iron heads, or which carried at their extremities some inflammable composition. The largest engine of this kind threw darts six feet in length which, at the distance of a hundred paces, would pierce through several men. These catapults were generally made from the trunks of trees roughly fashioned ; and, having been bent by means of ropes and pulleys, the pieces of timber, when suddenly released, violently struck the darts that were placed in readiness upon stakes prepared for that purpose, and drove them forwards.

The *balista*, a variety of the catapult, was a machine for discharging stones. One or more large stones were placed in a kind of wooden bucket suspended from the end of a beam which, after having been elevated, fell by a simple contrivance, and projected to a distance the contents of the bucket.

In the middle ages, and after the invention of the cross-bow, instead of catapults for the purpose of discharging bolts or arrows of great size, they used arblasts or cross-bows, which had power proportioned to the magnitude of the bolts. This bow was drawn by pulleys and cords, and in fact it was a tower or fortification cross-bow (*arbalète de tour*). The Artillery Museum at Paris possesses two of these formidable engines—*balista bows* (*arcs de balista*), as they have also been called ; one is made of a hard fibrous wood, which has the appearance of the wood of the palm-tree, and the other is of steel.

Ancient artillery, as may clearly be seen, could never have led the way to the introduction of modern artillery. They have really nothing in common, and it is not possible for the one to be considered the development of the other.

The art of composing or compounding inflammable substances, which eventually led to the production of gunpowder, and consequently to the invention of ordnance, is at least as ancient as the art of constructing such engines as the *balista*. At all times, in war, arrows have been discharged which were provided with some inflammable or combustible substance fixed to their heads ; and of substances such as these a principal ingredient has always been pitch. The Greeks of the Lower Empire are well known to have invented a

s

celebrated composition of this kind, which has been identified with them under the title of " Greek fire." We now know what was the composition of this once mysterious substance, which, after all, has not proved to be either very wonderful or very ingenious. It was a mixture of oil of naphtha with pitch, resin, and vegetable oil and grease, to which compound were added various metals in the form of powder. Of this " Greek fire," the Greeks, as we have said, were the inventors; but for its reputation it was indebted to the Arabs, and to the manner in which it was used by them in their conflicts with the western barons in the Crusades. After all, however, it now is admitted that " Greek fire," while certainly it inspired great alarm, did not inflict much serious injury.

At the time of the first crusade, and perhaps still earlier, the Chinese, when searching for fresh inflammable compositions, had already discovered that singular combination of substances which eventually was destined to revolutionise the art of war. It now may be considered to have been clearly established that to the Chinese belongs the honour—if honour it be—of having first introduced nitre or saltpetre into a mixture of charcoal and sulphur. The mixture of the two last-named substances they had made from very early times, and they had added various other substances from time to time; but they had not thought of nitre, which forms the distinctive element of real gunpowder, and imparts to the composition its explosive force. The Chinese appear to have made use of their discovery chiefly for manufacturing fireworks. Thanks to their communications with China, the Arabs were not long before they learned the art of making gunpowder; and, as it would seem, at the first they made petards with it—that is, they made objects such as " crackers," which would explode in a case. From such a use of powder as this, to putting it with a projectile into a tube for the purpose of discharging the projectile, a very long step had to be taken. It was by the

Arabs, once more, that this step was taken; and thus, with justice, they may claim to have performed a more important part in the invention of artillery than the Chinese themselves. But at this point we fall back into the obscurity which envelopes the invention of gunpowder; or, more strictly speaking, from that obscurity at this point we are unable to extricate ourselves. It still remains unknown by whom the first cannon were made—the time, the place also, and the manner of their original construction. All that we are able to assert with certain accuracy is, that in the year 1338 there was a cannon at Cambray, from which arblast-quarrels were discharged; that in the year following, 1339, at the attack on Quesnoy there were several cannon of the same kind; and, again, that similar pieces of artillery were present and in use, in 1342, at the siege of Algesiras; and so forth from that time onwards. Contemporary historians make mention of this novelty in warfare in a manner which proves them to have regarded it simply as a curiosity of no great value or importance—a proof that the cannon, at its first appearance on the field, not only did not produce any great effect, but also that it altogether failed to presage its own subsequent career. This is a circumstance that explains itself. The original cannon, of very small size, which discharged darts or small leaden balls, at most of three pounds in weight, was looked upon as neither more nor less than a substitute for the siege-arblast (*arbalète à tour*), or as a fresh engine of the same class, more noisy indeed than its predecessors, but not more calculated to do mischief. The many tales that have been told of the overwhelming terror caused by cannon on their first appearance, have been proved to be worthless fictions of later ages.

The earliest cannon of which we now have any knowledge were made of hammered iron, and consisted of tubes strengthened by rings; the tube was made open at both ends, and the charge of powder, with the projectile, was placed in a separate iron case or chamber, open in front, which was adjusted to one end of the tube and joined to it by iron wedges driven into an external case that enclosed the whole of what

1.   2.

Fig. 49.—EXAMPLES OF EARLY CANNON.

we may distinguish as the breech end of the gun. By this contrivance, the chamber containing the charge and the barrel were kept together in close contact at the time of the explosion ; and, in order the more effectually to secure this important object, an iron stirrup was passed round the external case. The chamber itself was pierced with a touch-hole, or *vent*, through which, when the piece was to be fired, a slender rod of iron at a red heat was introduced. Here, then, we have evidence that the idea of breech-loading formed a part of the original conception of the cannon itself.

The cannon, whether with a chamber, or without one and therefore formed in one solid piece, was mounted on a kind of trestle, or on a block of wood; or, when they were very small, several cannon were fixed side by side upon a timber frame, and the whole was called a *ribeaudequin*.

The circumstances which attended the first introduction of cannon would naturally suggest that some of them might be carried by soldiers, who might discharge them while held in their hands; and thus the origin of small arms appears to have been associated, from the very first, with that of cannon. We reserve for consideration, in another section of this chapter, the history of small arms from the time in which they assume characteristics distinct from those of their greater relative, and in themselves form a separate class of weapons.

The small scale on which the first cannon were made has been already noticed. Cannon of considerably larger size were speedily made; and others followed almost immediately, that were, indeed, enormous; so that the early cannon-makers appear to have carried their manufacture, at a single bound, from one extreme to the other. Towards the end of the 14th century we find that pieces called *bombardes* were in existence, which threw balls of stone weighing as much as 200 lbs. By the side of the pieces of field artillery then in common use, which threw leaden balls of one or two pounds' weight, the *veuglaires*, the *crapendeaux*, the *couleuvrines*, and the *serpentines*, in those days they used to drag to the field of battle bombards, not indeed such as discharged 200 lb. stone shot (which would not have been possible) but others that threw balls weighing from 50 lbs. to 80 lbs.; this, however, was accomplished only with very great difficulty; and, it must be added, that these heavy bombards proved to be of very little practical use.

The progress, accordingly, that was made in artillery during the 14th century, consisted only in increase of magnitude—very large cannon succeeded to very small ones. But that was not by any means an advance in the right direction. In order to render artillery really formidable, what was required, and what indeed was absolutely necessary, was the removal of certain imperfections and the introduction of certain improvements, all of them of primary importance, which we now will describe; thus we shall be the better enabled to understand the advances in the art of the artillerist, that we shall afterwards set forth.

Cannon made of hammered iron and hooped (or encircled with rings for the purpose of acquiring additional strength) did not offer sufficient resistance to the explosive force of the charge; and, consequently, these guns were constantly found to burst—they constantly proved themselves, therefore, to be deficient in that fundamental quality, sufficient strength. Gunpowder made with saltpetre that has not been well refined, instead of burning instantly, became ignited with comparative slowness; it smouldered, in fact, which greatly diminished its power of projection. Then, when some skilful powder manufacturer—one, perhaps, who was even too skilful—made a lively and quick-burning powder, he increased the chances that the gunners might be killed by the bursting of their own cannon. The system at that time was altogether vicious and bad.

A cannon, as is well known, has to encounter most severe shocks from the action of the explosive gases that are so rapidly generated within it by the ignition of the powder, and also by the equally violent pressure of the atmosphere which enters the cavity after the escape of the gases; this action, considered as one, is the *recoil.* Cannon are now constructed in such a manner that they are empowered to encounter and to overcome the recoil by yielding to it. The advantage of this is self-evident, since a body which gives way and yields to any sudden and sharp shock, does not experience the same disturbing effects which necessarily attend a firm and stubborn resistance. In the 14th century the cannon were made with the view to their overcoming the recoil by resisting it. The consequence was that, if the cannon of that period were not quickly out of order, it was solely the result, not of their own inherent good qualities, but of the weakness of the powder and the small weight of the projectiles. With such powder and such projectiles as are now in use, those old guns, with their cases and their backing of planks and wedges, would have been speedily destroyed, even if they had escaped self-destruction at their very first discharge.

Balls weighing 200 lbs. were fired, it is true, before the 14th century had passed away; and this is a fact which appears to contradict the statements that have just been made. But, then, what saved the bombard of those days from destruction was the massive and complicated apparatus by which it was carried and supported, coupled with the slow ignition of the powder, and the consequent comparative feebleness of the shock attending its combustion and the discharge of the projectile.

Other inconveniences resulted from the nature of the projectiles. The ponderous stone balls, which were generally employed in sieges, were easily crushed by their own action; nor were they able to batter down a wall of moderate solidity and strength. On the other hand, the small leaden cannonballs, while somewhat more effective against troops on the open field of battle, were but little superior to the stone balls in siege operations; and, since they were not well adjusted to

the calibre of the guns, and did not fit them well, they failed
both in range and in accuracy of aim.

The process of loading was very slow and tedious, and
particularly in the case of the great bombards. It was necessary to charge the chamber—a piece distinct from the body
of the cannon, and separated from it by the *volée*—then the
loaded chamber had to be brought to the body of the cannon
to be adjusted to it, to be securely fixed in its position, and to
have the iron stirrup run into its proper place; and, finally,
the piece had to be discharged. The discharge soon ceased
to be effected by means of the red-hot iron wire that has been
mentioned; because this method of firing, while both sufficiently expeditious and certain, was also dangerous, in consequence of the frequent bursting of the cannon. Instead of
the dangerous red-hot wire, in order to fire the cannon the
touch-hole was filled with fine powder that would ignite and
burn with great rapidity, and to this was joined a train of
slowly-burning powder, which was laid along the length of
the cannon; this train was fired at the end most distant from
the touch-hole, and while the fire was passing leisurely along,
the gunners had time to retire to a safe distance; and the
larger the cannon the longer would be the train, and the
gunners would have a proportionately longer time for their
movement out of the danger.

While treating of the dangerous nature of the early artil-
leryman's duties, we may consistently refer to a work of the
15th century, which contains, with much information that is
of no little value as a contribution to the early history of
ordnance, the following curious passage in a chapter entitled,
*Des conditions, mœurs et sciences que doibt avoir ung chascun
audit art de canonnerye.*" Of these "conditions, manners,
and sciences," which the author undertakes to set forth in
full in the course of his work, the first, and the chief and
most important of all he declares to be " to honour and to fear

and to love God, and have always before the eyes the fear of offending Him, more than the fear of all other men of war whatsoever. For, whensoever they fire a bombard, cannon, or any other piece of artillery, or that they desire to make use of gunpowder, their great strength and force constantly cause the cannon which they fire to burst; and, if the cannon itself do not burst, there always is a risk of being burned by the powder, if he is not very cautious, and does not use a good discretion for his own preservation and safety; of the which powder the vapour alone is really venomous against man, as presently we shall show; and it is to him an enemy more grievous and terrible than to all others, through its desire to kill and to destroy him by means of the great ills and mischiefs and damages that it does to him in its said vocation and trade." *Le livre du secret de l'art de l'artillerie et canonnerie*, p. 139.

The manner in which the earliest cannon were mounted made it a matter of the greatest difficulty to alter the direction in which even the small pieces were laid, while in the case of the greater cannon every alteration of the kind was altogether out of the question; and this alone was constantly enough to render the artillery useless. The early gunners were quick enough, indeed, in discovering means for raising and depressing their pieces, so as to change and regulate their elevation; but it was reserved for the 15th century to witness the introduction of any contrivances for altering the direction in which cannon might be pointed, and for varying their horizontal range.

It will be worth our while to glance at the machinery that was introduced in the 14th century for altering the elevation of cannon. The gun is laid upon two pieces of timber, resting one upon the other, of which the lower is fixed, and the upper (to which the gun is attached) is fastened at the end by a large bolt to the under, and on this bolt it can move as on a hinge. At the other extremity it is free. Thus this upper piece of timber may be raised, and with it the gun may be raised in such a manner as to have its angle of firing changed. Curved pieces of wood then are placed on each side, wherein there are holes to enable the gunners to maintain the desired elevation ; and in order for them to accomplish this, it is only necessary for them to pass a bolt of sufficient strength through the holes from one curved piece of timber to the other. The cannon, bearing on the bolt, would remain elevated towards the breech and depressed towards the muzzle at the desired degree of inclination. One caution only was necessary—and that was truly all-important—the gun, when thus elevated or depressed, must not receive a full charge, lest the recoil should destroy the whole apparatus.

At the present time, cannon move with ease on the field of battle ; they are transported with the utmost rapidity from one point to another ; and they may be pointed in any direction and at every elevation, with equal facility and security ; and, in fact, the great part which this weapon now plays in warfare depends even more on this faculty of swift and easy movement than on any other condition. It is certain that Gustavus Adolphus, who was the first to adopt this system on an important scale, by this great innovation alone accomplished almost a complete revolution in the art of war. In the 14th century, merely to bring up the cannon to the theatre of war was an operation sufficiently serious and difficult, and more particularly if one of the great bombards had to be dealt with. The gun itself had to be placed, for transport, on a vehicle constructed for that especial purpose. Then the gun-carriage had to be placed, in its turn, upon another vehicle, that had been provided to suit its particular requirements. And when all this had been done—and done not without severe labour and great trouble—the chances were that the whole might stick fast in the road, and remain immovable even in

the face of the enemy.; or, if this risk should happily prove to
have been unfounded, when on the scene of action the gun
would have to be removed, and the gun-carriage unloaded,
and the gun would have to be mounted in order to be fit for
service; and this by no means easy operation would have to
be accomplished by means of yet another heavy and cumbersome machine, called a *chèvre* (a goat), formed of a timber
framework, with ropes, and pulleys, and levers. After all
these things had at last been effected, we can easily imagine
that the gunners would not readily be disposed to entertain
the idea of moving and altering the position of a bombard in
face of the enemy. In action, accordingly, the cannon, after
it had reached its destined position, was almost inoffensive
(except, perhaps, to the gunners), since, when once the range
of its fire had been ascertained by the enemy, it was a simple
affair for them to avoid it. In sieges, of course, one of these
old bombards, when fixed in its position, was more efficacious;
and so, as a general rule, the early use of artillery, and especially
of what may be distinguished as heavy artillery, soon became
almost exclusively restricted to siege operations.

The first really important modifications, the first genuine
improvements, effected in the closing years of the 14th century,
took place in the projectiles. The stone balls that were used
in sieges were hooped with iron; and they were found at
once to be more effective against walls than the simple balls
of stone. But to form cannon-balls by the process of casting
them, was not then to be thought of—it was still held to be
simply an impossibility. This operation, which now appears
so simple, was altogether beyond the powers of the workers
in metal who flourished in those days. On the other hand,
as if to show that their genius and their abilities were by no
means to be despised, those same artillerists invented firing
with case-shot and firing with heated shot; and they made
experiments with parabolic shot, or bombs, and they even

attempted to introduce hollow shells, that would burst after they had been fired from the guns.

These experiments and attempts were not all attended with the same success. The case-shot, that were formed of pieces of iron or stone bound together by a kind of cement which broke up in the act of the discharge, and the inflammable balls, which were stone kernels surrounded by combustible compositions, very nearly fulfilled the purposes that they were desired to fulfil, so that so far the enterprising inventors had tolerable reason to be satisfied; but the red-hot stone balls, that they wanted to use as we now use red-hot shot, in causing the cannon to explode too soon, were found to be so excessively dangerous to the gunners who had to discharge them, that they were laid aside as impracticable; and the same fate attended the hollow projectiles, which either *would* burst in the gunners' hands, or *would not* burst at all.

Meanwhile, an important innovation was introduced into the construction of the cannon. Bronze cannon were cast. These were found to be decidedly stronger than the guns that were made on the old system, as was proved by their enduring the shock of stronger charges and heavier projectiles. Still, comparatively strong as these bronze cannon unquestionably were, there always existed some degree of apprehension lest they should burst. This arose in a great measure from the discovery of the true proportions of the copper and tin not having then been made; nor was it known how to conduct such experiments as would lead to the discovery of this proportion. In this matter, as in many others, they worked, if not actually in the dark, certainly in a dim twilight, and sometimes the result was truly disastrous. The cast bronze guns, however, gradually grew into greater favour, and the wrought-iron guns in proportion were held in lighter esteem; and yet, some of the latter are found to have been in use even to a very late period.

Next, the gunpowder had its turn. The art of purifying the saltpetre at length was acquired; and thus it became possible to charge stronger guns with more active powder, and the consequence was that the projectiles generally acquired an increased velocity and a greater power.

Towards the middle of the century, improvements were introduced into the machine that was used for carrying the cannon; or, in other words, the cannon were then for the first time mounted on what may fairly be called *gun-carriages*. It would be at once tedious and unnecessary to attempt to describe the various forms that the carriages assumed in different countries, or as they passed through all their successive modifications and improvements; it is sufficient, indeed, to state that in every instance, from the time of its first adoption, the gun-carriage was provided with wheels, so that horses could be attached directly to the cannon itself, without the necessity for any independent means for transport. In the monuments of the period some gun-carriages may be seen which resemble small cars, in which the gun forms an integral part of the machine—such is the case with the early Swiss artillery. Others of these early carriages, again, have *trails* (*flasques*), after the manner of modern gun-carriages—they have, that is, the two lateral pieces which issue from the flanks of the cannon, and descend in its rear to the ground, and are curved with a greater or a lesser curvature.

About the same time was invented a means for elevating or depressing the gun, which would have somewhat the effect of a modern "sight;" or, at any rate, in order to accomplish this, wedges of wood were placed, like so many pads, beneath the breech of the gun, in a greater or a lesser number, as it might be desired to depress the muzzle more or less. A more ingenious machine, but also one that was more complicated, was added, in order to obtain that important object which has already been noticed—changes in the horizontal range of a gun. This contrivance acts upon the small beam which supports the cannon in such a manner that, in addition to its faculty of elevating and lowering the gun with itself by means of bolts passing through the " bows " or curved side-pieces, it works in a grooved beam at its fixed extremity, and thus while that extremity moves towards the left, the gun is carried towards the right; and, by reversing the movement, a reciprocal action is obtained.

This contrivance is sufficiently easy in its application, and it is not in that respect that it can be considered faulty; but its real fault, which is so great that it absolutely destroys every possible advantage in it, arises from the fact that it renders the gun immovable, because such a carriage as this can have no wheels.

It was during the reign of Louis XI. (A.D. 1461—1483) that the first seriously important advance was made. Iron cannon-balls were then cast. This had previously been considered impossible, in consequence of the imperfect condition of the metallurgic art. In the first instance, indeed, an error was permitted, in a singular manner, to lessen the advantages of the new invention.

The original casters of cannon-balls were not content to produce balls of less dimensions than the old familiar spherical masses of stone, which they proposed to supersede. The result was that, when loaded with these enormous iron balls, the cannon burst much more readily than before; or, if attempts were made to obviate this by charging the guns with powder of inferior quality, the projectiles moved slowly and were incapable of producing any important effects. This was an error in judgment that was soon corrected. It was speedily ascertained that it was altogether a mistake to cast iron cannon-balls of any such extravagant magnitude, since velocity of movement would more than compensate for any diminution in weight. From the moment of this discovery, the rule of feudal despotism may be said to have been overthrown; and with its overthrow the haughty lords of castles, who for too long a time had oppressed the common people, would feel the necessity for submitting to the altered state of things.

About the same period, also, the difficult problem of overcoming the recoil of cannon was satisfactorily solved. For some time the artillerists had been on the track which would lead them to this much-desired discovery, and at length their efforts were crowned with success. Whoever has examined a cannon with any degree of attention cannot have failed to observe the two solid cylindrical appendages that project on each side of it, somewhat more than one-third of the length of the gun from its breech, and are embodied in its mass. These projecting appendages, called *trunnions* (*tourillons*, pivots), are placed at the point where the gun receives almost the entire impulse of the recoil, and they convey it to the trail of the carriage, by which it is met and overcome. This arrangement, combined with the backward movement that the form of the carriage concedes to the gun, deprives the recoil of all that strength which had been productive of such injurious and dangerous effects.[85]

These new inventions were seen for the first time to have been carried out with anything like complete success on a large scale in a park of artillery, when Charles VIII. of France (A.D. 1483—1498) crossed the Alps and marched into Italy, with a view to conquer the kingdom of Naples. Paul Jove, in his history of his own times, has informed us of the profound impression that was produced in Italy by the formidable aspect of this French artillery force, which, however, failed to be productive of any very great results.

From the time of Charles VIII. (the end of the 15th century, that is to say) to our own times, at any rate until the introduction of rifled cannon (*canons rayés*), there has been no invention for the improvement of ordnance which can be compared in importance with those that have just been described; unless, perhaps, it be the invention of the mortar, of which we presently shall have occasion to speak.

Under Francis I. (A.D. 1515—1547), and under Henri II. (A.D. 1547—1559), instead of that multitude of cannon of various sizes that it was customary to bring upon fields of battle, and which did not permit any precision or certainty in calculating the effects of artillery practice, in the French armies the excellent idea prevailed of adopting and adhering to a small fixed number of sizes for cannon.

Here follow, introduced for curiosity, the sizes of the six regulation cannon, to which the whole of the French artillery were restricted by Henri II.

1. The *cannon*. The weight of the projectile varied from 33 lbs. 4 oz., to 34 lbs.

2. The *great culverin*. The weight of the projectile from 15 lbs. 2 oz., to 15 lbs. 4 oz.

3. The *bastard culverin*. The projectile from 7 lbs. 2 oz., to 7 lbs. 3 oz.

4. The *middle culverin*. The projectile 2 lbs.

5. The *falcon*. The projectile 1 lb. 1 oz.

6. The *falconet*. The projectile 14 oz.

It was ordained that the bronze with which the vents or touch-holes should be lined, should be made with the fixed proportions of 100 parts of copper and 10 parts of tin.

During the course of the second half of the 16th century, in Germany, the *mortar* was invented. This is a species of cannon, short and of large bore, from which, at an elevation more or less approaching to the vertical, large hollow bursting projectiles, called *shells*, are discharged. These shells contain a chamber, within which powder is carefully placed; and this powder is fired, at the moment the shell itself reaches its destination, by means of a fusée or slow-match inserted through a small opening pierced through the shell, which opening is called,

not a touch-hole, but an *eye*. At the present time, for the purpose of firing shells (causing the powder enclosed within the
shells to explode, and consequently to burst the shells) in
France a small wooden cylinder is driven firmly into the eye ;
and this cylinder is traversed by a small channel, which is
filled with priming powder—a powder, that is, which
smoulders instead of burning briskly and rapidly. The shell
is placed in the mortar in such a position that the eye faces
the mortar's mouth ; formerly it was supposed that if a shell
were so placed, its fusée or priming powder would not ignite,
and that consequently the shell would not explode.

Since the introduction of mortars two distinct modes of
firing them have been in use. They have been discharged
with either a single fire or a double fire. That is, in some
cases the shells were constructed to be fired by the act of the
explosion of the mortar, and thus a single firing accomplished a twofold effect—it discharged the mortar, and in so
doing it caused the shell-priming to ignite. In the other case,
the gunner lighted the fusee of the shell with one hand, while
with the other hand he fired the mortar from which it would
be discharged. In single firing, the eye of the shell, charged
with a metal fusée, and either primed with powder or provided
with a match, was turned inwards towards the chamber of the
mortar, through the misapprehension that then prevailed (as
has been stated) concerning the ignition of the priming or
match ; the consequence was that the explosion of the mortar
would force the fusée into the shell and would fire the powder
within the shell instantaneously, so that the shell would burst
while yet it was inside the mortar. The danger to which the
gunners were thus exposed soon led to the abandonment of
the system of discharging mortars by single firing.

Until about the middle of the 17th century mortars were
invariably discharged by double firing. The process of loading, while this system of firing prevailed, was very slow and

tedious. After the powder had been placed in the chamber
of the mortar, it was closed-in by a wooden board or shutter,
made to fit the bore of the piece ; then this board was covered
with turf; and, over the turf, again, earth was placed; and,
finally, on the earth the shell with its live (or lighted) fusée
was made to rest in such a manner, that it was only partly
enclosed within the mortar. All this required time.

The introduction of the mortar into France was not
effected until several years after its first appearance as a distinct
piece of artillery. Hence, it was not earlier than the year
1634 that the use of the mortar was formally recognised in
the French armies, after a series of conclusive experiments
that had been conducted by an engineer, a native of England,
named Malthus, in the presence of French officers who had
been appointed to witness these experiments and to record
their results. It was at the siege of Lamotte, in Lorraine,
that French mortars for the first time appeared in action
before the enemy.

Another difficulty that presented itself when the mortar
was first invented, was the discovery of some effectual means
for obviating the disastrous effects produced by the recoil.
These effects were most serious, and also most difficult to deal
with, when a mortar was placed at the inclination nearest to
the vertical, that is, at an angle of 45 degrees. It is not possible for a piece elevated at such an angle to yield to any
recoil. The construction of the gun-carriage at that time
caused the trunnions of the gun, or mortar, under the excessively violent action of the recoil, to blow up the cap-squares
or plates which secured them to the carriage. This grave
inconvenience was remedied by causing the breech of the
mortar always to rest on a solid bed of timber, which received
and was able to resist the shock. Towards the close of the
17th century, the two problems, which at the first had
rendered the use of the mortar both difficult and dangerous,

had been solved in a manner that was considered to be completely satisfactory; and, from that time, accordingly, the regular and general use of this arm may be said to have commenced. The changes that have been made in the construction and use of mortars since that same time have been few in number, and of comparatively little importance.

About the same period that witnessed the invention and introduction of the mortar, a piece called a *howitzer* (*l'obusier*) came into use in England, by which hollow bursting projectiles were discharged in a horizontal direction, like solid shot from an ordinary cannon. In France, the same difficulty that was experienced in discharging mortars by a single fire, caused a prolonged hesitation with reference to the use of the howitzer. There was the same danger that the ignition of the shell might cause the bursting of the howitzer, as it might cause the bursting of a mortar. The solution of this problem in the one case was evidently also its solution in the other; and, therefore, with the adoption of the mortar, the adoption of the howitzer followed as a matter of course. Since that time, the use of the howitzer has continually increased; and, now, at the present day, unless some unforeseen change should create a revolution in our military system, it is evident that the artillery in modern armies will comprise larger numbers of pieces that discharge hollow projectiles—larger numbers, that is, of howitzers—than of cannon that discharge solid projectiles.

The 18th century witnessed the accomplishment of two most important innovations, which it will be sufficient for us here to mention only in a very few words, since they refer, not so much to the pieces of artillery, as to the organisation and regular working of the artillery service.

Lieutenant-General de Vallière reduced to five the number of the various calibres of the French artillery. We have seen that by Henri II. their number had been fixed at six; but

since his time, and especially under the disastrous influences
of the religious wars, the calibres of the French artillery had
again become almost as varied and unsettled as they had been
in the 14th and 15th centuries.   This same officer also for
the first time laid down definite rules for the construction of
gun-carriages; and he fixed the proportions of the metal alloy,
which should be used to line the vents of the French
artillery.

Lieutenant-General de Gribeauval divided the *matériel* and
the entire force of the artillery service into four distinct sections,
and to each one of them he assigned its own special duties;
thus, by this general the artillery of France were divided into
field artillery, siege artillery, artillery for the defence of
fortifications, and artillery for coast defence.   The guns
themselves, the gun-carriages, the ammunition tumbrils, the
teams of horses, and indeed every detail, in each of the
divisions of the artillery, were defined and worked out in
becoming combination with great skill and judgment, in
accordance with the nature of the particular service that
would fall to the lot of each division.   This system, adopted
in 1765, continued in force throughout the wars of the
Republic and the Empire; it has continued to be in use in
France until the year 1825; and men competent to form an
opinion on such a matter have attributed to it, in no slight
degree, the successes which in modern times have shed a lustre
over the armies of France.

A complete picture of the development and progress of
artillery in France up to the year 1789 could not be drawn
and coloured-in faithfully without our giving here a description of every discovery, and of each progressive step in the
course of discovery, that has taken any part in forming and
establishing that new science, so completely unknown to the
ancients, which we may entitle the "balistic science"—the
science, that is, of military projectiles—but this would supply

materials for a book, which would be altogether distinct from our present project. We now are content, with a view to demonstrate the profoundly scientific character of modern arms, to record in so many words the problems of which the solutions in greater or lesser degrees have produced that balistic science which we have mentioned, and to refer to the great names that present themselves to us in the course of the history of these discoveries.

When working out his investigations on gravity, Galileo, in the first instance, determined by calculation that a projectile, discharged from the mouth of a cannon, in its flight must of necessity describe a parabolic curve, always supposing that it moves *in vacuo*—in a void space, wherein it encounters the action of no opposing or disturbing forces. For a long period of time artillerists relied upon this principle, without allowing themselves to imagine that the resistance of the atmosphere was competent in any degree to affect the flight of projectiles. In England, Robins,[86] and after him, Newton, demonstrated the complicated effects that resulted from the action of this fluid; and they showed that the numerous contingencies which generally were attributed to the variable quality of gunpowder, in reality were caused and determined by atmospheric agency.

Blondel and Bélidor, in France, discovered and taught to the artillerymen of their day certain methods for calculating the different powers that they might assign to the same cannon, by means of various charges of powder. Robins, whose name we have already mentioned, was the inventor of an instrument constantly in use, and of very great practical importance, in the treatment of artillery; this is the *balistic pendulum*— an apparatus, constructed in accordance with the very complex laws that determine the transmission of shocks, which indicates the velocity of projectiles, and proves the relative strength of various kinds and qualities of gunpowder. In general terms this instrument may be defined to consist of a species of case or buffer of cast-iron, within which the cannon-ball is received and its flight is stopped, together with a pendulum, properly so called, that is disposed in such a manner as enables it to measure, and by its oscillations to declare, the velocity and force of the projectile.

The name of Robins naturally leads us to refer to the grandest invention and improvement of modern times in connection with artillery, the rifled cannon (*canon rayé*), because that eminent scientific artillerist foresaw and predicted the revolution which at some future time would certainly result from his inventions. To speak more correctly, indeed, the rifled cannon was invented at that time, and the principle of rifling was known to be no less applicable to the bore of a cannon than to the barrel of a gun ; but then, in those days leaden cannon-balls were discharged from the rifled ordnance ; nor was it supposed to be possible to form from any other metal cannon-balls which would be capable of adapting themselves, like those made of lead, to the grooves of the rifling. So long as it was considered to be a positive necessity that leaden projectiles should be used exclusively for rifled pieces, it also was found to be equally necessary to apply the process of rifling only to pieces of small calibre. Robins predicted that so long as this problem concerning the projectiles for rifled ordnance remained unsolved, the process of rifling would be but rarely applied to pieces of artillery ; but, on the other hand, it was his firm conviction that a solution of this problem would make its appearance in due time ; and he also believed that a military supremacy, at any rate of a temporary duration, would be at once the consequence and the reward of this discovery.

The problem was solved at last in France ; and the advantages which resulted from that discovery in the Italian wars are well known. As Robins had predicted, a method was eventually discovered, by means of which cast-iron cannon-balls might be used with complete success in rifled cannon. This was done by attaching to the cast-iron cannon-ball some other substance, which might accomplish for the cannon-ball what was altogether beyond its own capacity, and might traverse and be grasped by the grooves of the rifling. The discovery consisted, first, in determining this principle; and, secondly, in working it out successfully.

The ball for the rifled cannon, accordingly, is made of cast-iron, in form both cylindrical and conical, closely resembling a common rifle-ball, but hollowed after the manner of shot discharged from howitzers, and it is also pierced with holes, into which are screwed bolts made of pewter or of some comparatively soft metal alloy. These bolts, which expand under the action of the heat of the gases that are generated at the moment of the explosion, are forced into the grooves of the rifling, and thus the iron projectile receives, and carries with it from the mouth of the gun, the full influence of the rifling. A ball of this kind, weighing eight pounds, which is discharged by a gun of comparatively small calibre, has a maximum range of about 5,000 yards, or two miles and nearly seven-eighths; its point-blank range is 2,000 yards, or 240 yards more than a mile; and then, if at that distance the ball should touch the ground, it would have a rebound of from about 750 to 850 yards, or not very far short of half a mile.

At this point we may glance back, and may measure the distance that is traversed (in a course, unhappily, most deplorrable) between the rifled cannon and the javelin of the Homeric heroes—certainly we shall not desire to carry the comparison still further back.

Since the era of the Italian war, which demonstrated conclusively the power of the new arms, a fearful emulation has sprung up amongst the nations of the earth, each one seeking to surpass every other in the possession of artillery endowed with the most terribly destructive powers. All recent inventions, however, together with the numerous pretensions to invention that have sprung up on this side and on that, amount to no more than rifled cannon with modifications and accessories that are more or less happy and successful. For example, to adduce the most celebrated piece of recent artillery, the English " Armstrong " is simply a rifled cannon of a heavier calibre than the French rifled ordnance.[87]   It is loaded at the breech, and its admirers boast of the perfection of the apparatus for closing the breech (obtuvateur) after the gun has been charged, and which prevents the escape of the gases at the time of the explosion ; but, the closing apparatus is not the only thing that is important in a rifled cannon, when it is in action on the field of battle.   The French officers who saw the Armstrong gun in active service in the campaign in Cochin China agree in the opinion that the French rifled artillery, if they had less range, were more easily moved and more rapidly worked ; and, consequently, they had a compensation for their inferiority on one point by their superiority on another.   The French rifled cannon can be carried into almost every imaginable position ; and often, in Italy, the Austrians discovered, when they least suspected any such mischance, that they were within the range of French rifled guns that were firing upon them from positions which they might well have supposed to have been altogether inaccessible to artillery.

It remains for us now to direct attention to the fact that, at the present moment, amongst military men of reflection and experience throughout the world, the grand question for consideration is simply this : which of these two classes of artillery is the more valuable and important, because on the whole the more effective ; the rifled cannon of comparatively small calibre, which is easy to handle and rapid in movement ; or the enormous and complicated gun, also rifled, with projectiles of terrible power and tremendous range. The French artillerists prefer the smaller guns, and hold those in the highest estimation which in every respect are most distinguished by their simplicity. The contrary opinion obtains with the Americans. They delight in cannon that in their vast proportions are like mastodons amongst the lesser animals; breech-loaders, furnished with more than one barrel also—monster revolvers, in a word, powerful enough to discharge cast-iron mountains. While awaiting the complete realisation of their ideal of artillery, the Americans use (at sea, it is true; since on land they admit the present necessity for being content with somewhat smaller pieces) cannon having a bore of 15 inches, which throw shot weighing 400 lbs. " Heaven protect me," adds M. Lacombe, " from yielding to any desire to prejudge this question, but involuntarily my mind carries me back to the enormous bombards of the 14th century, and I cannot forget how short-lived was their existence !

The cannon, like every other offensive weapon, has received decoration. We do not now speak of fanciful pieces of artillery, such as may be classed with childrens' toys in consequence of their small size, of which characteristic examples may be seen in the Cluny Museum, at Paris, and elsewhere; but we refer to real cannon, which are fit for use and have been used in war. In the case of these arms, it rarely has happened that the ornamentation, whatever may have been the nature of the decorative designs, has been carried along the whole length from breech to muzzle. Instead of this, custom (without any definite or recognised reason for its existence) has restricted the ornamentation, as a general rule, only to certain parts of the gun. The gun-carriage, it may be added, has also often been considered to be worthy of artistic adornment. Thus the handles, *anses* (when in use in England called *dolphins*), are not unfrequently made in the form of the body of some living creature; for example, in

Button.

Breech.

Reinforce.

Trunnions.

Chase.

Muzzle.

Fig. 50.
DECORATED SPANISH
CANNON
(Paris Museum)

Fig. 50 they appear in the form of two dolphins. The "button" or boss of the breech, especially, has been regarded as a favourable object for decoration; and, accordingly, it has been sculptured in the form of a Medusa's head, a lion's head, a lizard, &c. It is upon this part of the gun that the artist generally preferred to display the choicest and the most original of his compositions.

The armorial insignia of the sovereign furnish a subject, ready at hand for the appropriate decoration of the cannon of every realm. Decoration such as this is generally displayed on the *reinforce* (*renfort*) of the gun, between the *trunnions* and the actual *breech*; and, sometimes, but less frequently, it appears upon the *chase* (*volée*). These technical terms by which, in both French and English, the different parts of a cannon are distinguished, are explained by Fig. 50. Along the length of the chase of cannon, however (the space, as will be seen, between the trunnions and the muzzle), various subjects represented by engraving are much more common.

We now will specify a few of the most beautifully decorated specimens of cannon that are preserved in the collections of the Artillery Museum at Paris.[88]

No. 29 in that museum is a cannon of the reign of Louis XII. (A.D. 1498—1515), which on its reinforce bears the figure of a porcupine casting its quills, the badge of that king.

Nos. *33, 34, 35,* and *36* : Cannon of the time of Francis 1. (A.D. 1515—1547). They bear the crowned salamander, the badge of Francis I. ; and they have strewn over them the initial of the king, the letter F, and fleurs-de-lys.

No. *39,* a gun of the same period, has a more original decoration by a cordon in salient relief, twisted after the manner of a spiral. The 16th century, amongst other things, delighted in twisting cannon from the trunnions to the muzzle, or in covering that part of them with panel-work.

No. 44 : The button of the breech in this cannon is in the form of a wolf's head.

No. 47 : A cannon of the time of Henri II. (A.D. 1547— 1559). The surface is divided into eight panels; the decoration consists of the initial H crowned, the cipher of Diana of Poitiers, with her crescent encircled with bows and true lovers' knots.

No. 49 : The chase represents a dragon's head, from which the mouth of the piece issues forth. It is a cannon of the age of Charles V.

No. 60 : In this cannon, which is a German production, the chase ends in the head of a dragon covered with scales.

No. 20 : This is one of the most beautiful specimens of decorated cannon that can be seen in any museum. It is of wrought-iron, and is represented in Fig. 50. The reinforce bears, in relief, the royal arms of King Philip V. of Spain. The " anses" are formed, as we have seen, like two dolphins. At the commencement of the chase is a small mask of singularly beautiful character, from which a band of rich foliage is carried in the direction of the muzzle, and terminates in a medallion. The muzzle-mouldings are adorned with an indented band, in which richness and simplicity are admirably combined. All these decorative accessories are executed in relief with a delicacy and finish that are truly surprising.[89]

PART II.

THE GUN AND THE PISTOL.[90]

ALREADY we have said some few words concerning the
origin of the gun—the small-arm.   In the first instance, and
at the starting-point, this weapon is not distinguished by any
peculiar qualities or characteristics of its own from the cannon
—the gun first appears as simply a small cannon.   As there
was a culverin which was fired in a kind of carriage, so also
there was a culverin which was fired in a man's arms—in fact,
a hand-culverin.   Such weapons as these were in use at the
end of the 14th century.   They then were called *sclopos*, from
which after a while came the terms *sclopette* and *escopette* (the
"carbine") ; and then, as some consider, from the same source
came the *muschite*, which gave its form to the word *mousquet*,
or " musket." These terms appear to have been local designa-
tions, applied in various places or at different times to the very
same weapon, but not the distinctive names of certain varieties
of that particular weapon.

Whatever may have been either the weapons of this class,
or the names by which in the 14th century they were known,
thus much is certain, that the arms which have been preserved
in museums, together with those that are represented in contemporary monuments, show that in the 15th century three
distinct types of the culverin were known and recognised : 1.
A small cannon placed upon a kind of stake shaped to receive
it, to which it is attached either by cord bandages or by bridles
of iron.   The gun itself is of wrought iron, and it is pierced
near the breech by a touch-hole which expands externally ; in
this is placed the priming, which is fired by a match carried
for that purpose at his belt by the culverineer. Two men were
generally required to serve one of these culverins ; of whom
one carried it, prepared it for action, and levelled it, and the

other (who, we may believe, also assisted his comrade in various ways) with his match discharged it. 2. A small cannon, in all respects resembling the last, except that at the breech it is of the same size as its own gun-stock, and also that the breech is constructed in such a manner as to form a socket for the reception of one end of the gun-stock. A culverin of this description is represented in Fig. 33, No. 1. 3. A culverin generally carried by cavalry; it is a very short little cannon, which is lengthened to the rear of its breech by an iron stock. It is held by the left hand—not so much supported, however, by that hand, as directed by it, since it really is carried by means of a kind of fork that is fixed on the pommel of the saddle.

At the end of the 14th century, considerable bodies of troops were in existence who were specially armed with portable culverins. Thus, at the battle of Morat, the Swiss army contained not less than 6,000 culverins.

In the time of Francis I. (A.D. 1515—1547) the *arquebus* was invented in Spain. In this new weapon, the cannon, or barrel, is much longer than in its predecessors; but what constitutes the true novelty is the appearance of a piece of machinery for firing the priming, while the arrangement of the priming itself is very greatly improved. In the arquebus the touch-hole is pierced, not at the top, but on the side of the barrel, and above a small *pan*, or *bassinet*. In this pan is placed the priming, which then is covered by another plate (a *pan-cover*, or *couvre-bassinet*) that moves on a hinge. The match, grasped between the jaws of some nippers named *serpentin* (the *cock*, that is—or, rather, the prototype of what became the cock in a gun-lock), is made to fall upon the pan by means of a trigger. In order to discharge his piece, the arquebusier had to uncover the pan, to adjust the match in such a manner that when falling it should exactly reach the powder, and, finally, to blow upon the match in order to make it burn more brightly. There is still a long interval inter-

vening between this arquebus, with all its improvements, and
the Prussian needle-gun of to-day.   In those days of Francis I.
the *cartridge* even was unknown—that is to say, it had not
then been discovered that by placing the powder and the ball
in a small case the gun might be charged by a single movement.   The arquebusier carried a flask for the ordinary
powder, a bag of bullets, and a small case containing the
priming-powder.

The *musket* speedily followed, after the arquebus had made
its appearance.   It differs from its predecessor only in its
magnitude and its proportionate power, both its calibre and
its charge being more than double those of the arquebus.
Consequently, the musket was considerably heavier than the
arquebus, so that it was necessary to place it, when about to
be discharged, upon a forked rest (*fourquine*) furnished at its
extremity with a point to fix it steadily on the ground.   The
musket and the arquebus were employed simultaneously in
the French armies, but only in comparatively small numbers.
When the celebrated Montluc made his first appearance in
the field, under Francis I., the arblast still continued to be
held in much greater esteem than fire-arms.   This is shown
very clearly in the following characteristic passage, in the
original written in quaint old French :—" I must observe,"
says Montluc, " that the troop which I commanded consisted
of crossbowmen, or arbalestriers only, since at that time there
were in our nation no soldiers armed with the arquebus.
Only three or four days before, six Gascon arquebusiers,
deserters, came over from the enemy's camp to our army ;
and these men I kept with me, as I had the good fortune on
that day to be on duty at the gate of the town ; and also one
of these six men was from the Montluc estates. I wonder, however, that it could have been the will of Providence that this un-
lucky instrument should have been invented! I myself still bear
about me the marks that it has left, which even now cause

me to suffer much weakness.   And brave and valiant men
were killed with it in such sad numbers; and it generally
happened that they were struck down to the ground by those
abominable bullets, which had been discharged by cowardly
and base knaves who would never have dared to have met
true soldiers face to face and hand to hand.   All this is very
clearly one of those artifices, which the devil employs to
induce us human beings to kill one another."—*Michaud* and
Poujoulat, page 9.

From contemporary writers, and particularly from the
works of Montluc, it appears that at that time fire-arms, in
consequence of their strangely imperfect construction, offered
very few advantages, if any, over cross-bows; and, in fact,
the arquebus, as it would seem, was introduced at all only
from the hope that its noise and fire might terrify the enemy's
horses, and perhaps (it must be confessed) that it might have
something of the same effect upon the enemy themselves.
The cross-bow soon disappeared; and the year 1535 found
the French army without a single cross-bowman in its ranks.

Already in Germany a *wheel-lock* (*platine à rouet*) had
been invented.   In this new piece of machinery, the match
was superseded by a piece of flint, fixed close to a plate
or disc of steel, having a fluted surface, which when made
(by the pull of the trigger) to revolve rapidly, struck sparks
from the flint and threw them down upon the powder in the
pan.   This new invention led to the introduction of the
pistol, which, without doubt, in its earliest form, was that kind
of short arquebus, holding a middle place between the true
pistol and the genuine arquebus, that bore the name of
petronel (*pétrinal*).

Great was the astonishment of the French soldiers when,
at the battle of Renty, in 1554, they saw the German horsemen charge the infantry in deep squadrons, and, at some paces
from the lines, halt and fire their pistols rank by rank, and

then turn bridle. Both the weapon and the manœuvre of those horsemen were new to the Frenchmen. They charged in line, having the support of both second and third lines, each one at its proper interval. After a while the French borrowed from the Germans their weapon, the pistol; and they also adopted the method in which those same Germans used their pistols in action.

The first pistols had very short barrels. The stock, towards its extremity, made almost a right angle with the barrel, and the pommel or butt-end was a ball of extravagant size. Subsequently, the stock was lengthened towards the butt, and its direction conformed much more nearly to that of the barrel.

The new invention of the wheel-lock was applied, at once, as well to the arquebus and the musket, as to the pistol. These weapons thus improved were very costly; and, under Henri IV. (A.D. 1589—1610) there were in the French armies very few soldiers who were provided with them.

In the earliest French specimens of wheel-locks, the pieces which produce the rotatory motion are fixed on the outside of the lock itself. The next step caused these pieces to be enclosed within the cavities made for that purpose in the gunstock, and thus they became invisible. The wheel-lock continued to be in general use until about the year 1630, when the use of the lock à la Miquelet, or true gun-lock, a Spanish invention, began to prevail. By this contrivance fire is conveyed to the priming-powder in the pan by a guncock, which holds in its grasp the flint; this, when falling, is made to strike against a movable steel pan-cover, which is caused to fall back and to leave the powder open to the sparks, by the same blow from the flint that produces the sparks. This gun-lock, which is so well known, constitutes the distinctive characteristic of all flint-guns; which even now, in some remote regions, continue to be in use. The new lock was not by any means readily adopted in the French army. It was objected to it, what was quite true, that the sparks from

the flint (from the *fusil,* whence, by a very common abuse of
language, which consists in giving to an entire object a name
taken from one of its parts, the weapon has derived its desig-
nation) sometimes fell by the side of the priming-powder, and
not upon it, and that consequently in such cases the piece
would not be discharged. Hence, the experiment was tried
of making *musket-fusils*—guns, that is, having a double firing
apparatus, or both match-locks and flint-locks. And thus it
was not till the beginning of the 18th century that the flint-
lock musket finally drove the match-lock from the field. The
wheel-lock musket must always be considered to have been a
weapon of an exceptional order.

We must pass on to the commencement of another
century—that 19th century which still continues to be in the
course of its progress—before we meet with any other modification of considerable importance in portable fire-arms. It
was about this time that the *percussion-lock,* which was
destined to supersede the flint, as the flint had superseded the
match, was invented by Alexander Forsyth, a Scottish gunsmith. Percussion-guns are universally well known. These
excellent weapons still continue to be in very general use.
They are only waiting, however, until they all shall have
yielded their places to the *breech-loader,* which carries the
perfection of gun-making a grand step in advance, even
beyond the percussions themselves. In the percussion-lock,
the ignition of the charge within the barrel is caused by the
fall of a hammer upon a cap, which is a very small copper
cylinder lined with a fulminating matter.

Some few words are desirable in this place upon the
fulminates with which the caps are charged. These volatile
chemical preparations, at once so dangerous and so valuable,
for which the comparatively slight degree of heat that is produced by a blow is sufficient to disengage their elements and
to cause them suddenly and violently to ignite, are obtained

U

from gold, silver, platinum, and chloride of potash. The
discovery of these remarkable salts took place in 1785—1787;
and it is due to the distinguished French chemists, Fourcroy,
Vauquelin, and Bertholet, who immediately devoted their
attention to the consideration of the most advantageous means
for applying their discovery to the improvement of fire-arms.
But it was the Scotchman, Andrew Forsyth, who, as we have
said, first succeeded in making a tolerably good gun that was
to be fired with a fulminate. His invention, made known in
France in 1808, excited amongst the French gunsmiths an
emulation which found its expression in the production of
percussion weapons of strangely diverse forms. Not one of
these guns was free from some serious drawback. It was not
till the year 1820 that the true *percussion-gun* (*fusil à capsule*)
was first made in England; and it soon found its way into
France. The cap, a minute thimble in form and appearance,
closed at one end and open at the other, and having attached
to its interior at the bottom a film of fulminate, was crushed
at that time exactly as it is now, between a hammer and the
point of a nipple (*cheminée*).

At the time that it was desired to introduce the new percussion musket into the French army, the unfortunate idea
was conceived by the French gunsmiths that some apparatus
ought to be added by means of which the cap might be
placed on the nipple without any help from the hand. A
complicated series of locks were thus produced, of which the
only effect was to prejudice the percussion system. And so it
was not until about 1840 that the French gunsmiths, when at
last they were content to submit to the simple principle of
adjusting the cap on the nipple by the hand, produced a
thoroughly serviceable weapon, suited as well for the use of
the sportsman as for the more serious duties of the soldier.
From that time the flint-gun has been superseded in the
French armies by the percussion-gun.[91]

We now for some time have been observing how, during a prolonged period, the efforts that were made by the spirit of improvement (the sensible efforts at any rate) were exclusively directed towards the one point of the firing-apparatus—the single aim was the discovery of some more effectual means for igniting the priming-powder. It was not until later times that the gun itself attracted attention, and efforts were made to give to it increased capacity and greater precision. This did not occur, however, in consequence of any deliberate neglect of the weapon itself, since we have proof that the principles of all the modern improvements had been discovered some centuries ago ; but then, the means at that time were wanting for the proper application of those principles, and for their consistent development.

In order to enable a bullet to move freely in a gun having a smooth-bore barrel, it is necessary that the diameter of the bullet should be just so much less than that of the bore of the gun-barrel as will permit its movement to be perfectly free. This difference between the two diameters is the *windage* (*vent*). Windage is the primary cause of default in the exact precision of the aim. A second cause of this same default arises from the fact that every leaden bullet contains a minute hollow, produced by the condensation that takes place with its cooling after it has been cast. It follows from this that the centre of gravity in the projectile does not coincide with its own true centre of dimension. These drawbacks from its efficiency had been observed from the early infancy of the gun ; and, as far back as the 15th century, an effort was made to obviate them by precisely the same means that in our own times have succeeded so well. The process that was devised for this purpose, was to *rifle* the interior of the gun-barrel with two or three sunk grooves, and then to drive in the bullet in such a manner into the barrel that it would be forced into the grooves of the rifling, which would completely destroy all windage.

The first rifle grooves that were made were parallel with
the axis of the gun-bore; but in Germany spiral grooves were
soon made, exactly as they are made in the French rifles of
the present day. If it should be asked, from what motive the
rifle grooves were made to assume a spiral line, we reply that
the projectile has been proved to have both a longer and
a truer flight when it moves rotating on its own axis. Even
before the first invention of fire-arms, in the palmy days of the
cross-bow, in the 14th century, this important fact was ascertained, and efforts were accordingly made to impart to the
cross-bow bolts a rotary movement, by arranging the feathers
with which they were flighted in spirals upon the bolt-shafts.
Spiral grooves in rifles are another and a more effectual means
for arriving at the same result. We see that the principles
which govern our modern arms may be traced back sufficiently far; consequently, we well may feel surprise that the
invention of guns of long range and exact precision should
have been delayed until our own era.

During the course of the 17th and 18th centuries the
rifled gun and carbine were used for military purposes only as
exceptional weapons, and for the equipment of certain corps
specially appointed to act as riflemen, and whose numbers were
comparatively small. In 1793, a rifled carbine was given to
the officers and non-commissioned officers of the French light
infantry. This carbine required too much time for loading,
in consequence of the necessity of forcing down the ball by
blows struck with a mallet on the ramrod. It had but a poor
range, and its chief merit consisted in its precision. It was
laid aside about the close of the first empire.

In 1826, a new mode for forcing the balls into rifles was
suggested by Captain Delvigne. A kind of recess, of less
diameter than the bore of the rifle, was formed at the breech
of the barrel, and called the " chamber." This chamber was
filled with the powder of the charge. The ball, when driven

down to the bottom of the barrel, rested on the rim that jutted out and encircled the mouth of the chamber. With the ramrod the ball, as it rested on this rim, was driven into the grooves of the rifling, which could be accomplished much more rapidly than by the former use of the mallet. This weapon, however, had its disadvantages to set off against its advantages. It was found that the ball was driven, in a greater or a lesser degree, into the chamber under the blows of the ramrod, and thus the powder was compressed in a manner that caused a recoil very disagreeable to the rifleman ; and, besides, the axis of the ball by this process was not necessarily identical with that of the rifle. This weapon did good service, nevertheless, since it led to a series of experiments, that were conducted with all the method and exactness which characterise the spirit of modern inquiry. The result of these experiments, which was not reached without certain failures, enabled the inquirers to determine what length of rifle-barrel and what charge of powder produce the best effects. It was also demonstrated that no advantage was obtained by increasing the number of the grooves, as was done at first; and, accordingly, the number of the grooves was reduced to six. The grooves themselves were to be cut to a depth a little exceeding one-tenth of an inch (three French millimétres), so that the balls should not enter the grooves to their full depth ; and in their section the grooves were to be rounded hollows. At last, after numerous experiments, and after having tried various contours for the rifling, and particularly the parabola, it was decided to form the grooves in the barrel after the manner of a cylinder very considerably elongated. We have not attempted here to enter into any discussion of technical details ; and, indeed, we have been careful to avoid even the slightest appearance of exceeding the limits of a simple and strictly popular sketch; our object has been, not to produce a scientific treatise, but to show in a few plain words how truly scientific is the character of modern arms. It is this quality, it may be observed in passing, that secures for modern arms that deep interest, which in the arms of earlier ages is attracted only by their appearance, by the beauty and gracefulness of their forms, and by the rich splendours of their decoration. The early arms and armour were the works of artists ; those of our own times are the production of men of science.

The experiments, the researches, and the inquiries, of which we have just briefly spoken, led, as their first practical result, to the production of a rifle on what was known as the *Pouchara system ;* but of this, it will be unnecessary for us to give any particular description, because it very speedily was superseded by the *Minie* rifle. The distinctive peculiarity of the Minie consists in its having fixed within the barrel at the breech and in the axis of the barrel a small iron pillar, which may receive the rifle-ball, and act as a rest to support it, while the ramrod causes it to bite the grooves of the rifling. Instead of the old spherical ball, also, with the introduction of the Minie rifle a cylindrical ball was introduced.

After repeated experiments, this Minie rifle was accepted in 1846 as the regulation weapon of the French regiments of *tirailleurs ;* and, at the same time it was determined that the length of the barrel should be thirty-three inches and rather more than three-fifths of an inch, and the calibre or diameter of the bore a very little less than seven-tenths of an inch (by French measurement, severally, 0^m, 868 ; and 0^m, 017). The Minie has four grooves, each of which would complete a spiral revolution in six feet six inches ; so that in a barrel which is not quite three feet in length, the grooves of the rifling of necessity do not complete a single revolution. The charge of powder is $40\frac{1}{2}$ grains. The ball, which in form is an oval cylinder, weighs a very little more than 47 grains (47·02 grains) ; and the barrel is provided with a movable

" sight," which slides in a groove, and has a graduated elevation, and thus regulates the aim for various distances not exceeding 1,200 yards.

In 1857, all the regiments of the French army received rifled arms in place of the old smooth-bore muskets. The regulation rifle of the line, which was adopted at that time, however, is a weapon of much simpler construction than the Minie. It has no pillar-rest for the ball within the barrel, but a result similar to that produced by the Minie pillar is obtained from a hollow formed in the base of the ball itself. Upon this hollow the gases act with great force at the moment of the explosion, so that they cause an expansion of the ball itself at its base, and thus it is compelled to bite the grooves of the rifling. Balls of this same order have been adopted for the Minie, in consequence of their completely successful action; the pillar, therefore, has been removed from the Minie barrels.[92]

There remains but one more step to be taken in advance, and then we shall have arrived at the latest and most perfect of the improvements which modern science has been enabled to devise for the weapon of the soldier. This step completes the rifle by converting it, from being a muzzle-loader, into a breech-loader. The reputation to which the " needle-gun " of the Prussians so suddenly attained, rendered it imperative that some corresponding improvement should be introduced into the weapons of the French army; and, accordingly, the " Chassepot rifle " has just taken the place of the Minie, and has become the regulation weapon of the whole French army.

Breech loading is not by any means a novelty in gunnery. The wheel-lock arquebus was sometimes made upon this system, and there are examples in the Artillery Museum at Paris. And cannon, as we have already seen, in the first instance were planned and, indeed, invariably constructed on the breech-loading principle. Consequently, the adoption of this same principle at the present day is in reality nothing more or less than a return to the primitive system. To attempt to trace all the changes and modifications in the application of the principle of breech-loading, and to follow and give descriptions of them, would far exceed our limits, neither would the inquiry possess much attraction for general readers; we shall rest content, therefore, to notice the *Lefaucheux* breech-loading fowling-piece, which in France is held in the highest esteem by sportsmen ; and, as a type of the military breech-loader, we may adduce the Prussian *needle-gun*, which has lately commenced its career with such extraordinary *éclat*.

The principle of the Lefaucheux gun is generally so well known that it is unnecessary to give a very minute description of it. The under-guard (*sous-garde*) of the barrel, formed of two pieces of iron having a joint, is maintained in a right line by a rigid metal plate which supports it. This plate may be made to revolve on its axis with a horizontal backward and forward movement, by the action of the hand, when it withdraws its support from the under-guard, which forthwith yields and severs the breech from the rest of the barrel. The chamber which is to receive the cartridge thus is exposed, and the piece is loaded. The cartridge itself at its base is provided with a large cap, from which projects a pin or small nail ; this fits an opening in the breech of the gun, and the hammer strikes it and so fires the piece. As a matter of course, after the cartridge has been adjusted to its position in readiness for firing, the breech of the barrel is restored to its proper place, and the rigid plate is returned to fulfil again its original duty, before the finger touches the trigger.

The mechanism of the needle-gun is sufficiently simple. The gun-barrel at its base has a channel or lateral aperture, rounded at its anterior extremity, which is continued, gradually becoming narrower, to the breech, and the breech itself is open. It is by means of this aperture that the cartridge is placed in the barrel. The cartridge contains a small conical ball, a charge of ordinary powder, and some priming-powder is placed between them. Thus, at the open end of the barrel a small hollow cylinder is introduced, which is surmounted by a kind of key. This key is fitted to the little channel, of which we have spoken, so that it may move freely along it; and, as it moves, the cylinder that is attached to it moves with it into the barrel. When the cylinder fills, and therefore closes the lateral aperture, the key is inclined to the left; and, in this position, held fast in the angle of the aperture, the key cannot recoil, nor can the cylinder move out of its position. Thus the gun is loaded. The cylinder, as we have said, is hollow, but it is not empty. On the contrary, it encloses a spiral spring, that is held back by a little ring attached to the cylinder; to the head of this spring is fixed a needle, which advances with the forward movement of the spring. When the trigger is pressed, the spring is released, its forward movement takes place, and the needle is made to advance and to traverse the case of the cartridge until it strikes the priming-powder and causes the explosion. This famous needle at once recals to remembrance the mechanism of a toy for children, very common in France, and with which all are familiar.

The diameter of the chamber that contains the cartridge is somewhat greater than that of the bore of the barrel; and, therefore, at the time of the explosion, the ball in its passage bites the grooves of the rifling. This increases the range and confirms the precision of the weapon, which is also fitted with sliding and elevating sights for directing the aim. With this needle-gun from ten to twelve shots may be fired in a minute, whilst in ordinary guns in the same space of time not more than two or three rounds can be discharged.

This breech-loading rifle, in addition to its other valuable qualities, possesses the important feature of escaping from that division of the barrel by a backward and forward movement which prevails with the generality of breech-loaders—as it does, for example, in the Lefaucheux. To breech-loading military rifles constructed on the Lefaucheux system it would be impossible to add the bayonet; or, at any rate, the use of the bayonet in actual conflict would be almost certain to lead to an involuntary complete separation of the two parts of the piece, and the consequence would be that the weapon would altogether cease to be serviceable.

The first drawback from the excellence of the needle-gun arises from the danger that the needle may break. In that case it becomes necessary to unscrew the cylinder, and to adjust another needle to the spring. In anticipation of such an accident the Prussian soldiers always are provided with one or more spare needles. The operation of unscrewing and of fixing the new needle is not very long; but still it may be supposed that it would to a soldier be much too long when face to face with the enemy. Another fault in this gun is that it heats rapidly; and, therefore, in order to escape from the risks inseparable from over-heating, it is desirable not to fire with any extraordinary rapidity, which practically amounts to a voluntary surrender of one of the special advantages that distinguish the weapon.[93]   On the other hand, with reference to the extraordinary rapid fire of the needle-gun, it must be kept in remembrance that it is no easy matter for a soldier to carry such a supply of ammunition as would be amply sufficient for the consumption of such a gun. In the Prussian army it is considered that a supply of sixty rounds of ammunition is quite as much as ought to be carried by any one soldier; and, indeed, the weight of sixty rounds is so great that the balls have been reduced to the smallest consistent dimensions, and they are sensibly smaller than those that are fired by ordinary guns.[94]

The practice of decorating the arquebus, the musket, the rifle, and the several varieties of fire-arms, has led to the pro-

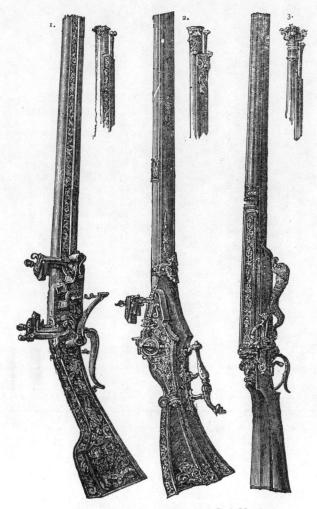

Fig. 51.—THREE EARLY MUSKETS. Paris Museum.

duction of many remarkable and admirable examples of what may be correctly designated the art of the gunsmith. In the case of decorated weapons of these classes, however, as a general rule, the ornamentation is excessive, so that the effect produced is by no means satisfactory or agreeable. In these over-elaborate compositions, each detail in itself is frequently eminently meritorious, and yet from the whole, as a whole, there result lines that are complicated and wanting in gracefulness. And, in addition to this, it is but too commonly the fact that, in highly-decorated fire-arms, the decoration has had the effect of very seriously detracting from the practical efficiency of the weapon.

A common form of early decoration consists of small slabs of ivory, or mother-of-pearl, which are cut out in almost every imaginable variety of forms, as dogs, birds, deer, flowers, trees, and human figures, and these are inlaid on the gun-stock; and this inlaying or incrustation is sometimes carried to such excess that the surface is very nearly covered over, and the wood itself almost disappears. Formerly, decorative figures of all kinds were carved upon the solid wood itself; and this was done in such comparatively high relief that the gun-stock must be considered to have had its surface made sufficiently rough to be grasped securely by the hand. When the chasing, and the other decorative processes that deal with metal-work, are applied only to the breech and the muzzle, to the sight, to the lock, and to the trigger-guard, this is all very satisfactory, and the ornamentation must be considered to bear the impress of sobriety and good taste; but, unfortunately, it is not at all uncommon to find guns completely covered, both barrel and stock, with uninterrupted ornamentation in high relief. Engraven designs may be executed without reserve, and with excellent effect; and gun-barrels may be covered with engraving without in any degree detracting from the simplicity of the leading lines.

The three muskets that are represented in Fig. 51 form parts of the collections in the Artillery Museum at Paris. No. 1 is an example of excessive ornamentation produced by carving in relief, with deeply-sunk hollows interspersed amongst the raised work. In No. 2, the decoration is produced by inlaid work, and the effect is decidedly more pleasing and praiseworthy. And No. 3 is a matchlock musket, once in the possession of Cardinal Richelieu.[95] We are not able to describe this remarkable weapon in more expressive words than those which have been used by M. Penguilly l'Haridon, in the catalogue of the museum :—" The barrel, cut and squared towards the base, chased and partly gilt, exhibits three oval medallions, representing, in relief, warriors in ancient armour. The sight is formed of two rams' heads coupled together. The upper part of the barrel, formed like a fluted column, supports a capital in which are introduced four caryatides in full relief. The lock, decorated throughout with chasing on gold, has a head of Medusa in high relief. Beneath the gun-stock, which is of cherry-wood, is a boldly sculptured figure of a dolphin. Above, where the barrel joins the stock, is a beautiful mask of a man's face, surmounted by a shell; and on the shoulder-plate of the butt may be seen the three chevrons with a cardinal's hat, the armorial insignia of Cardinal Richelieu."[96]

APPENDIX.

REMARKABLE EXAMPLES OF ARMS AND ARMOUR IN VARIOUS CONTINENTAL MUSEUMS.

Fig. 52.—HEAD OF STAFF OF PETER THE CRUEL.

Fig. 53.—HELM OF XIMENES.

Fig. 54.—SHIELD OF XIMENES: A.D. 1437—1517.
Both in the Royal Armoury, Madrid.

No 2.

No. 1.

Fig. 55—PARTS OF TWO SWORDS IN THE ROYAL ARMOURY, MADRID.
1. Sword of Gonzalvo di Cordova, A.D. 1453—1515. 2. Sword of Don John.

X

Fig. 56.—MEDUSA SHIELD: a Work of the 16th Century.   In the Royal Armoury, Madrid.

Fig. 57.—PERSIAN SHIELD. In the Imperial Russian Museum.

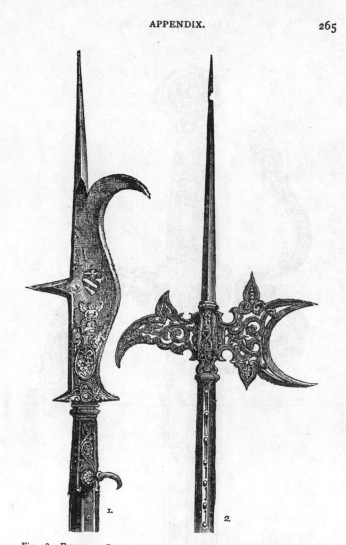

Fig. 58.—Enriched Shafted Weapons. In the Artillery Museum, Paris.
1. A Fauchard. 2. A Partisan.

Fig. 59.—THE MASCARON SWORD. Royal Armoury, Madrid.

Fig. 60.—Armour of Gonzalvo di Cordova : A.D. 1453—1515. Royal Armoury, Madrid.

Fig. 61 —Moorish Adargue : 15th Century.

Fig. 62.—ITALIAN HELM OF THE 16TH CENTURY.

Fig. 63.—ITALIAN SHIELD OF THE 16TH CENTURY.
Both in the Artillery Museum, Paris.

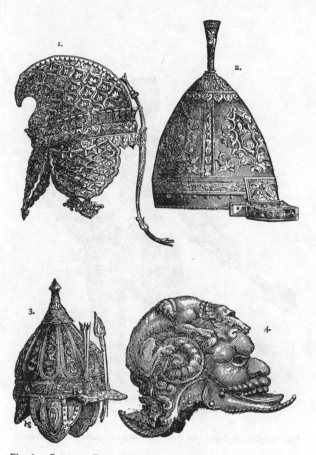

Fig. 64—GROUP OF FOUR HELMS IN THE RUSSIAN IMPERIAL MUSEUM.

1. Italian Helm   2. Mongolian Helm.   3. Persian Helm.   4. Russian Helm.

Fig. 65.—POLISH ARMS AND ARMOUR. In the Imperial Russian Museum.

Fig. 66.—GROUP OF MONGOLIAN ARMS AND ARMOUR. In the Artillery Museum,
Paris.

Fig. 67.—GROUP OF JAPANESE ARMS AND ARMOUR.   In the Artillery Museum,
Paris.

Fig. 68.—GROUP OF FOURTEEN EXAMPLES OF SHAFTED WEAPONS. In the
Artillery Museum, Paris.

1 6, 7 Military Flails. 2. Marteau. 3. Axe. 4, 8. Fauchards. 5. Corsesque.
9 Military Fork. 10. Halberd. 11. Partisan. 12, 13. Guisarmes.

Fig. 69.—Group of Two Swords and Three Early Bayonets.

1, 3, 5, Bayonets. 2. Spanish Sword. 4. Italian Sword. All in the Artillery
Museum, Paris.

NOTES.

———◆———

NOTE 1, *p*. 1.—In the infancy of nations, the same implement which would be applied to the ordinary requirements and uses of every-day life, would also doubtless serve the purpose of the hunter in the chase ; and in the time of strife, the very same implements, with some additions probably suggested by the exigency of circumstances, would become the weapons of a barbarous people.

NOTE 2, *p*. 4.—It is quite possible that some of the statements in the text relative to the distinctive characteristics of various primæval objects in flint, may be considered, even by many experienced archæologists, to be speculative, or, perhaps, purely fanciful. The study of these certainly very curious relics of remote ages has been pursued with great earnestness and proportionate success on this side of the Channel, where the flint weapons and implements have been found in great numbers and no inconsiderable variety.

NOTE 3, *p*. 7.—See Note 2.

NOTE 4, *p*. 8.—The sketch of the "Stone Period," given in Chapter I. in the text, is to be regarded as a *sketch* only ; so that it has not been proposed to enter with any minuteness into details, or, indeed, to deal with the "Period" at all from an archæological point of view. Stone "celts," and every variety of implement or weapon of the same class or period, are constantly found in England. The term "Dolmen" denotes certain Celtic tombs, which consist of a large nearly flat table-stone, raised entirely from the ground upon two or more (but not more than four) stone props or upright blocks.

NOTE 5, *p*. 9.—In the *Athenæum* journal, No. 2,121, published June 20, 1868, there appeared a communication dated from "Shanghai, China, April 21, 1868," and bearing the signature of "Thos. W. Kingsmill, Corr. Sec. of North China Branch of the Royal Asiatic Society," which contains much information that bears directly upon the considerations that are set forth in the text.

In the ancient sacred Scriptures there is no evidence to show of what metal the swords of the warriors of Israel were made. In the Old Testament, however, iron and brass (or bronze) are mentioned together on several occasions ; as in Genesis iv. 22 ; Deuteronomy xxxiii. 25 ; 1 Samuel xvii. 5—7 ; and 2 Chronicles xxiv. 12. The spear-head of Goliath of Gath (B.C. 1063) was of "iron," while his defensive armour—"helmet, target, greaves"—was of "brass ;" 1 Samuel xvii. 4—7. But the spear of that son of the giant, who, in after days, when "girded with a new sword, thought to have slain David," was of "brass ;" 2 Samuel xxi. 16.

Plutarch has recorded the discovery of a brass or bronze sword and spear head in the tomb of Theseus.

Plato says ("De Legibus," XII.), that "iron and brass are instruments of war"—that is, that weapons of war were formed of both those metals.

Polybius assigns to the Gauls (B.C. 223) leaf-shaped swords of bronze, while the swords of the Romans were of iron. It must be added, however, that swords of iron which correspond with the description of the bronze swords given by Polybius, and of a date long anterior to Roman dominion, have been found in Switzerland.

The poet Virgil, who must have known of what metal those arms were made that were ancient in his days, speaks of the brazen swords and javelins that were in use when the Trojan settlers established themselves on the soil of Italy—

" *Æratæque micant peltæ, micat æreus ensis.*"

("Glitter their brazen spears, and their swords made of brass are bright.")

ÆN. vii. 743.

And, once more, Pausanias asserts that all the ancient weapons were made of brass. Iron began to supplant brass in the 5th century B.C.

NOTE 6, *p*. 10.—It will not be forgotten, when reading this passage, either, on the one hand, that the text does not profess to deal (and, therefore, does not deal) with early British military antiquities ; or, on the other hand, that numerous relics of the early military antiquities of Britain are preserved in our own museums and other collections.

NOTE 7, *p*. 11.—Numerous examples of ancient Assyrian arms and armour, all of the greatest interest, are represented in Mr. Layard's admirable volumes.

NOTE 8, *p*. 11.—Every variety of body-armour that was in use amongst the ancient Assyrians is exemplified in the slabs, and numerous examples are engraved in Layard. Some curious scale-armour closely resembles certain well-known mediæval examples ; and some Assyrian figures wear defences almost identical with the camail of the 14th century. Some original iron scales of Assyrian scale armour are in the British Museum, with Egyptian brass scales, and Roman scales (some found in Britain) of bronze.

NOTE 9, *p*. 12.—The Assyrian sculptures contain many examples of swords, but they all are of the same type and general character.

NOTE 10, *p*. 13.—The bows and arrows, with the quivers of the archers, that appear in the Assyrian sculptures, are very numerous, and they are rendered with the greatest care. Some of the largest figures have the bow, arrows, and quiver, and they give every detail on quite a large scale. As a general rule, the arrows do not appear to have the large proportions when compared with the bows, as it is stated in the text.

NOTE 11, *p*. 14.—On many occasions, in the Assyrian slabs, siege operations with battering engines in action are depicted.

NOTE 12, *p*. 16.—Numerous examples of British bronze "celts" are in existence, showing several varieties in their forms, and also in the arrangements for fixing them to their shafts. Some have loops cast in the metal, through which cords or fibres may be passed, for the purpose of lashing them securely to their shafts. The forms of these celts are generally very graceful and elegant. The original *moulds* in which they were cast have also frequently been found.

The *torque*, the military ornament and token of honourable distinction, generally made with a twist in metal, and formed of gold, silver, or bronze, may consistently be mentioned here in connection with the British bronze celts. Very interesting treatises on both the "celt" and the "torque" will be found in the "Archæological Journal ;" on "Celts," by George du Noyer, in vol. iii., pp. 1 and 327 ; and on the "Torque," by Samuel Birch, in vol. ii., p. 368, and vol. iii., p. 27.

NOTE 13, *p*. 16.—Many fine examples of ancient bronze swords have been found in Britain, and are preserved in our national and other collections.

NOTE 14, *p*. 18.—The helm decorations of the Gauls. mentioned in the text as the "horns and wings," may be considered to have been in favour with the early German races also whenever they wore any head-pieces. The ancient usage has left remarkable tokens of its existence in the mediæval heraldry of Germany, from whence these same tokens have come down to our own times.

NOTE 15, *p*. 20.—The Roman arch, which stands about a quarter of a mile from Orange, a town in the Department of Vaucluse, in the Roman-Corinthian style of architecture, is profusely adorned with sculptured representations of ancient naval trophies. From the circumstance that of the original inscription there remains the one word MARIO, it has been surmised that the arch may commemorate the victory of Marius over the Teutones, B.C. 102 ; if so, the arch itself is a work of a a considerably later period.

Circular British shields, ornamented with bosses and studs, have been found, and fine examples are in the British Museum and in the Meyrick Collection.

NOTE 16, *p*. 24.—The long swords that were in use at certain periods in the middle ages, were adjusted, as it would seem, by their sword-belts in such a manner that they hung at the warrior's back when he was on foot, the hilt rising above his left shoulder.

In addition to the great sword of his warriors, Homer mentions their wearing a weapon of the same class, but of a smaller size: so that in respect to their weapons those ancient heroes closely resembled the knights of the middle ages, when they were armed with lance and sword and misericorde.

NOTE 17, *p*. 24.—The helm of Achilles, notwithstanding the omission of any such detailed description of it in the Iliad as is accorded to his shield, may reasonably be supposed to have been a work of art no less worthy either of Vulcan, or the son of Thetis. By an accidental error in the French text, it would appear that Homer had altogether neglected even to mention the "divine" helm of his semi-divine hero.

Note 18, *p.* 31.—The shields of warriors, and also of warrior-divinities, that are constantly represented in the paintings upon ancient Greek vases, though they are some centuries later than the Homeric era, may be advantageously compared with the descriptions of defensive armour that are given with such minute care in the Iliad.

Note 19, *p.* 35.—In the French original text, M. Lacombe, speaking of the Greek bow of the Homeric era, says, "Il est d'assez petite dimension, tendu par le moyen d'un nerf;" and, again, he speaks particularly of "la petitesse de l'arc" of Pandarus; but the language of the Iliad seems scarcely, if at all, to sanction this view of the very small size of even the most famous bows that the Greeks took with them to Troy.

Note 20, *p.* 36.—In the graphic description, given by a contemporary chronicler, himself an eyewitness of what he describes, of the siege of the castle of Caerlaverock, on the Scottish border, by Edward I. of England, in the year of grace 1300, not the least remarkable feature of the narrative is its close resemblance to the fighting passages in the Iliad. The soldiers of the great mediæval Plantagenet almost reproduce, before the walls of the northern border fortress, the scenes and the incidents of which, something like 2,000 years before their time, Homer sang under a warmer sun in his "tale of Troy divine." In the matter of stone-throwing in the heat of battle, the acts of the ancient and the mediæval combatants might be described in the very same words.

Note 21, *p.* 37.—Homer gives a fine, though brief, description of the helm of Hector, and of the terrors of its waving plume.

The helms represented on the painted Greek vases are no less worthy of study than the shields; and, if they do not actually exemplify the helms of the Homeric age, they certainly are in a striking manner suggestive of what those early helms must have been.

Note 22, *p.* 39.—With the dialogues of the Homeric combatants, as preludes to actual conflict, compare the disdainful words addressed to his youthful antagonist by Goliath of Gath, together with the magnificent reply of the son of Jesse.—1 Samuel xvii. 43.

Note 23, *p.* 45.—Upon the shields of the Greek warriors and warrior divinities which are represented on the painted vases, are blazoned a great variety of devices, which certainly may be considered to constitute an ancient heraldry. These devices include human figures, lions, horses, bulls, wild boars, dogs, birds, dolphins, scorpions, serpents, leaves of plants, chariots and chariot-wheels, sacrificial tripods, bows, rostra of ships, &c., with discs and fanciful figures. See Fig. 71, at *p.* xvi.

Note 24, *p.* 47.—See Note 21.

Note 25, *p.* 50.—Second in interest and value only to Assyrian and Chaldean histories of the successful invasions of Israel and Judah, with a sequel to the latter containing the conqueror's account of the return of the Jews from their seventy years' captivity, all of them contemporaneous with the events themselves, would be a Persian contemporary history of the great Greco-Persian war.

Note 26, *p.* 53.—It is scarcely necessary for me to refer to the famous sculptured groups of the fighting Amazons, once decorations of the Parthenon, and now preserved amongst the most precious treasures of our British Museum.

Note 27, *p.* 58.—The triumphal columns of the Emperors Trajan and Antoninus at Rome, were severally erected A.D. 114, and shortly after A.D. 161, in which year the Emperor Antoninus died. The column which bears the name of the latter emperor was the work of M. Aurelius and the senate. The Emperor Traja died A.D. 117.

Note 28, *p.* 60.—See Note 15. The device on the Roman shields is apparently what, in accordance with the language of mediæval heraldry, would be entitled the badge of the "thundering legion." The legions had distinctive names, and this is one of them. The device is a thunder-bolt, such as the French imperial eagle now grasps in his talons.

Note 29, *p.* 62.—The *sandals* and the *caligæ* (leggings, or military half-boots) of the Roman soldiery, must be included in their equipment.

Note 30, *p.* 63.—The *cippus* is a monumental memorial, generally a column, or a broken column, adorned with sculpture. The title of *legio primigenia* was borne by three of the Roman legions—the 2nd, the 15th, and the 22nd legions.

Note 31, *p.* 65.—The two great Romans, P. Cornelius Scipio Africanus (who was at Cannæ, B.C. 216), died B.C. 183; and P. Æmilianus Scipio Africanus, died B.C. 129. The Greek historian, Polybius, from whose works an important passage is quoted in the text, was the contemporary of the younger Scipio, and died B.C. 124, at the advanced age of 82.

NOTE 32, *p.* 69.—The great defeats of the Macedonians by the Romans under T. Flaminius and Paulus Æmilius, at Cynocephalæ in Thessaly, and Pydna in Macedonia, took place severally B.C. 196 and 168.

NOTE 33, *p.* 75.—In consequence of the close connection that existed for so long a time between the inhabitants of our own island and the Romans, the arms and armour of imperial Rome possess an especial interest for us, and they may be most consistently associated with the earliest chapters in the history of British civilisation. The arms and armour of the Romans, indeed, during many successive generations, were the arms and armour of the Britons also. In his Life of Julius Agricola, who was appointed to the command in Britain, A.D. 78, Tacitus tells us that, under the administration of that able officer, "the sons of the British chieftains began to affect our dress;" and we may feel sure that those youthful Britons were not less ready to adopt Roman arms and armour than they were to conform in their dress to Roman fashions and usages.

NOTE 34, *p.* 77.—See Note 23.

NOTE 35. *p.* 78.—The usage still obtains of making shields in the Renaissance style of art, for the purpose of display or decoration, and sometimes in order thus to produce a work of high art that may become an honourable trophy or testimonial. The shield form, however modified, is peculiarly adapted for the advantageous exhibition of artistic powers ; and, at the same time, notwithstanding the complete and long-sustained severance between every variety of portable shield, and the requirements and usages of modern warfare, the power of old association still causes a fine shield to be regarded as not altogether an anomaly in our own times.

NOTE 36, *p.* 81.—The remarks in the text upon the Homeric ægis are singularly suggestive of the practice, adopted late in the Middle Ages, of fixing additional plates on the left side, for the defence of the bridle arm, while the sword arm was left comparatively free for action.

NOTE 37, *p.* 85.—The friends of Dandie Dinmont (and where is he without friends?) will not forgive me if I fail here to refer to *his* fish-spearing, as it is described in the autobiography of his specially valued friend, Colonel "Guy Mannering."

NOTE 38, *p.* 85.—For minute and full descriptions of the weapons and war appliances of the African races and tribes, I refer with much pleasure to the "Natural History of Man," one of the popular and copiously illustrated works by the Rev. J. G. Wood, M.A., that are deservedly held in high estimation.

NOTE 39, *p.* 86.—With the statement concerning the restricted use of poisoned arrows amongst savage races, compare what is recorded in p. 94 as to the application of poison by Fredegonde, and as to the poisoned daggers of the Franks. The large knives that are sometimes found in early Anglo-Saxon graves, have a single edge, and near the hilt are two grooves, apparently for the reception of poison.

NOTE 40, *p.* 87.—The Australian *boomerang* certainly is one of the most remarkable of known missiles, both in itself and from the extraordinary skill that is displayed in the use of it. Nor is it much less remarkable that a weapon possessing such singular qualities should be known and used only by the aborigines of Australia. It is to be understood that it is not always the intention that the boomerang should return in order to inflict its blow, though such in general is the case. The weapon also is made to assume many modifications of its curved form. In section it is boldly convex on one side and has a very slight convexity on the other side.

NOTE 41, *p.* 87.—The *kris*, the keen dagger-knife of the Malays, and their formidable *sumpitan*, or blow-tube (the simplest form of instrument for applying compressed vapour as a propelling agent), together with the *tomahawk* and the *scalping-knife* of the Red Indians of North America, though not specified in the text, must have their names set forth (amongst others) in a catalogue of such "savage" arms as possess individual characteristics and are well known.

NOTE 42, *p.* 88.—It is not possible to bring to a close the slightest and most concise sketch of "savage" arms without an expression of admiration for the ingenuity, skill, and perseverance that are almost invariably shown in their manufacture ; and also for the extraordinarily happy facility with which their makers have evidently made the most of simple and limited means. By an intuitive faculty also, as it would seem, the savage weapon-maker discerns and applies to his own purposes some of the great principles on which nature works. And, again, the ornamentation of savage arms claims a becoming tribute of admiration, often as well deserved because of the intrinsic beauty of the decorative designs, as from the patient labour and the dexterity of hand with which the designs have been executed. It must be added that the minute surface carving that is lavished upon the shafts of lances, and on war clubs of all kinds, besides its adornment of the weapon, was designed to have the practically useful effect of giving firmness to the grasp.

It is worthy of remark here, that the stone axes, hammers, lance-heads, and arrow-heads that were made and used by the primitive races, who were our own remote predecessors in the occupancy of Britain, resemble very closely the weapons of the same early periods that are found in various parts of the globe, as in Australia, New Zealand, the Pacific Islands, Mexico, &c. Thus we perceive that, under whatever sky he may have been born, in his primitive state man has availed himself of the same natural resources throughout the habitable globe.

NOTE 43, *p.* 93.—The historian Agathias, who wrote in Greek, flourished about A D. 535 ; he was the continuator of Procopius, the interval between the works of the two authors being only fifteen years. Nearly a century earlier, that is, about the middle of the 5th century of our era, Sidonius Appollinaris wrote concerning the weapons and the war usages of the Franks.

It is remarkable that Procopius, writing only fifteen years before Agathias, makes no mention of the *angon* as a Frankish weapon. He says that the foot-soldiers of the Franks were armed with axes, swords, and bucklers only. The Frank axe he describes as having a broad blade and a short haft ; and he says that a *shower of them* would be certain to *cleave the shields* of the enemy, and to render them defenceless. Sidonius Apollinaris speaks of the remarkable skill of the Franks in casting or hurling the axe. Thus, the Red Indian of the north in the New World has been unconsciously imitating the Frank of the Old World, when he dashed his deadly tomahawk with unerring dexterity against his enemy.

The description of the *angon* given by Agathias is so minutely exact that it must be accepted as the expression of his own personal observation. At the same time it can scarcely be supposed that this remarkable weapon had been introduced, adopted, and brought into general use amongst the Franks, so as to supersede the use of the axe as a missile, within the brief space of that fifteen years that elapsed between the narratives of Agathias and his predeeessor. It will not fail to be observed that both axe and *angon* are said to have been used with precisely the same object—to deprive the enemy of the defence of his shield, and to expose him unprotected to a blow from another weapon. Thus it is probable either that the *angon* was the favourite missile of some particular tribe amongst the Franks, while the other tribes still threw their axes ; or, that the *angon* was the weapon only of certain corps (as we now should say), or of certain picked men distributed throughout the Frankish armies, the axe still being the characteristic missile of the main body.

The arms of the Anglo-Saxons, of which so many examples have been found, with other relics also of great interest, in the graves of that race in different parts of our island, in many respects closely resemble the weapons of the Franks of the continent, and not unfrequently they are identical with them. In addition to weapons also, in Anglo-Saxon graves, the *umbo*, or central boss of a shield, is frequently found.

The *axe*, or *francisca*, from which they took their name, was always a favourite weapon (whether as a missile or to grasp in the hands in order to deal a blow) amongst the Franks ; and it was also a weapon held in high esteem amongst the Anglo-Saxons. Examples of an elegant taper form have been found in Saxon graves in Kent, though not in such numbers as have been discovered in the Merovingian cemeteries in France. It is just possible that more than one *francisca* that was buried in Kent may once have been the weapon of a Frank who had found his own grave on this side of the Channel ; or these relics may have been trophies of Saxon prowess, and so interred as honourable memorials with the remains of the deceased warriors.

In the tomb of Childeric (A.D. 458—481), accidentally discovered at Tournay, in 1653, were the skeleton and trappings of a horse, a spear-head, a sword having a single edge, and an iron axe head, not double-edged, but a true tapering *francisca*, resembling those often found in France and sometimes in England.

The term *bipennis*, originally denoting the Asiatic double-edged axe, in the course of time was accepted as the common name of all war-axes, whether with single or double-edged blades.

NOTE 44, *p.* 94.—Fredegonde, the wife of Chilperic, and the mother of Clothaire II., who, if chroniclers do not deal with her unjustly, was one of the most remarkable examples of successful iniquity that ever wore the human form, was born A.D. 543, and died A.D. 597. We have no reason to suppose that dirks and daggers that had been deliberately poisoned were weapons in habitual and systematic use amongst the Franks. It is bad enough to be obliged to believe that, even if exceptional and not customary and general, the use of such weapons could have existed amongst the Franks at all. (See Note 39.) We may not forget the attempt (recorded by Bede in the 9th chapter of his second book) to assassinate Edwin, King of Northumbria, by a poisoned dagger that was sufficiently long in the blade to pass through the body of the loyal Thane and to wound the king. The knives of the Franks are reproduced in the dirks of Scotland, with the knives that garnish their scabbards.

NOTE 45, *p.* 97.—English readers will not fail to observe that the French character of the opening portion of this chapter is maintained throughout the entire chapter, and that the subject is treated in the text as it is seen from a French point of view. This French sentiment is not by any means without both interest and value for us in England. We require to know in what light mediæval arms and armour, as they were specially in use in France during the middle ages, are now regarded by a French writer who treats expressly of them. At that period our country was kept in close contact with France, and in many particulars there existed a certain degree of conformity in the military equipment in use at the same time in both countries ; and the decided differences that also were then in existence, in order to their being thoroughly understood and duly appreciated, require to be shown from a comparison of what arms and armour really were in those days in both France and England.

The use also in England of a French technical nomenclature for all mediæval arms and armour, renders it the more necessary that we should be familiar with the pieces of armour and the weapons in use in France, which may have given their names to the corresponding (and yet, it may be, not identical) pieces and weapons in England.

Again, it appears to be highly desirable for us in England to become familiar with the distinctive forms, the details, and the general characteristics of French arms and armour, that we thus may be enabled readily to distinguish French from English representations of armed figures and combats in illuminated MSS. The MSS. themselves being written in the French language, as well when the writers were Englishmen as when they were Frenchmen, without a knowledge of the arms and armour of both nations it is scarcely possible to determine to which nation the artists who executed any particular illuminations may have belonged. Thus, contemporary illuminations may appear to be altogether at variance amongst themselves, or to militate against the evidence of monumental effigies, and even against that of actual relics of the armourer's craft ; whereas the difficulties and the contradictions vanish at once, when it is ascertained that in some of the examples French arms and armour are represented with the same discriminating fidelity, which in other examples characterises representations of the arms and armour of England. For example, M. Lacombe has recorded that military gauntlets were unknown as pieces of armour in France earlier than the reign of Charles VII., A.D. 1422—1461 ; but we know that in England gauntlets were constantly worn a century and a half before the close of the reign of that French sovereign. It is obvious that numerous and by no means unimportant mistakes and misapprehensions must result from the want of a familiarity with so singular a difference in contemporaneous usage.

NOTE 46, *p.* 106.—That the Bayeux Tapestry is an original work of the age to which it professes to belong—that is, that it was executed in the reign of William the Conqueror, may be considered to be established beyond all question. There also is a very strong probability that the actual execution of the tapestry was accomplished, at any rate in part, by the hands of the Conqueror's queen, Matilda herself. In any case, however, it may be consistently assumed that the design for the tapestry (including all the details of arms, armour, costume, and other accessories) was drawn out for the fair worker or workers by some professional artist, well qualified to perform such a task ; and it is also more than probable that the original design may have been very decidedly more artistic than the tapestry itself. In fact, the tapestry may fairly be considered the most successful attempt that it was possible to make, to imitate with a needle a design that had been drawn with a pencil · and thus whatever artistic imperfections may exist in the tapestry, they in no way affect its character for accuracy of representation. The internal evidence of the tapestry itself is conclusive in its own favour ; and this evidence receives the most complete confirmation from the illuminations in contemporary MSS. and from the writings of the Anglo-Saxon poets.

It will be observed that some of the lances represented in the tapestry have barbed heads. (See Note 43.) Some of these barbed heads are long and slender, while others are both shorter and broader.

Axes of two distinct varieties are shown ; some with short and curved hafts, doubtless missile-axes ; and others having long and straight hafts, which apparently would be used in hand-to-hand conflict. The heads of the axes of this second-class (like those of the former class also) have a single edge, and they are generally fixed quite at the top of the haft. These long-hafted axes appear to have been used (as spears were also occasionally used) in those days as insignia of rank and authority, without any necessary or direct reference to warfare—precisely as, in later times, swords were worn by gentlemen in compliance with the usage which had made the presence of that weapon a necessary accessory of a gentleman's costume. Thus, in the tapestry, where Harold is represented having the crown offered to him, the great Thane who makes the offer holds in his hand an axe having a haft certainly five feet in length, while Harold himself holds a somewhat similar axe, of which the length would be four feet. In other parts of the work axes of the same kind appear in the hands of both Norman and Saxon soldiers.

Bows and arrows appear to have played a much more important part at the battle of Hastings than M. Lacombe has assigned to them.

In addition to the long mail tunic, the "twisted warbyrine" of Beowulf, the Anglo-Saxons at Hastings wore body-armour formed of pieces of leather cut into the shape of scales, and arranged in overlapping rows. "It was most probably copied from the Normans," says Planché, "for, in the Bayeux Tapestry we perceive it worn by Guy, Count of Ponthieu, and Odo, Bishop of Bayeux; and it continued in use in England as late as the 13th century." Some characteristic battle-scenes, nearly contemporaneous with the Norman invasion, are illuminated in the MS. also in the British Museum, marked *Cott. MS. B A.* The combatants in these illuminations have very large swords.

NOTE 47, *p.* 108.—In the Parham collection of arms and armour is represented a nasal helm, showing that protection for the face wh ch is universal in the Bayeux Tapestry.

NOTE 48, *p.* 109.—The last sentence in this paragraph does not occur in the French version. Until some years after the close of the brief reign of Richard I., over which the personal reputation of the lion-hearted king has cast so brilliant a reflected light—that is, until about the middle of the 13th century—it is probable that except in the districts furthest to the East) a general uniformity prevailed in the arms and armour that were in use throughout Europe. The first great and decided changes, which were modified in accordance with the tastes and requirements and the climate of different nations, grew out of the Crusades. It is certain that those remark-able enterprises exercised a very powerful influence upon the equipment, both defen-sive and offensive, of the Western chivalry ; and, in like manner, without any doubt, the traditions and usages that the Crusaders brought back with them from the East were adapted by them to the varying circumstances of their several homes.

Not many examples of original mail armour—the true mail, formed of interwoven rings fixed with rivets—are still in existence of a date earlier than our Richard I., A.D. 1189—1199; and, indeed, genuine examples of that era are "few and far between." In the remarkably fine armoury at Parham, the seat of the Hon. R. Curzon, is preserved a coif or hood of mail, a relic of extreme rarity and great interest ; it still retains its original leather lining. It is difficult to assign even a proximate date to this remarkable example, which might have been made and worn at any time from about the middle of the 12th century until about the middle of the century following.

It is worthy of special remark that the numerous fine examples of oriental mail defences that of late years have been brought to England (and particularly the mail armour worn by the Sikhs in their fierce but unavailing struggle, of which there is a singularly characteristic collection in the Tower armoury) appears to be identical in manufacture and general treatment with that mail of the 12th and following centuries, which the warriors of western Europe brought from the Crusades and subsequently established amongst themselves.

NOTE 49, *p.* 110.—M. Lacombe is of opinion that all the changes in the form and character of pieces and suits of armour were based upon such changes in the fashion of the ordinary costume, as were adopted at any particular time by men who were of a rank to entitle and require them when armed to wear armour. This opinion, derived (as it would seem) from the unquestionable usage at the time of the decline of armour, in its general application cannot be accepted without reserve. Indeed, until after the complete establishment of the steel panoply of plate in the 15th century, it would not be by any means easy to demonstrate as a fact that armour had ever accepted its distinctive features from suggestions made by existing fashions in civil and ordinary costume. A certain degree of general resemblance may have existed, and must have been expected to exist, between the equipment of the same man when armed and when without his armour, and particularly in the matter of the surcoat (whatsoever might be its peculiar form) that he would wear over his defences ; but, anterior to the second half of the 15th century, this general resemblance must be considered to have arisen quite as much from the influence of armour upon costume, as from the influence of costume upon armour. It is certain that ladies of rank delighted to assimilate their costume in some particulars to the knightly equipment of their time ; thus, we find the wimple of high-born dames to have been adjusted in such a manner, in connection with their coverchef or veil, as to disclose their features very nearly in the form of a triangle, precisely after the fashion of the mail coifs and the camailed basinets of their lords. And, in like manner, the strange adjustment of the knightly belt about the hips from about 1330 to about 1400 was adopted by the ladies, and introduced into their costume. It would not be difficult, I think, pursuing the same course of inquiry, to derive from knightly appointments and .decorations both the very effective style of dress long in favour with mediæval ladies, and also their acceptance of heraldic insignia as suitable for the adornment of their own proper costume.

The really important point for consideration in connection with any inquiry into the successive changes in arms and armour arises from *their relative bearing and influence upon one another.* From the earliest and rudest age down to the present day, a contest for the supremacy has always been maintained between the weapons that would wound and kill, and the defences that would protect and save. As long as any form of defensive equipment would prove equal to accomplish its own avowed purpose in a satisfactory manner, and would really defend the wearer when in actual conflict, so long would men be content with that equipment and gladly would accept its protection. But it is never thus with weapons. The instant that men find their arms in any degree powerless to cope with the existing armour, and to pierce through whatever opposition may be presented to their attack, that instant they commence devising some means by which their weapons may become more powerful and efficient. Then, and not till then, when the arms beat the armour, the armour in its turn is strengthened. And so the struggle goes on. The stronger armour is but a challenge to produce arms that will prove to possess still more formidable powers; and these arms, once more, call forth from the armourer fresh evidences of the existence of reserved resources. The final result is, that the offensive weapons become too strong to be effectually resisted by any such armour as men are able to wear and to endure : and then armour subsides into being only a memory of the past. Thus it was that gunpowder disposed of the panoply of steel ; and thus, before that great revolution in warfare had been accomplished, armour gradually increased in strength, and unwieldiness, and weight ; and arms, if they did not continually become more formidable, certainly always aimed at enlarged capacities for destructiveness. This same struggle in our own times has been renewed under conditions that are truly tremendous. We do not, indeed (at present at any rate), attempt to encase our men in defences that might profess to be Armstrong-proof and Snider-proof; but the old contest is waged over again in the old fashion, between cannon and armour-plates—between projectiles of enormous powers and almost superhuman destructiveness, and ships and batteries sheathed in massive iron. There appears now, indeed, to remain but little more to be accomplished on either side—unless, perhaps, the cannon and the projectile should attain to a *maximum* of efficiency which would render all resistance impossible, and so put an end to warfare altogether.

NOTE 50, *p.* 111.—The dislike for the armour of the middle ages entertained by M. Lacombe culminates in the aversion with which he regards the great helm—the "heaume" of the mediæval chivalry. And yet, massive and ponderous as it certainly was, this mighty head-piece was in true keeping with both the feeling and the usages of the times. Nor was the great helm either an unknightly or an unseemly piece of armour. It will be remembered that the heaume was actually worn only at the moment of the charge, or while the combatant was in the thick of the *mêlée* : it then was placed *over* the smaller basinet, and it rested on the shoulders. In English monuments this heaume is habitually represented placed beneath the head of armed effigies, for which it forms a befitting pillow. In the Parham Collection is a characteristic example of the tilting helm of the 15th century. See a valuable notice of the helms in his armoury at Parham, by the Hon. R. Curzon, in the *Archæological Journal,* vol. xxii., p. 1.

NOTE 51, *p.* 112.—In many English effigies, and also in numerous illuminations, the padded and quilted garments, known as either a *haqueton*, or a *gambeson*, which were worn under the mail armour, and formed an important secondary defence, are very plainly represented.

NOTE 52, *p.* 114.—The additional defences described in the text were placed over the mail armour earlier in France than there is any existing evidence to show that they were in England.

NOTE 53, *p.* 115.—The mediæval shields used in England are admirably exemplified in monumental effigies, from the long *kite*-shaped shield to the almost triangular shield of the *heater* shape. These shields generally retain their armorial blazonry ; and it is at least probable that originally such blazonry was always displayed upon them. Of the earlier and larger shields fine examples may be seen in the series of effigies in the Temple Church, London. (These effigies, it is true, have been restored ; but they retain their shields in their original size and form.) The brass to Sir R. de Bures, at Acton, in Suffolk (A.D. 1304), has a good and characteristic shield of the period when the 13th century passed into the 14th. The fine effigy in alabaster of Prince John of Eltham, younger brother of Edward III., in Westminster Abbey, displays a splendid shield, with the armorial ensigns admirably executed in rather low relief ; it is represented in Fig 70, and the date is A.D. 1336.

Fig. 70 —SHIELD OF PRINCE JOHN OF ELTHAM.

NOTE 54, *p.* 116.—The series of French royal monumental effigies, in the Abbey Church of St. Denis, near Paris, is very numerous, and it ranges over a long period of time ; and, notwithstanding the *very complete restoration* that all the earlier and specially interesting effigies have recently undergone, these works must still be considered to be of great historical importance and value. So thoroughly complete, indeed, is this restoration, that not a vestige remains of any original work which may be accepted as unquestionably untouched. Consequently, it would not be possible to recognise in any one of those remarkable sculptures a certain authority upon "Arms and Armour," without some corroboration, such as a cast taken from the original before the restorer had touched it ; or, at any rate, without a trustworthy drawing or other representation (of the same rank as Stothard's etchings of our Temple Church effigies) also executed *previous* to the restoration. I carefully studied the St. Denis effigies last summer ; and if I had before entertained any doubts on the subject of the restoration of early effigies, even the shadow of any such doubt had passed away some time before I left that grand Abbey Church, the Westminster Abbey (to our own Westminster—THE Abbey, as we rightly call it, *proxima, sed proxima longo intervallo*) of France.

NOTE 55, *p.* 117.—In England, in the middle ages, three distinct classes of military heraldic flags were in general use, each class having a distinct and well-defined signification.

1. The *Pennon*, the ensign of knightly rank, small, pointed, or swallow-tailed, and charged with a badge or other armorial device, was displayed by a knight upon his own lance as his personal ensign.

2. The *Banner*, square or oblong in form, larger than a pennon, and charged with a complete coat of arms, was the ensign of a sovereign, prince, noble, or knight banneret, and also of the entire force attached to his person and under his immediate command.

3. The *Standard*, introduced about the middle of the 14th century, large, of great length (its size varying with the owner's rank), appears to have been adopted for military display rather than for any specific significance and use in war. Except in royal standards, the standard had the cross of St. George next to the staff, and the rest of the field displayed various badges accompanied with a motto. See " English Heraldry," p. 254 ; and " Heraldry Historical and Popular," third edition, p. 286.

NOTE 56, *p.* 117.—I may here consistently remark on the very great value of our English mediæval effigies, whether sculptured or engraven, as contemporaneous authorities which exemplify and illustrate not only *varieties* in arms and armour, but also their *details*. A complete armoury of swords, for example, down almost to the close of the 15th century, with their characteristic varieties of sword-belts, showing every detail of form, ornamentation, and adjustment, is preserved in these admirable national works.

NOTE 57, *p.* 119.—In the introduction to his " Monumental Effigies," Stothard has given an excellent treatise on mail armour, as it was worn in western Europe ; and, since the publication of his work, the subject has attracted no little attention. It does not appear, however, that we have much certain knowledge concerning the mail armour of the western chivalry before their return from the Crusades. In fact, the term " mail," when applied to defensive military equipment in western Europe, must be regarded as simply a general conventional name for any kind of garment that was strengthened with studs, rings, or small plates of metal attached to its surface. Unfortunately, no authority is given for the very complete description in the text of the Saracen mail-armour at the time of the Crusades, and for the account of its excellence. M. Lacombe appears to consider that both Crusaders and Saracens were armed alike, except so far as the existence of a palpable superiority in the Saracen equipment, arising from the greater skill with which it had been made. It would be interesting to learn in what direction further information on this point might be sought, with a probability of finding it. See No. 48.

NOTE 58, *p.* 122.—The statement in the text concerning the comparatively small loss of life in the battles of the 12th and 13th centuries requires to be accepted with some caution ; and it ought to be subjected. not only to a careful investigation of authentic data, having reference to both mediæval and modern batt'es, but also to a variety of circumstances that bear on both sides of this question. Whatever may have been the loss of life in the battles of the 12th and 13th centuries, in those of the 14th and 15th centuries the loss undoubtedly was very great. And, as the art of war has gradually been perfected in modern times, it is equally certain that the increased destructiveness of the weapons that have been brought into use has tended rather to diminish than to increase the amount of destruction that has actually been accomplished. With the most improved weapons of precision and long-range projectiles, a great and severe loss may be inflicted suddenly and within a very short space of time ; but, on the whole, in modern battles the tremendous power of their weapons does not by any means necessarily imply that the combatants now inflict and suffer heavier losses than attended the conflicts of the olden time.

NOTE 59, *p.* 122.—It can scarcely be admitted that M. Lacombe is justified in his use of personal epithets, when he contrasts the " little modern foot-soldier" —" *le petit fantassin moderne*," with "*l'enorme baron*"—the " enormous baron" in full panoply of the middle ages. Modern French foot-soldiers, generally speaking, in their stature and in the slight structure of their hardy and athletic frames, are certainly "little" enough ; nor, in our own service, is the standard of height very elevated "in the line ; " still, these modern facts do not necessarily magnify the bulk of the mediæval warrior, until he attains "enormous" proportions. On the contrary, so far as the argument rests on the testimony of armour, the question concerning the relative sizes of the men now living and their predecessors of the middle ages, is decided in direct opposition to the views expressed in M. Lacombe's comparison. The existing suits and pieces of mediæval armour, that certainly were habitually worn in their own times, and which as certainly have no exceptional qualities, are *much too small* to be worn now by men of moderate average height and size. In fact, we have reason to believe, as a general rule, that the mediæval knights and barons were very far from being "enormous," and that the once popular theory of the physical degeneracy of modern generations reverses the fact. The ideal image of a "man in armour," and more particularly of an armour-clad "baron," seems to have an inherent tendency to assume colossal (or, at any rate, "enormous") proportions—somewhat like the figure of the "king," whose greatness is typified in Egyptian hieroglyphics by his being represented as equal in stature to at least half a dozen of his subjects; still, in point of fact, it is more than probable that very small was the number of even the most potent of the old "barons," who in physical magnitude could have taken rank with either the "Cent Gardes" of the French empire, or our own Life Guards.

The French term *fantassin*, signifying "foot-soldier," is evidently derived from the same source as the word "infantry;" and both lead us back to the times in which foot-soldiers were neither more nor less than attendants (and very generally hired servants who attended) on the knights and mounted men-at-arms. These attendants for the most part were young men or lads—in Latin *infantes*, and in Italian *fanti*, or *infanti*. And, when massed together, these youthful knights' attendants became "infantry;" and, still retaining the original form of the name, though without a trace still existing of the original condition of his prototype, the "little" French "foot-soldier" of to-day is a *fantassin* still.

NOTE 60, *p*. 123.—The descriptions of the arms and armour of the 14th century given in the text, in accordance with the original work, must not be considered in any way or degree applicable to England.

NOTE 61, *p*. 124.—The great war between Edward III. and Philip of Valois commenced in the year 1340, when the English sovereign asserted his title and right to the crown of France, and maintained that he was *ipso facto* King of France. In that same year the armorial ensigns of France and England were marshalled quarterly upon the same shield by Edward III. Sandford, however ("Genealogical History," edition of 1707, p. 160), states that on March 1, 1339, Edward III. promulgated and used a new Great Seal, bearing the legend, KING OF FRANCE AND ENGLAND; whereas, in the document of that date, to which the seal was appended, the style of the king was, "Edward the Third, by the Grace of God, King of England and France."

NOTE 62, *p*. 125.—Strictly French in their authority and application are the statements in the text, which ascribe to the example and influence of the Free Companies a "revolution in arms and armour;" and the descriptions, which accompany these statements, while strictly applicable to France, have no reference to our own country.

The armour worn in England during the second half of the 14th century, and the well-known *jupon* of that period, do not appear to have attracted the notice of M. Lacombe. A *plastron*, or small breast-plate, at that time was constantly worn by English men-at-arms *under* their mail hauberk. See Chapter XII.

NOTE 63, *p*. 128. – M. Lacombe's dislike for the great "heaume" of the mediæval warriors has already been noticed in Note 50. He does not advert to the modifications in the adjustment of the *camail*, not its *lacing*—at first exposed, and then covered—eminently characteristic matters of detail in English armour.

In this place also I must particularly caution English readers to observe that in the text, which follows the French original, no clear distinction is drawn between the armour of the second half of the 14th century and that of the first half of the 15th century, as such a distinction would be drawn by an English writer who based the leading statements of his essay on English armour. And, further, in like manner, the French author does not arrange the armour of the entire 15th century into well-defined groups, each having its own period, as an English writer certainly would do. The *lance-rest* is not mentioned by M. Lacombe.

NOTE 64, *p*. 129.—I have been very careful to give a strictly faithful rendering of this paragraph, since it sets forth in so explicit a manner what, in the judgment of a living French writer, could be effected about the middle of the 14th century by such infantry as the English and Genoese archers against mounted men-at-arms.

M. Lacombe appears thoroughly to appreciate the effect upon the English mediæval foot-soldiers of the superior social position enjoyed by them, in comparison with the position of their contemporaries who formed the infantry in the armies of France and of other continental countries. From the days of Magna Charta, in England the commonalty had shown that they were not to be despised, and they were not despised. With an aptitude and a love for manly exercises, the yeomanry of England was sturdy and muscular; and, moreover, the English yeomen were cherished and trusted by the English nobles. These were the men who enabled the Edwards and Henrys first to dispense with foreign mercenaries in their own armies, and then to beat them when they appeared under hostile banners. It was an honour to command and even to fight side by side with such men. Their services were of great value, and they were highly valued accordingly. And, above all, between themselves and the king and his nobility there existed a cordial sympathy and a mutual confidence. "Nothing," says Froude (' History of England,' vol. i., p. 60) "nothing proves more surely the mutual confidence which held together the government and the people, than the fact that all classes were armed." In war, in those days, the archers of England were the best infantry in the world; but, then, their famous long-bow acquired its reputation in no slight degree from the fact that, in peace, archery was the favourite national pastime of the English yeomanry. Very different from this was the condition of the commonalty in France. There nobility was rampant, and arrogated exclusively to itself the profession of arms. The people, despised by the nobles, and at once trampled down and distrusted by them, were purposely made unfit to become good soldiers. Accordingly, a French writer (Brantôme) has recorded of the native infantry of his country that, until the 15th century, it was composed of the very lowest and the most degraded dregs of the populace. And even if, in spite of every adverse circumstance, those unfortunate men chanced to fight well, their courage and success at once aroused the jealousy of their own men-at-arms, who actually would charge and beat them down as if they were enemies. Thus, while in the one country a martial spirit was earnestly cherished, in the other it was rigorously repressed; and while the English archer had his natural manly qualities developed and matured, while he himself was highly esteemed and his services were suitably acknowledged, the French foot-soldier was conscious that for *him* to possess and exhibit any true military qualities was simply to imperil his own life.

The archers wore iron head-pieces, and sometimes breast-plates or mail shirts; but generally their principal defence was their thickly quilted tunic.

NOTE 65. *p.* 135.—M. Lacombe has omitted all notice of armour for the defence of horses. The protection of their war-horses from injury or mischance was to the mediæval knights a matter of such vital importance, that they provided for their defensive equipment with the most scrupulous care. The accoutrements of the knight's war-horses have the general name of " bardings ;" and an armed charger is accordingly said to be "barded." This horse-armour came into use in England in the second half of the 13th century; and its use was continued until about the middle of the 17th century.

NOTE 66, *p.* 135.—Whatever may be the nature of the inferences drawn from the Homeric descriptions of the chariots of the Greeks at the siege of Troy, the chariots of antiquity appear generally to have been destined to fulfil other duties on the field of battle besides that of simple locomotion. The chariots of Egypt and Assyria mentioned in Holy Writ, were strictly war-chariots; and the existing remains of both Egyptian and Assyrian art confirm the warlike character of the chariots, and exemplify their use in actual battle. Again, it is not possible for us to forget the war-chariots of our remote predecessors in the occupancy of this island, with their scythe-armed axles, of which Cæsar, after his manner, has bequeathed to us a vivid description.

NOTE 67, *p.* 137.—The *pavise*—which may be regarded as a kind of portable intrenchment—was in use in England—that is to say, it was in use by English soldiers —as early as the first quarter of the 15th century. See the end of Note 64, and Fig. 81. Examples of the pavise are given in the fine MS. in the British Museum, marked "Cotton. MS., Julius, E. IV., 219 and 225."

NOTE 68, *p.* 146.—The armour that is described in the text from page 146 to page 152 inclusive is French armour The text contains no description of the true plate armour of England. The engraved figure bearing the number 28, and entitled a French knight of the time of Charles VI., A.D. 1380—1422, however accurate in representing the French armour of that period, does not convey any idea of such a suit of armour as was habitually worn in England, either during the forty-two years of the reign of the French king, or at any other period. See Chapter X.

NOTE 69, *p.* 151.—*Sollerets*, formed of articulated plates of steel, and having mail to guard the instep-joint, were in general use by English knights from about the middle of the 14th century. After about the year 1500, the *solleret* was superseded by the *sabbaton*, which was cut off square and was very broad at the toe.

The statement in the text, that military *gauntlets* were unknown in France until the era of the seventh Charles, appears very singular to those who are familiar with the military effigies of England. The actual gauntlets (I see no reason to doubt *their* accepted authenticity) of our Black Prince, who died in 1376, hang in Canterbury Cathedral above his monument, whereon reposes his noble effigy, with similar gauntlets upon the hands. This is not the earliest effigy with gauntlets. It will be observed that the gauntlet, which is a glove provided with defences of steel plates or scales, and with formidable little knobs or spikes (called *gads* or *gadlyngs*) on the knuckles, is quite distinct from the *mail mitten*—in reality a prolongation of the sleeve of the shirt of mail, which at earlier periods mediæval warriors were able to draw over their hands at pleasure. The true gauntlet was introduced in England as early as the time of Edward I., or about A.D. 1300.

NOTE 70, *p.* 152.—In England in the 15th century the *gorget* was a collar of plate armour, which at first superseded the camail, and subsequently assumed various modifications. A gorget of plate is represented worn *over* the camail, as early as 1347, in the brass to Sir Hugh Hastings, to which I have already referred.

The *basinet* was worn in England early in the century; but several varieties or modifications of the *helm* were introduced before the 15th century had reached its close.

NOTE 71, *p.* 155.—For a notice of the *passe-gardes*, and the various additional plates that were introduced into English armour at late periods of its history, see Chapter X.

NOTE 72, *p.* 155.—See Notes 49 and 62. The fluted, puffed, and other highly decorated armour in use in England in the 16th century was evidently made in imitation of the costume worn by the nobles and gallants of the day. Such a direct and indeed servile imitation of textile fabrics in metal is in itself a very decided sign of decadence in armour. It is not by any means a necessary inference from the undoubted imitation of dress in the armour of the Tudor era, that a similar imitation was prevalent, or even existed at all, in earlier periods when true art was flourishing.

NOTE 73, *p.* 162.—With the increase of decoration and of elaboration of details, and with the contemporaneous addition of extra plates to the suit of armour, the decline of the armourer's art and craft in England may be considered to have kept pace, until at length the era of true armour in our country came finally to a close.

It will be observed that the *morion*, and the *burgonet*, together with the *pike*, the *halberd*, the *partisan*, and the *bill*, and other pieces of armour and other weapons also that were in use in France, were well known and were in habitual use at the same period in England. We appear, moreover, to have introduced more than one additional modification of weapons of the halberd and partisan class, which are not represented in Fig. 68, page 273.

There is also one continental weapon of the same order not included in the group in Fig. 68, which I think must have been accidentally overlooked by M. Lacombe, since it certainly may claim a place amidst its formidable (or formidable-looking) confederates that compose his group. The weapon in question is the *morgenstern*, a club or mace having a long and strong stock, like the shaft of a halberd, surmounted by a globular or oval head of hard wood, bound about with three or more bands of iron, each of which bands bristles with iron spikes; and another spike, somewhat longer than the rest, projects at the top. It was used in the 16th and 17th centuries in the defence of breaches and walls. At the end of the fourth chapter of his "Legend of Montrose," Sir Walter Scott mentions this weapon after such a fashion as this:—Major (then Captain) Dalgetty, *loquitur*, "It's a pity he should be sae weak in the intellectuals, being a strong proper man of body, fit to handle pike or morgenstern, or any other military implement whatsoever." A remarkably fine specimen of a Swiss morgenstern is conspicuous in the collection of my friend, Mr Ricketts.

NOTE 74, *p.* 163.—Early in the 15th century the Swiss showed that a *pike*, 16 or 18 feet in length, in strong hands, was the most effectual weapon to check the charge of a body of horse.

The pike, which never had been regarded with favour by French soldiers, was abolished in the armies of France in 1703-4; and it is probable that it ceased to be used in our own army at about the same time. The plug-bayonet was introduced into the English army in 1672; and in about a quarter of a century the musket and bayonet could not fail to supersede the pike. It would seem that the dislike of the French for the pike arose in a great measure from the fact that they were not physically as strong as the well-fed English yeoman.

It is remarkable that, while the bayonet (now rendered almost useless by long-range projectiles) has fairly driven the pike from the ranks of modern infantry, the old knightly weapon, the *lance*, has reappeared and is held once more in high esteem amongst the cavalry of every European nation.

NOTE 75, *p.* 164.—Shields are not represented in English effigies later than a little after the middle of the 14th century. Targets, however, sometimes were used in more modern warfare ; and in Scotland, as is well known, the Highland target was retained in use as late as till "the '45."

NOTE 76, *p.* 166.—The *bayonet,* which was invented about the year 1650, was adopted in France in its simplest "plug" form about 1675, or about three years after it had been introduced into the English army. It is obvious that, very shortly after this weapon had been brought into use, efforts would be made to discover some means for fixing it firmly to the muzzle of the musket without obstructing the free action of the musket itself. Accordingly, as early as 1689, bayonets were attached by means of two rings to muskets, by Macay in Scotland ; and thus, while the bayonet remained fixed, the musket could be fired. This contrivance is said to have been known and adopted on the continent at least eleven years before 1689. The great improvement of the "ringed bayonet" did not secure for it either a general or a ready adoption. The next and the final step was to substitute a socket for the two rings. This was effected at the commencement of the 18th century, when the "socket bayonet," in its general character identical with the weapon in its present method of adjustment, came into general use in the armies of both England and France. (See a valuable illustrated paper in the "Archæologia," xxxviii., 422. See also "British Army," ii., 314.)

NOTE 77, *p.* 167.—The Swiss and German pikemen certainly were excellent and thoroughly efficient soldiers ; still, they never were opposed to the archers of England, or, possibly the opinion that those pikemen were "the best European infantry" might have been somewhat qualified. At any rate, in our own times we have the satisfaction that a French officer of high rank, and concerning whose competency to form and to express an opinion on such a subject there can be no doubt, has pronounced our own to be "the best European infantry." "The English infantry," said Marshal Bugeaud, "is the most formidable in the world ; *it is heaven's own mercy that there is not more of it !*"

NOTE 78, *p.* 170.—It will be understood that the swords described in the text are French, and—with the exception of the *rapier*—not English weapons. Swords of foreign make, however, at this period were very commonly imported into England. There are some remarkable rapiers of immense length in the South Kensington Museum.

NOTE 79, *p.* 177.—The gigantic two-handed sword was occasionally in use in England. Every visitor to Westminster Abbey will remember the tremendous weapon, seven feet in length, and weighing 18 lbs., which, as legends tell, was carried before the victorious Edward III. in France. Possibly such swords as this of Edward III. were designed rather for display in processions than for use in battle. The two-handed swords of the Swiss, as I need scarcely add, are famous in history.

NOTE 80, *p.* 178.—From a very early period the productions of the sword cutlers of Spain have deservedly enjoyed the very highest reputation. The blades of Toledo stand first ; and, second only to them are those of Zaragoza. Italy, also, has long been famous for swords as well as for armour. The steel of Milan is proverbial for its rare excellence, as the Milanese armourers are for their skill in working it ; and again, Florence is another celebrated seat of the most skilled armourers. In England, and more particularly in Scotland, the name of Andrea Ferrara as a sword-smith is second to none. It appears that this famed artificer—concerning whom very little is really known beyond the excellence of the blades that have a just right to bear his name—was born in Italy about the year 1550 ; and, being of a family of hereditary armourers, with his brother Giovanni he seems to have established himself in Spain. By what means the name of Andrea Ferrara became so familiar in Scotland is not known. The fine, highly-tempered, keen-edged blades of Damascus for upwards of a century have ceased to be produced at that long-famous sword-making city. It must be added that the fame of Toledo is in some degree due to the Moors, who, before the first thousand years of the Christian era had passed away, had introduced there, not only their peculiar system of Damascene ornamentation, but also the Damascus mode of tempering the steel.

The swords of Cologne were held in high estimation as early as the 13th century. At an early period Bordeaux was celebrated for its swordsmiths. Nor was our own country without its skilled craftsmen, whose weapons were worthily considered to possess the highest qualities; the English swords of the 15th and 16th centuries, indeed, are remarkable for excellence. In the 16th century, also, the German swords of Solingen enjoyed a world-wide reputation ; and in the 17th, Nuremberg was remarkable for its sword-hilts. Amongst the many perhaps equally skilled producers of weapons in various countries in our own times, a place of honour must be assigned to the mountaineers who inhabit the range of Kara Dagh, on the shores of the Caspian, who from time immemorial have been famous for their manufacture of both armour and weapons.

NOTE 81, *p.* 179.—With the sword, a smaller weapon of its own class has been universally worn and used from the earliest times. This weapon, the *dagger*, is specified by name as a *misericorde*, in France, in a charter of Philip Augustus, A.D. 1194; and, in England, in the statute of Winchester, A.D. 1285. From about the middle of the first half of the 14th century the *misericorde* is constantly represented in English effigies, whether sculptured or engraven ; and, like the sword itself, it is shown to have been sometimes secured to the person of the wearer by a chain fixed to the hilt.

Amongst the varieties of weapons of the dagger class, M. Lacombe has not included one, well known in Italy, in the design and construction of which a murderous ingenuity is carried to the highest pitch of refinement. This poignard has an *expanding blade*. When the blow is struck, the blade is thin, keen as a razor in both its edges, and acutely pointed ; but, after the stab has been inflicted, a concealed mechanism causes the blade to open—that is, smaller blades spring forth which instantly change the first minute puncture into an internal gash of ghastly extent. A specimen may be seen in the South Kensington Museum ; and in the collection of Lord Boston is a German misericorde, about 1540, which has the blade perforated with two channels on each side for poison.

NOTE 82, *p.* 180.—The Scottish usage of carrying a knife or knives in the sheath of the dirk, or attached to the leggings, is well known. As an example, I may specify a beautiful dagger, now the property of Mr. Kerslake, that appears to have been worn by King Charles I. when he was Prince of Wales. The hilt has the plume of three ostrich feathers, and a knife and fork are inserted in the sheath.

NOTE 83, *p.* 182.—The "Hussars" mentioned in the text are singularly suggestive prototypes of the "Zouaves" of the present day.

NOTE 84, *p.* 213.—In his treatment of the comprehensive and copious subject of "Modern Arms," the plan and extent of his book required that M. Lacombe should write in a concise manner, and as briefly as possible. The few "Notes" that I propose to add to this portion of the present volume, for the same reasons also must necessarily be both concise and brief.

"Artillery," says Sir Sibbald Scott ("British Army," ii. 166), "a word derived from the old French *artiller* ('to fortify'; from the Latin *ars*), in its general signification denotes all kinds of missile weapons, with the engines used in propelling them. In the modern acceptation of the term it is appropriated to the larger sorts of fire-arms: in mediæval times it naturally referred more generally to bows and arrows and their appurtenances." Sir Sibbald then proceeds to quote from Stowe's "Annals," that writer's definition of "artillery," to the following effect:—it is the *"ars telorum mittendorum*—the art of shooting in long-bows, cross-bows, stone-bows, scorpions, rams, catapults, as also (and especially in this age) in cannons, haselisks, culverings, sakers, faulcons, minnions, fowlers, chambers, muskets, harquebusses, calivers, petronils, dags, and such like ; for this is the artillery which is now in most use and estimation."

The earliest engines for discharging projectiles—in all probability the projectiles were stones of great weight—were invented early in the world's history. One thousand years before the Christian era it is recorded of Uzziah, king of Judah (2 Chron. xxvi. 15), that "he made in Jerusalem engines, invented by cunning men, to be on the towers and upon the bulwarks to shoot arrows and great stones withal." These engines were the *balista*, originally designed to throw stones, and the *catapulta*, arrows; the *espringal*, *trebuchet*, *mangonel*, &c., all having one purpose, but each one distinguished by some peculiarity either in its construction or operation. Then names of animals were given to these pieces of ancient artillery, under the idea that such names would denote the possession by the engines of certain qualities peculiar to the animals so called ; thus, the *scorpion* discharged small envenomed darts; and the *onager*, a machine for hurling stones, had its name from the wild ass of the desert, which, on being hunted, was said to fling up stones with its heels at its pursuers. As the Middle Ages advanced efforts were made to improve the various military engines, but without any great success, until at length gunpowder was universally admitted to be the one supreme propellant.

The use of gunpowder in Europe, however, "did not prove so decisive for those who first availed themselves of it as to mark distinctly in history the precise time when its practice first took place." (Colonel Chesney on " Fire-Arms.") The first mention of cannon in England is in June, 1338. The first allusion to cannon by Froissart occurs in 1340, and then he appears to take it for granted that they were well known. Edward III. certainly had cannon in 1346; and it may be assumed as certain that he used them at Crécy in that same year. (See "Archæological Journal," xix., 68.) In 1378, Richard II. had 400 pieces of artillery at St. Malo. From the commencement of the 15th to the middle of the 16th century, the use of artillery is mentioned in various sieges for defence as well as for attack ; and the besieging batteries consisted of bombards of both large and small calibre, the latter being designed to sustain an uninterrupted fire during the intervals required for reloading and discharging the former. From the middle of the 16th century for a considerable time the improvements in artillery chiefly consisted in rendering the guns more easily and expeditiously movable. In 1500, Louis XII. was able to move his artillery from Pisa to Rome, 240 miles, in five days ; and his light pieces were taken rapidly from one point to another in a battle. Francis I. had 74 pieces of ordnance in Italy in 1515. And in 1556 the Emperor Ferdinand marched against the Turks with 42 heavy and 127 light pieces of artillery. Such is a glance at the early progress of this powerful arm, which, in the early part of the 17th century became of greatly increased importance under Henry IV. of France, Maurice of Nassau, and Gustavus Adolphus. "Although retaining too many calibres," says Col. Chesney, "the artillery of Gustavus Adolphus was admirably organised, embracing as it did limbers, carrying canister shot and other kinds of ammunition ready for action ; and, what was no less important, having the allotment of a proportion of reserve artillery, in addition to that destined to accompany the troops during their movements in action. Moreover, this distinguished commander was the first who fully appreciated the importance of causing the artillery to act in concentrated masses, and who well understood the saving of life consequent on taking into the field a due proportion of this arm."

Gunpowder may be traced up to a very early period—certainly to the 7th century before our era—in China ; and it is probable that the knowledge of it was brought to Europe from the Chinese through the Arabs, or perhaps direct by the Venetians. Or, brought by the same means, it might have come to our quarter of the world from India, where a noisy propellant powder was known as early as the time of Alexander the Great—this is recorded by Philostratus. Ctesias and Ælian both speak of Indian combustibles ; but a distinction must always be observed between the ancient *inflammable* compounds (such as might be used in peace for fireworks, or for causing conflagration in war) and those which have a propellant and explosive power. In China, *jingals*, or small cannon, were in use three centuries before Christ, and probably much earlier. In some of the northern parts of China very ancient breech-loading jingals, with movable chambers for the charge and projectile, may still be seen. There is an authentic record of the use of cannon in China, A.D. 757 ; and again A.D. 1232. In the year of our era 1200, cannon-balls were employed in warfare in India ; and cannon were certainly known and used in the peninsula of Hindostan in great numbers long before they were known in Europe. Sulphur and nitre are found in great abundance in both China and India ; in the Sanscrit, gunpowder is *aigmaster*—"weapon of fire ; " but, though the true propellant compound was certainly known in very ancient times in Hindostan, there exists in that country no positive historical record of the invention of it.

In the manufacture of gunpowder the proportion of the ingredients has varied considerably at different periods. At first the three ingredients appear to have been mixed in equal parts. In 1410 the proportions were—nitre, 3 parts ; sulphur, 2 ; and charcoal, 2. In 1520—nitre, 4 parts ; sulphur, 1 ; and charcoal, 1. And now, in England, the proportion for military gunpowder is 100 parts—75 nitre, 10 charcoal, and 15 sulphur.

It is remarkable that *all the ancient and early cannon, whether in the East or in Europe, were breech-loaders;* they were composed of two distinct pieces, the "chamber," and the " chase " or barrel.

As the cannon gradually became larger, it was necessary to strengthen or *reinforce* them ; and then they were formed of longitudinal bars, arranged like the staves of a cask, and hooped over, the whole being of wrought-iron. Several most characteristic examples of these early guns were recovered in 1836 from the " Mary Rose," which sunk at Spithead in 1545; she was found to have been armed with large brass 32-pounders, 18-pounders, together with ancient bar and hoop guns.

In the Rotunda at Woolwich there is an excellent example of a gun of the 15th century, the calibre 4¼ inches. The Woolwich and the Tower collections also contain many early guns of different periods, calibres, and styles.

In 1439, James II. of Scotland was killed by the bursting of one of his guns at the siege of Roxburgh Castle. The great Scottish bombard, known as "Mons Meg," now at Edinburgh Castle, 16 feet long, and made of hooped staves, was used in the sieges of Dumbarton and Norham in 1489 and 1497. The first discharge with "a peck of powder and a granite ball nearly as heavy as a Galloway cow," is *said* to have carried off the hand of Margaret Douglas, the " Fair Maid of Galloway," as she sat at table with her lord in Threane Castle, and then the ball went *through the castle!* (See "Archæological Journal," x., 25.) At Mont St. Michel, in Normandy, are two bombards, left there by the English in 1423, of which the larger now weighs about 5¼ tons, and it would throw a granite ball 19 inches in diameter, and weighing about 300 lbs. The remarkable gun at Dover Castle, known as "Queen Elizabeth's Pocket Pistol," and which is popularly supposed to be able to "send a ball to Calais Green," was cast at Utrecht, A.D. 1544, and was presented to Henry VIII. by the Emperor Charles V. ; it is 24 feet 6 inches in length, and the calibre is only 4⅞ inches. The two pieces of ordnance now standing on the parade-ground in the rear of the Horse Guards, in London, consist of a French 13-inch mortar, brought from Cadiz, and of a Turkish gun, 16 feet long (originally it was 20 feet) taken at the battle of Alexandria ; this gun was placed in its present position March 21, 1802. See Col. Chesney's "Observations on the Past and Present State of Fire-Arms ;" and Sir Sibbald Scott's "British Army," ii., 161—257. See also "Archæologia," xxviii., 373, for a notice of some ancient guns found in 1839 in Lancashire.

NOTE 85, *p.* 229.—The subsequent introduction of *trunnion* shoulders was an improvement of very great importance, which enabled the gun to be placed firmly and steadily on the carriage, while at the same time it could move freely upon the axis formed by the trunnions themselves.

It has been reserved for an English officer of our own time, Captain Moncrieff, to convert the recoil of a heavy gun from being a dangerous and sometimes a destructive condition incidental to the use of artillery, into a powerful agent for protecting both gun and gunners while in action, and also at the same time for increasing in a truly remarkable manner the efficiency of the gun itself. Captain Moncrieff's system provides that the cannon to be used should then only be raised above the level of the parapet of a battery, when it is in the act of being discharged. The recoil, by a beautifully simple and thoroughly effective contrivance, causes the gun to sink down out of sight behind the parapet, and in so doing the gun elevatesa counterpoise ; and, in its turn, this counterpoise raises the gun when, after it has been loaded and laid (and by means of the Moncrieff *reflecting sight*, it can be laid while below the parapet), it is again ready to resume its firing position. This is accomplished almost without any strain—certainly without any serious strain—to the gun-carriage, or to the foundations of the works which constitute the standing and working place of the gun in the fort or battery. It will be observed that a gun worked on this admirable system is laid and fired, not through the opening of an embrasure, but above the upper line of the parapet—that is, in technical phrase, it is laid and fired *en barbette*. Thus, embrasures are dispensed with, and the line of a parapet may be unbroken ; and, more important still, by this means the greatest possible extent of lateral range is obtained. But the advantages of the Moncrieff system extend far beyond even these most important points. It actually enables heavy artillery to be employed without any fort or battery whatever, by simply placing the guns in pits dug in the ground, so that the natural surface of the ground itself becomes the crest of a parapet. This would not have been possible, had the necessity for solid foundations for the gun-platform still remained. Captain Moncrieff does not require solid foundations. In one of his gun-pits a heavy gun can be worked, easily and in safety, with very simple appliances. When down in the pit in the loading position, not only is the gun out of sight with all its detachment, but there is no visible mark of any kind for the aim of an enemy. For a few moments the gun must be raised into the firing position and fired ; but even then not a man needs to be exposed, and at the very instant of firing the gun spontaneously disappears below the surface. Thus the recoil, no longer a shock but changed into a power, is absorbed by the counterpoise ; and in the counterpoise it lies latent until it is permitted quietly to put forth its strength that it may perform its appointed duty. Like the fly-wheel of a steam engine, this is indeed a triumph of combined science and skill. At present it would be altogether premature to anticipate what results may be effected by Captain Moncrieff's invention; thus much, however, is certain, that this admirable system marks the commencement of a

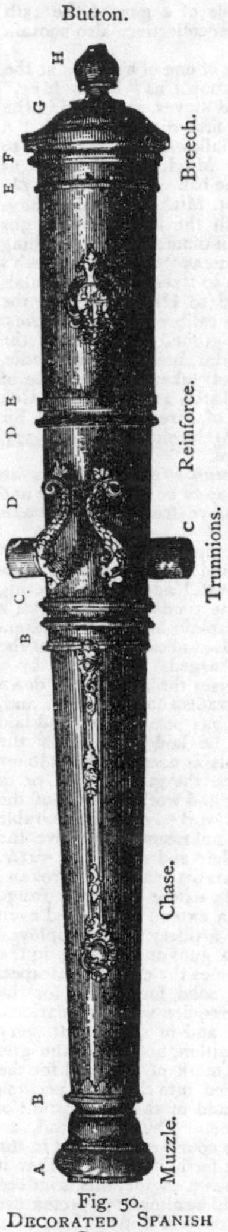

Button.

H

G

E F

E

D E

D

C D

C

B C

B

B

A

Breech.

Reinforce.

c

Trunnions.

Chase.

Muzzle.

Fig. 50.
DECORATED SPANISH
CANNON
(Paris Museum).

new era in the history of heavy artillery, and that it places Captain Moncrieff in the front rank amongst the eminent masters of practical science in his own or any other age. The Moncrieff system appears to be no less available at sea than on shore—in a word, it *reverses the turret system.*

The *hydraulic buffer*, to check recoil in heavy ordnance, the invention of Colonel Clerk, R.A., accomplishes its proposed object with complete success.

NOTE 86, *p.* 235.—Benjamin Robins, the eminent scientific English artillerist, whose researches and experiments, conducted with such remarkable ability, skill, and perseverance, effected so much, and led the way for the introduction of the more recent improvements in gunnery, died in the year 1742. His able works continue to be regarded as possessing the highest authority. And, as if in anticipation of his name, at the siege of Caerlaverock by Edward I., in 1300, a propellant engine called a *Robinet*—"*quod dicitur Robinettus*"—the peculiarity and special use of which are unknown, is recorded to have played its part amongst the other pieces of early "artillery" that were employed on that memorable occasion. (See Note 20.)

NOTE 87, *p.* 238.—The text is a faithful translation of the French. It is scarcely necessary to remark that this French estimate of the "Armstrong" is very far from being accurate ; or to state that "Armstrongs" are made of every calibre, and that they are no less distinguished for ease and rapidity of movement than for range and power.

NOTE 88, *p.* 240.—The representation of the Spanish cannon (Fig. 50), which I repeat here in order to avoid the necessity for reference to another page, may be used as a diagram to assist in explaining the technical names that are given to the several parts of our own pieces of ordnance. A is the *muzzle* ; B to B the *chase* ; C C the *trunnions* ; D to D the *second reinforce* ; E to E the *first reinforce* ; F the *vent-field* ; G the *cascable* ; H the *button.* In this Fig. 50 the trunnions are plain, solid, cylindrical masses, of uniform diameter throughout, and without "shoulders." The "handles," or *anses*, made in the form of dolphins, while they continued to be attached to guns, were technically called *dolphins*, in consequence of their general (but not universal) form ; they have ceased to exist, however, in all the more recent guns. The hollow of a gun is the *bore* ; the end of the muzzle is the *face*; and the aperture of the muzzle is closed by a *tompion.* The *sights* for the aim, and the various appliances for charging the gun at the breech have also their appropriate distinguishing names. The touch-hole is the *vent.* The trunnions are secured to the carriage by *cap-squares.* That part of the carriage which extends to the rear of the gun, and rests on the ground when the gun is in position, is the *trail*; and, if this is solid and in one piece, it is a *block-trail*; but, if divided so as to be double, it is a *bracket-trail.* The ammunition is carried with field-guns in a *limber*—a kind of cart having two wheels, to the back of which the end of the trail is attached when the gun is in motion ; the gun itself with its carriage, when thus "limbered up," and with its limber, forms a single four-wheel vehicle. It will be observed that, when in motion, the gun is dragged along reversed, with its breech towards the limber and the horses, and its muzzle pointing down towards the ground. The old system was to discharge the gun by igniting the touch-powder with a *port-fire*; but now the discharge is effected by either *percussion-tubes, quill-tubes,* or *friction-tubes.*

NOTE 89, *p.* 240.—Cannon are cast in England without much of decorative accessory. Decorated examples, however, but generally those which were cast in foreign countries and have found their way to resting-places in England, may be seen in our national arsenals and armouries.

NOTE 90, *p.* 242.—My "Note" upon the second part of this chapter must of necessity be restricted within very narrow limits.

The relationship which existed between the cross-bow and the catapult would naturally suggest the construction of some miniature form of cannon, which might be portable, and which accordingly might be carried and used by individual soldiers as their personal weapons. In accordance with a natural suggestion such as this, hand fire-arms, or small-arms, were invented in the 14th century; but so slow was the progress of the successive improvements which ultimately developed the long latent qualities of these weapons, that they were not brought into general use until nearly three centuries after their first invention.

The *hand-cannon* soon gave place to the *hand-gun,* which, in its turn, was superseded by the *arquebus* or *harquebus.* This weapon, discharged by means of a trigger, was evidently designed after the model of the arblast or cross-bow, to which it bore a decided general resemblance, except in the substitution of the barrel for the bow.

Hand-guns were known in Italy in 1397, and in our own country they appear to have been used as early as 1375. A century later they begin to be more frequently mentioned, and they also appear in illuminations, about the same time that the invention of the arquebus took place—that is, as the 15th century was drawing towards its close. The Swiss, according to De Comines, had the arquebus at Morat in 1476; in England, in 1485, one-half of the Yeomen of the Guard, then first established, were armed with this weapon; but in France it was not adopted till after 1520, notwithstanding the presence in that country of a strong body of arquebusiers with Henry VIII. at "The Field of the Cloth of Gold" in 1518. The Tower Armoury contains fine specimens of the arquebus of the time of Henry VIII.; one, with the date 1537, and ornamented with a crowned Tudor rose and the initials H. R., appears to have belonged to the king himself; this weapon, like the other early examples of its class, is a breech-loader.

The *haquebut* is an arquebus with a curved stock; and a *demi-haque* is a small haquebut.

The *musket,* a larger, heavier, and more powerful modification of the arquebus, was in use in Italy about 1530, and in France about 1570; and it probably found its way into England about the same period, since it certainly was well known in this country before 1590. At first, in consequence of its weight and size, the musket was fired from a rest. The names of animals were generally bestowed upon ordnance, as the *falcon* and its diminutive the *falconet,* and so forth; and as the musket was the most important of small fire-arms, the name of the smallest of the birds of prey might be very consistently given to it—the *musket* is the male young of the sparrow-hawk.

The *caliver* and the *fusil* are lighter varieties of the musket. In the armoury at Penshurst, in Kent, there are preserved no less than twenty-eight examples of the early musket and of the caliver; some have round barrels, and in some the barrels are canted to the muzzle; the barrels of several are enriched with scroll-work chased upon them, and on three there is the date 1595; one also, which is more richly ornamented than the rest has, with the date 1595, in relief the motto RIENS SANS DIEV. These, probably, are the earliest known specimens of the weapons of their class; but, as a matter of course, numerous other specimens exist in various armouries.

The *carbine,* or *carabine,* is a short caliver with a large bore; and the *blunderbus* (or *thunderbus*) is still shorter, and has the bore still larger. The *musquetoon* is another variety of comparatively light musket.

The true miniature arquebus is the *pistol,* which has been supposed to have derived its name from the circumstance that its calibre corresponded with the diameter of the coin—the pistole. Apparently it was common in Germany in about 1512; was adopted by the French cavalry in about 1550; and reached England a few years later. Occupying a position half-way between the arquebus and the pistol is the *petronel,* which was known in our country as early as 1580; and again, at the same period, the *dag,* which is a long pistol with a curved stock, appears amongst our countrymen.

In the first instance, the hand fire-arm was discharged by means of a *match,* or a coil of thin rope, held in the hand. The first improvement, which is coeval with the arquebus, is the *match-lock*—a simple contrivance for holding the match in a curved *cock*, or *serpentine*, and causing it to fall, at the pull of the trigger, on the priming-powder. The matchlock itself was very greatly improved about the middle of the 16th century. The *wheel-lock*, introduced a little before 1510, and said to have been invented at Nuremburg, was designed to obviate the great inconvenience of the match method of firing ; by a simple mechanism, a small grooved wheel of steel was made to revolve rapidly in contact with a piece of pyrites, or native sulphuret of iron, which was fixed into a " cock-head," and the sparks thus produced fell upon the priming in the pan. The earliest known specimen, bearing the date 1509 with the armourer's mark, is remarkable from having two cocks ; by this arrangement, if one piece of pyrites should break or in any way fail, a second would be at hand and available. This most curious wheel-lock is in the collection of Mr. Pritchett, F.S.A. The wheel was wound up, or "spanned," like a watch, with a key, or *spanner*.

The *snaphance*, *snaphaunce*, or *flint-lock*, succeeded towards the close of the 16th century, probably about the year 1580. Evidently suggested by the wheel-lock, it substituted a piece of flint for the pyrites, and instead of the wheel it had a rough plate of steel. The pull of the trigger caused the flint to strike the steel plate, and by that same act the pan was uncovered, so that the priming-powder might be exposed to receive the shower of sparks that would fall upon it. It seems to have been a Dutch invention, and to have by no means a dignified origin ; for this lock is said to have been brought into use by certain marauders, who by the Dutch were called " snap-haans," hen-snappers, or poultry-stealers—these worthies could not afford wheel-locks, and the lighted matches were liable to lead to their detection ; so they devised their own *snaphance*, little suspecting, doubtless, that their ingenious invention would be universally adopted, and would maintain its supremacy during the greater part of three centuries.

While the wheel-lock was still without any rival, its liability to miss fire led to the invention of a double kind of lock, which combined the two principles of the wheel and the match, so that if one should fail, recourse might be had to the other. This idea is claimed by the French for the great Vauban, and locks which combine two methods for firing bear his name ; still, there appears to be good reason for believing that the compound wheel-and-match lock was made in England earlier than the time assigned by French writers (after the year 1692) to what they designate " the invention of Vauban." This compound method of lock construction was also applied to combine the match and the flint systems in one lock. In order to fire the piece with the match held in the serpentine, the pan-cover is perforated to admit the match to pass through it to the priming ; and, on the other hand, the priming-powder was protected from the burning match, while the flint was available, by means of a sliding-lid which closed the perforation in the pan-cover. (See " Archæologia," xxxi., 491.)

In addition to the fire-arms already described, there was one of a formidable character, a kind of blunderbus, called a *dragon*, which gave to the troops who used it the name " dragoneers," whence was derived the well-known term " dragoons ;" "Grenadiers," again, were soldiers who threw small shells or *grenades*. Hand-*mortars* also were introduced towards the close of the 16th century, for discharging similar small shells, but they were never used to any extent.

When small-arms were first used, the soldiers carried their powder, priming-powder, and balls in flasks and bags. After a while—about 1550—*bandoleers* were introduced, consisting of shoulder-belts from which were suspended a series of small cases, each containing a charge ; numerous examples may be seen at the Tower, Woolwich, and especially at Hampton Court. About a century later *cartridges* were invented ; and then cases, called *patrons*, were provided, each of which would contain a small group of cartridges.

I have already noticed the remarkable circumstance that the early small-arms, like the early ordnance, were (at least in some instances) *breech-loaders*; and now I have to add that they also were sometimes *revolvers*. In the Tower Armoury, for example, there is a *match-lock revolver*, the date of which is about 1550. It is singular that M. Lacombe should have made no mention of revolving arms, except in an indirect allusion to American ordnance ; but how much more remarkable still, that the suggestive qualities of those old breech-loaders and revolvers should have remained unnoticed, actually from century to century !

Locks, as it is well known, have been applied to ship-guns.

The discovery of detonating powder by the French chemists, which is mentioned in the text, led to the adoption of the *percussion-lock* and a *cap*—a grand step in advance towards the perfection of fire-arms. The "needle" and the various achievements of recent science and skill, with the rifling of the gun-barrels, have almost, if not altogether exhausted the resources of gunsmiths, and produced weapons so perfect that any decided further improvement would seem to be scarcely possible.

The *rifling* of gun-barrels may be considered to date in England from about the end of the 16th century ; but the earliest patent for rifling is dated in the year 1635. (See Colonel Chesney's "Observations on Fire-Arms," p. 258; Sir S. Scott's "British Army," vol. ii., pp. 250—327 ; and "Archæologia," vol. xxii., p. 59, and vol. xxvi., p. 241.)

NOTE 91, *p.* 248.—It is scarcely necessary for me to observe that the English percussion-lock guns of every class and variety, whether rifles or smooth-bores, breech or muzzle-loaders, are at least equal to the best that have ever been produced in any other country. And, in like manner, the *Snider* rifle (the invention of an American, but a weapon now naturalised amongst ourselves), the *Whitworth*, the *Lancaster*, the *Enfield*, the *Henry*, and various other English rifles, while in the *Chassepot* and the *Needle*, and others of foreign production—not forgetting the American *Spencer* repeating carbine—they may have rival weapons, can concede to none a just claim for superiority.

NOTE 92, *p.* 253.—Col. Chesney ("Past and Present State of Fire-Arms," p. 267) gives a minute description of the Minie rifle-ball, together with an explanation of the system of loading with that projectile from the muzzle. The important points are the elongated and conical form of the ball, and the cause of its expansion in the act of firing the piece. A deep cylindrical hollow is sunk in the ball at its base, which is closed with a capsule or small thimble of sheet-iron. This capsule is made to sink to about one-third the depth of the hollow in the ball. When the rifle is loaded, the ball is placed in the barrel with this capsule downwards and next to the powder. The leaden ball itself exactly fits the bore, without filling or in the slightest degree entering the grooves of the rifling. "In firing, the explosion, as a matter of course, forces the iron thimble up into the conical hollow of the ball, before the *inertia* of the ball itself has been overcome (before the ball moves, that is), and thus, by increasing its diameter (by causing the ball to expand), it forces the lead into the grooves of the bore so completely, that the whole base of the bullet is exposed to the action of the powder without allowing the slightest windage, or any diminution in the explosive force of the powder, by which so much of the impetus is lost in common rifles."

The *needle-gun* is loaded at the breech ; consequently the ball, which has a peculiar form, is so much larger than the bore of the barrel that it becomes rifled in its passage, without any necessity for expansion. The "needle" is made to pass through the charge of powder, and to cause the explosion of some fulminant which is placed between the gunpowder and the ball ; thus the charge is *fired from the front*, which ensures a more perfect ignition, than when the fire is given at the lower extremity of the charge. The chamber, also which contains the charge is so constructed that there is an empty space behind the gunpowder, and this causes the recoil to be but slight.

It will be understood that elongated and conical rifle-balls are attended with this important advantage, that in consequence of their length they are considerably diminished in circumference without any loss of weight ; and, therefore, it follows that they can be discharged from rifles having comparatively small bores, which are much lighter and more easily wielded.

NOTE 93, *p.* 256.—Excessive rapidity in firing is not altogether free from drawbacks. Soldiers in action, who are conscious of their ability to discharge their rifles many times in a single minute, may be tempted by the very excitement of their own rapid firing to fire at random, to waste their ammunition, and even to expend all their ammunition prematurely as well as much too speedily. It is undoubtedly a matter of great importance that soldiers should be able to fire rapidly ; but it is of much greater importance that their fire should be steady, and delivered with a real meaning. The latest experience has shown that it is only under very rare and exceptional conditions that a soldier fires away more than half of his sixty rounds of rifle ammunition, even in the most hotly-contested action ; he *may* fire sixty rounds in a few minutes, and he *may* with almost equal rapidity expend a second supply ; but these are the exceptions to the rule of rapid firing, and not the rule itself.

NOTE 94, *p.* 256.—*War-rockets* are not included by M. Lacombe amongst the modern missiles and implements of warfare which he enumerates and describes. They have been proved in the Abyssinian campaign to be very formidable weapons ; and there can be no doubt that, in future they will be regarded with serious attention.

Z

Note 95, *p.* 260.—I find it necessary to follow the example of M. Lacombe in omitting all special reference to *marine artillery*, and to the application of modern science and skill to *naval warfare*. The subject, however, is equally important and interesting; and the existing usage of employing massive plates of iron for the defence of shipping, coupled with the extraordinary magnitude and power of the guns that are now constructed for the armament of ships of war, bring this subject into direct connection with a treatise on "Arms and Armour." The *turret-system*, also, possesses the strongest claims for such a careful and unprejudiced description in a popular form, as might make its true aim and purpose more generally known and better understood. I can only add that it is the very importance of these and such matters which, since it forbids a cursory and superficial treatment of them, excludes them from the fixed limits of the present volume

Note 96, *p.* 260.—The *Meyrick Armoury*, now exhibited at South Kensington, is rich in every variety of "Arms and Armour" in use from about the close of the 15th century. It is to be hoped that this truly magnificent collection will become the property of the nation.